A PENGUIN IN THE EYRIE

"A flock of Liberators, waiting to patrol the entrance to the Channel, when 'D' day comes" (see p. 151)

A PENGUIN IN THE EYRIE

AN R.A.F. DIARY, 1939–1945

HECTOR BOLITHO

WITH 19 ILLUSTRATIONS

LONDON
HUTCHINSON

Hutchinson & Co. (Publishers) Ltd
178-202 Great Portland Street, London, W.1

London   Melbourne   Sydney   Auckland
Bombay Johannesburg New York Toronto

First published 1955

Made and Printed in Great Britain by
GREYCAINES
(*Taylor Garnett Evans & Co. Ltd.*)
Watford, Herts.

TO

GRETA AND WILLY HOFFLIN

LIST OF ILLUSTRATIONS

INTRODUCTION

This book is derived from the diaries I kept during the war, from September 1939 to May 1945. I use the word 'derived' for several reasons. The entries, running into about a quarter of a million words, had to be cut, and edited, to bring them within one volume. Also, some episodes had to be clarified, as their meaning has become half-lost during the ten years that have passed since the war ended. And there were many passages in my diary, kept while I was a serving officer, which were subject to censorship that is no longer necessary.

My books, *War in the Strand*, and *Task for Coastal Command*, included a considerable part of what is published here, but they have long been out of print. Where I have modified or condensed parts of the narrative, they have been submitted for correction to the members of the R.A.F. concerned, if they are still alive.

The first title I chose for this book was *A Coward Among the Brave*, but I rejected this because it sounds affected. Yet it describes my part quite honestly, for I began the war as an Intelligence officer in the Air Ministry—then as editor of the *R.A.F. Journal*—in a state of continuous fear. I avoided danger whenever I could, disliked my duties when I was obliged to fly, and never emerged from the hundreds of air raids in London with any emotion but selfish gratitude that I was still alive.

The story falls into two parts: the first, describing my three years in the Air Ministry; and the second, my service with Coastal Command, as editor of the Command *Intelligence Review*. Then I came nearer to the eagles who were fighting, and I learned my lesson. I remained a penguin, still disliking my safe journeys in the air; but this nearer view of the R.A.F., moving towards 'D' day, when I was stationed with operational anti-U-boat squadrons, helped me to conquer my introspective fears.

I hope this theme emerges from my narrative.

There are gaps in the story because some of my papers were destroyed by a bomb and because there were periods when I was too busy, or too lazy, to write of what happened about me. I cannot vouch for all the dates in the diary because some entries have been written from pencil notes, made casually or in a hurry.

I wish to thank Marshal of the R.A.F. Lord Douglas of Kirtleside, Marshal of the R.A.F. Sir John Slessor, Air Marshal Sir Aubrey Ellwood, and Air Marshal Douglas Colyer, who were my commanding officers during the five and a half years I was with the Royal Air Force. Each of them has kindly checked the chapters describing what happened when I was under his command. I am especially grateful to Mr. A. J. Charge of the Imperial War Museum for his help with the illustrations, and to Mr. J. C. Nerney, Chief Librarian of the Air Ministry, who has saved me from many errors with his incredible memory and his wise advice.

HECTOR BOLITHO.

The Close,
  Salisbury, Wilts.

1939

September 3, 1939. Jack was kneeling on the floor, packing my things for London, and I was standing by my bedroom window. We heard Mr. Chamberlain say, *No such understanding has been received, and consequently this country is at war with Germany.* Jack glanced up for a moment and said, "Well, I suppose we are for it, sir." Then he went on wrapping my ties in tissue paper. I stood by the window for a little time, looking out over the fields. Nearer, the moorhens were pecking on the edge of the bulrushes and the white ducks were waddling past the red geraniums.

Pilots from Debden aerodrome, five miles away, were to take off for France. We had already agreed that when the war began some of their wives were to occupy my house. We had to move furniture and worry over what we could do with Mitzi, my old Austrian servant. With all her Viennese spirit and her declaration that Hitler was 'a beetch' and that she wished she had 'a streeng for his neck', she was now our enemy. I had to think of the possibility of her becoming the victim of resentment in the village. We wrote a note for Norman, the gardener, telling him to plant out as many vegetables as he could, and we cut sheets of beaverboard to black out the windows in the hall. We packed the superficial ornaments of the house, the Capo-di-Monte figures I bought in Rome and the jars from Petra . . . every unnecessary object, into cupboards. We found a luscious cobweb, with its fat spider, behind a tallboy which we were moving.

"Leave it for now," I said to Jack.

"Cobwebs'll hold the house together if there's a bomb," he answered.

It was a glorious day: the dahlias and roses were out in great splendour. I drove over to see 85 and 87 Squadrons at Debden. The loaded aircraft have been waiting for days, straining at their leashes in the field. I saw the containers with their ammunition—innocent enough objects to look at. I knew Debden aerodrome when it was a farm: I have seen it grow from the days when the indolent ploughman used to wave good-morning to me as I drove by.

Laurie[1] was magnificent. No fuss; cracking jokes in his merry Irish voice and halving the inner anxiety of everybody he talked to. Dickie Lee[2] brought me a pile of framed pictures to be stored in the attic of my house. They are the pictures a boy would gather: a photograph of his spaniel, something by Walt Disney, and water colours of static aircraft, painted against blue skies. We drank champagne, agreed that Hitler was a fierce bastard, and that the Poles were for it.

Three of the R.A.F. wives arrived to stay in my house, with their babies. Their husbands are to fly off at any moment now. Not a complaint or a murmur!

I walked around my garden, which I have made out of a bedraggled farmyard. I have poured more care into it than into my work. The hibiscus bushes were in flower. I paused on the edge of the field over which the same barn owl has flown in the summer evenings for six years, and by the tree in which the turtle dove has cooed its benediction over our lives. I paused for only a second, to wonder if this is to be the end of it all. Then to the London train; past Audley End, with the immense lawn sweeping up towards the solemn façade of the mansion. It is incredible that it might be bombed. Brigadier Bridge, one of the fathers of the British Council, was standing on Audley End station. We ate cold ham and salad together, on the train, and talked of Roumania and France. We held back from mentioning the war, although it was only an hour old. I did not hear the air-raid warning at 11.40. The journey past the fields and into the hot stinks of London was placid: the platform at Liverpool Street, the trembling air, the quickened feet and the men in new uniforms. The porter said: "Have you heard? There's been an air raid over the east coast and they've brought down a German plane." This turned out to be the first of what will no doubt be many false rumours, dancing from tongue to tongue.

1 Flying Officer R. L. Lorimer, killed in action May 14, 1940.
2 Fl.-Lieut. R. H. A. Lee, D.S.O., D.F.C., killed during the Battle of Britain.

I drove to Regent's Park to see Marie Tempest. I found her playing two-pack patience in her sitting-room, which was splendid and pretty with flowers. She told me that her theatre was already closed. She had gone down to the cellar with her gas mask, when the sirens sounded, an hour or so before. "Everybody was so kind. Basil Bartlett brought all his dining-room chairs down so that we could sit." Then she drew herself up with all her frightening courage and said that she would not leave London. I begged her to go to my house in Essex, or to Penzance, but she refused. She repeated the remark of my servant, "Well, we are for it." She reminded me of Queen Victoria at the time of the Fenian riots, with her secretary on 'his bended knees' begging her to leave Osborne. All she said was that she would 'not have it mentioned again'.

Marie Tempest gave me a new photograph of herself and wrote on it, 'Hector, War! September 3! Mary!'

I left the brave presence and carried my suitcases along Avenue Road, searching for a taxi-cab. I drove to my club and telephoned Sir Cyril Newall's secretary and offered myself to the Air Ministry. "Any job, any place," I said, with blind gallantry. Then to Belgrave Square, to stay with Viorel Tilea,[1] who was calm and optimistic. We took the key of the garden in the Square and walked under the trees, talking of peaceful things. Then to dine with Sandy Vereker and Ralph Howard, at the Ritz. London was already dark. There was a menacing beauty in the canyons between the high buildings: the crawling, subdued lights of the cars, the secret rustling of people, sucked from the outer darkness of the streets into the deeper shadows of doorways.

We ate well. "It might be our last good meal! Let's go the whole hog and have a partridge and a bottle of red wine!" Afterwards, we encouraged Noel Coward on to the platform in the restaurant, to play and sing to us. He strayed through old war songs, waltzes and tunes. Then we made him sing songs from *Bitter Sweet*. When I asked him what he was doing he said, *Intelligence*, in a voice that reeked of sealing-wax and invisible ink.

I slept at No. 1 Belgrave Square. At three in the morning

---

[1] The Roumanian Minister and an old friend.

there was an abominable warning. Viorel Tilea dragged me out of bed, made me put on my slippers and dressing-gown, and carry my gas mask down into the shelter. I insisted on brushing my teeth and combing my hair. I bruised my finger in the bathroom door and this put me in a foul temper. I was so tired that I clung to the brass railing as I tottered downstairs. I did nothing to show a brave British face to the Roumanian servants and the Italian chef. It all seemed such a bore, waiting, with the humiliating gas mask: a snout of rubber in a brown cardboard box. There was no raid.

September 4. In the afternoon Viorel and I went on to the roof to look at the balloon barrage. The hundreds of silver monsters caught the sunlight as they rode below the clouds. They were magnificent: they gave London a sort of carnival look and had no apparent relationship with bombers and death.

September 5. We were dragged out of bed again, at 6.45 a.m., by the air-raid warning. This time, I was awake. I brushed my teeth, dashed cold water over my face and head, grabbed my gas mask and made for the shelter, which is divided into three compartments. The lesser Roumanian servants sit in the far one, the butler and the Italian chef in the centre, and Viorel and myself alone in ours. Rather extravagant class-consciousness in the face of death.

The shelter is built under the pavement and I was able to creep up the steps into Belgrave Square. There one could enjoy the morning sunshine, superb and clear silver, and exchange a chat with the air-raid warden who seemed to enjoy blowing his whistle. He stopped a foolish young man on his bicycle and ordered him under cover. Then he pounced on a North Countryman who was crossing the road and said, "You must go down into the shelter." The man answered, "I've been down in bloody shelter for 'arf 'our and I'm tired of bloody shelter."

September 6. I returned to my home in Essex. The house, once

tranquil and orderly, is like a boarding house. I was bored so I
went down to the pub and ate alone. Mitzi whimpers, feeling
that she has no home and no country; that she hates Hitler and
wonders if she will be pitched into a concentration camp. The
police are reassuring; they have allowed her freedom within a
radius of five miles.

The refugees in the village turned out to be unwashed illiter-
ates from Whitechapel. Stanley, the village carter, found six fleas
in his clothes after bringing their paraphernalia of luggage from
the station. The radio told us that the evacuation of the London
children had been made without a hitch. Well, it is an unholy
mess here. There is bitterness already. But the villagers are rather
silly and emotional. Today, they were full of friendliness for me.
Some months ago, when there was a war scare, it was a different
story. Rodney Wilkinson[1] came to stay for the week-end and, on
Monday morning, he rose early and left for his R.A.F. station,
taking my shaving brush by mistake. He telephoned me from
Duxford and said that he would fly over the house and drop the
brush on the lawn. It sailed down, from the aircraft, in a brightly
coloured linen bag, in time for me to shave.

There was a lot of busy gossip in the village: the ultimate
story was, *a*, As my name ended in a vowel, I must be an Italian.
b, As I had been to Italy for my last holidays, I was obviously a
spy. *c*, The aircraft was obviously Italian, dropping messages to
me from Mussolini.

September 7. I rose very early. The house was still and dark, so I
moved the gloomy black-out curtains and looked down at the
orchard. It was so beautiful that I hurried out and walked
between the whitewashed boles of the trees. Great clusters of
apples weighed down the branches; wasps and bees were already
fussing among the fallen fruit. I picked some plums from the cool
recesses of a tree and walked down to the rose garden. The world
was mine for an hour.

[1] Squadron Leader R. L. Wilkinson, killed in action August 16, 1940.

B

September 8. To London, to the Air Ministry, to see Air Commodore Buss, Director of Intelligence. I am more or less promised a job. He talked of Trans-Jordan and of King Abdullah and King Feisal, whom we both knew. He agreed that if Feisal had been given a good English adviser, to be near him and whom he could trust, he would never have strayed into such mischief. . . . I like Buss. I could work with him.

I went down to the Savoy Hotel in the afternoon. The leaves of the plane trees on the Embankment caught the afternoon sun. There were many people, including American war correspondents, almost dragging the tapes out of the electric news machines, anxious for the latest reports. It was pleasant to hear their voices: one, a silky, Southern drawl that made me feel less a prisoner on this little island, which we may not leave for many a long day.

Later there came a telephone message from the Air Ministry, which has acted quickly. I am to go in, with a commission. *Intelligence*. There is great comfort in the word.

September 10. My first day in the Air Ministry. I could not sleep last night so I got up at seven and went into the street to buy some newspapers. I walked down Oakley Street, awakening memories of my arrival from New Zealand, seventeen years ago. I came at the end of the last war, to a flat here in Chelsea. I remember leaning over Battersea Bridge and seeing the river at night; Ellen Terry moving a curtain and looking into the King's Road, Mr. Lloyd George banging his gate in Cheyne Walk, and Mrs. Lloyd George knitting at a window.

I found a newspaper girl, on her bicycle. "I have to do it myself. All the boys have been called away," she told me. So I bought some papers and went back to bed, to read them. The news was cold and thin; like news of some other war, happening on the far side of a wall of years.

Once the Air Ministry decided to employ me, I was examined, physically, told to fill in nine forms, order my uniform, and begin work. I am to be part of a small, new section of Intelligence, with

David Garnett as my colleague and a fine old fighter as our chief: Brigadier-General P. R. C. Groves,[1] army trained and one of the early R.F.C. pilots, now serving as an Air Commodore.

David Garnett and I were shown into a room which we must share with Colonel Chambers, a very important person, judging by his manner; distinctly amiable, but mysterious. He bustled into the room with files marked SECRET, and VERY SECRET, which he locked into steel cupboards. David Garnett was bewildered, but charming. Shy, I imagine. But I was shy also. We read some secret files, but I understood very little of what was in them. So far, I am out of my depth.

September 21. News came, this afternoon, of the assassination of the Roumanian Prime Minister, Armand Calinescu, in Bucarest. Members of the Iron Guard shot him while he was in his car. I hurried back to the Roumanian Legation to see Viorel Tilea. The big London house was English no longer. The eyes of the Roumanian servant who took my hat were smeared with the marks of tears. Viorel Tilea was quiet. While I was with him the telephone rang, with a call from Bucarest. Apparently the assassins rushed back after their job was done, shot the men in the broadcasting station, and announced their bloody deed to the people.

It was only last March that I saw Calinescu in the palace in Bucarest: he followed me in after I had seen King Carol. He did not know that I was watching him as he ascended in the lift: rigid, cold, as if on parade. He was a brave, loyal man, and I could not help feeling sorry for King Carol, with one friend less in his struggle. He is not strong enough to stand alone.

November (*undated*). It is not easy for me, with my civilian sense of freedom, to accept the discipline of service life, even within the easy pattern of the Air Ministry. Air Commodore Groves is the greatest of gentlemen and he is especially kind to writers,

---

[1] Brigadier-General P. R. C. Groves, C.B., C.M.G., D.S.O.

being one himself. But he is a little deaf and this caused me two hours of distress a few days ago. I was standing before him and I must have mumbled my reply to one of his questions. He leapt to his feet and said, "You can't speak to me like that; I'll have you on the mat."

He shook a file of papers in my face, brushed my protests aside and said, "Come with me." His personal assistant was also in the room; he tried to explain that I had been misunderstood, but he failed.

The Air Commodore, still shaking his papers, led me to the office of the Director of Intelligence, who was, fortunately, away at a meeting. My master's fury did not abate; he said, "This is not the end of the matter; you will stay here until the D. of I. returns."

I had to sit down, like a scolded schoolboy, and wait. It was almost lunch-time and when I explained the disturbance to Flight-Lieutenant Baring, P.A. to the Director of Intelligence, he said, "You had better go and eat." I did not dare, so he gave me a bar of chocolate.

A few minutes later, Groves sent for me. His P.A. had explained and his indignation had changed back to his usual charm. He extended his hand and said: "I am sorry. I am a little deaf at times and I must have misunderstood you."

He was so kind that I smiled, but the sickness stayed, all day. In the evening, my office door opened. The Air Commodore looked in and said, "Will you come with me to the club for a drink?"

We drove to the United Service, where I was beckoned into a circle of highly senior officers, all of Groves's vintage. The talk was very much, "When I was in 'Pindi in '06." The way that Groves drew me, a wingless flight-lieutenant, into the conversation, and told the old warriors that he was so lucky to have me on his staff, made me very fond of him.

Among the great soldiers in the circle was Sir Ernest Swinton[1] who said to me: "I am pleased you are working with Groves. He's so upright he falls backwards."

[1] Major-General Sir Ernest Swinton, K.B.E., C.B., D.S.O., M.A., R.E.

December 6. The war is having one strange effect on me. I have lived in England almost twenty years: in most of my interests I am English, but I am becoming more conscious of my New Zealand origin and less absorbed in the land of my adoption. I am seeing the English people at a distance that was not possible before.

I find that my patriotism is different from that of most of the Englishmen about me. I have talked this over with Canadians and New Zealanders in London and they agree that it is not for England alone that one strains one's heart and one's hand. The feeling of belonging to the Commonwealth of Nations is strong in us. We feel all these things in a broader field of thought than the Englishman who, in his rather insular way, looks upon the dominions as colonies, and even has the effrontery to use the word. This ignorance must be educated out of him.

I have remained more raw and mutinous than I realized: with all my love for the English landscape, and my respect for the English way of life, my New Zealand birth makes me feel separate and apart. I still feel that, as the son of the son of a son, who sailed from England and dug his own acres in a new country, a century ago, I have the right to think for myself and to act upon the impetus of my own loyalties. I feel that I should love to turn my back on the old world when the war is over, and live on earth that does not give up Roman coins and Elizabethan ornaments and ancient spear-heads . . . the trappings of the dead.

December 21. I was duty Intelligence Officer last night, for the first time, and I was terrified. It meant that I had to sleep in the Air Ministry and open boxes of documents, brought in every now and then, from other Ministries in Whitehall. Frankly, I thought it very silly to entrust me with such a task. I was given a tiny key, on a slim chain, and Air Commodore Buss kindly said that I might sleep in his office as the bed is more comfortable than the others. I pleaded, "But what am I to do?" and was told, "Oh, deal with anything that turns up." This, with the war going on outside, made me wish to die, for my own sake rather than for England.

About 1 a.m. a telegram arrived. It was from the G.O.C. in C. Eastern Command to the G.O.C. London. A copy. It read more or less like this:

Text information received from source hitherto reliable that Hitler has decided on drastic air action against Great Britain. Raid by successive waves of bombers to be directed against Channel ports, naval bases in south, Thames Estuary and Woolwich. Source states attack may start before Christmas. At any rate before New Year.

I was alone, with the fearful document in my hand. I can grin about it now, but, at the moment, I expected to hear the enemy approaching. I felt that all the fate of Britain lay in my hot hands. Air Commodore Buss had said, "Deal with anything that turns up." How did I deal with this?

In the office is a terribly secret telephone. I rang my opposite number at the Admiralty and asked him a few guarded questions. He said that he was in a flap also as he had never done the job before. So he was no use.

Then I remembered that my friend, John Hawtrey,[1] was on duty in the War Room. I put my greatcoat over my pyjamas and went down the cold concrete stairs to find him. Hawtrey is an old hand, and he knows all the ropes. He took the telegram into the office of some high-up, beyond my approach, came back and said: "Do nothing. It is just confirmation of something that came in during the day. It's nothing for you to worry about."

Of course I worried, but I was none the wiser. I went back to the Air Commodore's room, holding the telegram and the secret key.

I must really have been a little dotty because I had a vision of Hitler himself climbing the back stairs of the Air Ministry and snatching the key from my hand. As I got into bed I put the chain and key about my ankle: I thought them safer there than under the pillow.

About three o'clock in the morning there was a knock on the door. I said, "Come in," and a young officer appeared. As he had read, *Director of Intelligence, Air Commodore K. C. Buss* on

[1] Ultimately Air Vice-Marshal J. G. Hawtrey, died October 26, 1954.

the door, he gave me a cracking salute. I was then sitting up in bed, in my pyjamas, and, having no idea of what King's Regulations would require of me in such circumstances, I said, "Good morning". Then he presented his secret box from which I had to extract the next secret paper. I must say that I felt very stupid as I turned down the bed-clothes and took the key from my ankle. The expression on his face was something to behold.

1940

January 1940. During a war it is our business to hate the enemy. I know Germany well: I have stayed with German families, worked in German libraries and tramped the German roads—the enchanting roads of the south, with apple-trees leaning over them. There are Germans of whom I became deeply fond and there are times when I find myself wondering over their fate. There was one with whom I used to stay in his fifteenth-century castle in Ober-Hessen. There was a peasant burgomeister with whom I shared sausages and schnapps; the old keeper of the museum at Herrenhausen, and the fat old woman who made *bratwürste* and sold them in the market square in Coburg; near the statue of the Prince Consort, where geraniums were planted every summer, at the expense of Queen Victoria. At the other extreme are men of noble families who brought the best wine from their cellars when I dined. I was very happy during ten summers, wandering over the beautiful country.

But I was never wholly certain of my friends: there was a gap in many of the relationships. One day, after walking in the woods, through the snow, I returned to a castle of noble size and luxury. My host, about twenty-five years old, was wearing high boots and when we arrived in the hall he sat back in a chair and rang a bell. A small kitchen-maid appeared and, while my friend sprawled in the chair, she went on her knees and drew off his boots, so that he should not soil his hands. He was ordinarily a very kind man, and imaginative, but I never felt quite the same about him again, after seeing the swagger with which he allowed the girl—she could not have been more than fifteen—to remove his boots.

Episodes of this kind separated me from my German friends. The gap widened when the National Socialists gained power. When I went to Germany in the spring before the war, my friends were in uniform and we no longer spoke the same language. The swastika flew over Rosenau Castle where Prince Albert was born: the miasma of the war was already rising and I felt, in my heart, that I would never laugh with them again.

(*My diary for the first eight months of* 1940 *was destroyed, along with other papers and books. There is thus a gap in my story, until the late summer. I think it better to leave it so, rather than attempt to bridge the narrative by merely recollecting what happened.*)

September 14. I am enjoying my first week of leave since the war began. You might think that this little Essex village had no links with the world outside, except that my gardener, devoted to the cinema, has named his daughters Marlene and Greta. On the edge of the village is my house, set in sixty acres of sugar beet and clover. On the first day I walked out and found that the crops had prospered. The sky was silver blue and a hundred white butterflies shimmered in the sun. The harvest was good and the world was calm.

Yesterday, the spell broke. The Hurricanes from Debden aerodrome rose above the trees that stand in the west. From the coast came fifty German bombers, with their fighter escort. Our aircraft, outnumbered by three to one, met them, almost over my house! But not all: forty-four of the enemy turned back towards the sea leaving only six to face the music.

Standing on the edge of field, I watched the terrible, quick battle overhead: the appalling sight of the first bomber hurtling down, into the clover. The second! The third, into a field towards Radwinter. All six were vanquished and the flaming pieces of fuselage made a dangerous rain over the houses. Two of our Hurricanes limped out of the battle and were destroyed.

The enemy parachutes fell slowly out of the fleecy clouds: lovely white parachutes, like gigantic chrysanthemums, with Germans swinging beneath them.

The hedges bristled with men of the Home Guard: old farmers, whose ancestors had polished their arrows against the Danes, ran across the fields with their rifles. The parachutes drifted gracefully over the willows and the Germans landed. Our oldest farmer peeped cautiously through the hedge; he waited for a second, to be sure the prisoner was not holding a grenade in his hand, then he crawled through and captured him.

I went to our village pub in the evening and talked with the farmer. He said: "That German! He wasn't more than eighteen years old. A boy, you might say. Trembling all over, he was."

I asked him then, "Did you feel that you would have liked to shoot him?"

He said: "Oh, no! He was a trembling sort of boy. So I took him back to my cottage until the military came for him. My wife made him a cup of cocoa. He couldn't speak English, you see, but he seemed to understand me when I said, 'Cocoa'."

We drank our beer and then he put down his mug and said: "You know, women are queer creatures. All my wife said was, 'You should have brought home the parachute as well. They're made of fine silk and it would have given me blouses to last until Doomsday'."

September 30. I have been to stay on a bomber station in East Anglia. At one end were the hangars with their great doors open; nearer were some twenty bombers—fabulous animals, waiting for the darkness that would release them for their journey over the Ruhr.

The members of a bomber crew are placid and silent: more like sailors than their fighter brothers. They were gathered about the empty fireplace, drinking glasses of beer. One of them, a New Zealander, was soon my friend. He was tall, and his body moved with the clumsy ease of a rugger player. We talked of the lakes and coast we know in our own country; of the white yachts of summer, and the glaciers up which we climbed in winter-time. I tried to make him describe his combats, but he just moved uneasily and offered me a cigarette. Nor would he talk much of what he felt about the enemy. Of the Germans he said, "We've got to fix them and that's all there is to it."

He made one remark that seemed casual at the time. I was

badly sun-burned on my shoulders a week ago and, while we talked, I must have moved my body within my clothes, for the sake of comfort. The New Zealander thought I was cold and said: "You'd better put on something warm if you are going to wait up for us to come back. It's as cold as ice here towards morning."

I explained that my trouble was not cold, but sunburn.

We stood, silent, in the crew-room. Evening had come and the steeple and the trees of the village were swallowed into the general darkness. We walked into the immense hangar and I watched the pilots change shape under the weight of the flying kit they put on. They looked immense and formidable. There was little said. They moved out to the darkness: there was a slim moon—enough to give life to the moving shadows. The bulky figures climbed into the big lorries that made their bodies seem more immense than ever as they stood up, against the sky. Then they moved towards the bombers: some of them were four-engine Stirlings, so colossal that it seemed impossible that they could ever mount on their wings.

The aircraft rose from the earth, in turn, over a period of an hour and a half: I stood in the shadows and watched them soaring, towards the Channel and the Ruhr. It was strange to be left alone, knowing that while I waited—a useless figure leaning against the wall of the hangar—the Stirlings would drop their bombs in the far-away country and return before morning.

The hangars loomed like cliffs about me and the great doors creaked under the pressure of the wind. The spaces were lonely and cold and the only point of life and colour was on the blade of a bayonet, where the sentry stood. He seemed barely alive, he was so still.

After an hour the padre came along on his bicycle: we sat on a log and talked. He told me of a pilot who was bringing his bomber back after an attack on Bordeaux, at night. Two hundred miles from home, 'something went wrong': after diving from 10,000 feet, into the sea, the pilot was flung to the end of the aircraft, unconcious. When he came to his senses again he realized that one of his ankles was broken. He hopped through the dark body of the bomber, to the escape hatch, and looked upon the sea, covered with flames.

The padre said: "There was one slim gap on the water where the petrol had not spread. He dragged the rubber boat from the fuselage and threw it out: then he dived into the strip of water, between the flames. As he swam towards the rubber boat, two other members of the crew appeared and climbed in. Just as the pilot was scrambling in to join them, he realized that the tide was carrying the boat towards the fire. He slipped back into the water, holding the rope from the rubber dinghy over his shoulder. With one arm and one leg he swam against the tide to keep the boat away from the flames. When they died down he crawled in. The pain of his broken ankle and his exhaustion were too much: he remembered no more until he woke some hours later and saw the searchlight of a destroyer moving over the water. He was saved, with the others, and brought back."

The padre stayed with me until the first gentle stirring of light came to the horizon. We walked past the sentry, gave him the password, and made our way to the landing-ground. The morning came, in great beauty: but it was still dark when the first three bombers appeared . . . we walked over to one of them —the second to land—and watched the crew climb down from the vast body of the aircraft.

Two more flew in; then three more. Their return was spread over a long time. We counted, anxiously. The morning light increased and birds began to twitter in the poplars.

Just as the sun rose, with shafts of light that set all the birds singing, the last bomber appeared—far away. It landed and the crew jumped out—among them my friend from New Zealand.

He came over to me as calmly as if we were meeting in a street. "Hullo," he said. "We've had a good night. I could see the fires miles away." Then he asked: "What have you been doing? Have you had any shut-eye?"

I said, "No."

Then came the sentence that shook me to the core. "Oh, by

the way, I suddenly remembered as we were coming near the coast—I've got some stuff in my room for sunburn. Come over to the mess and I'll give it to you before we turn in."

October 10. I am a countryman at heart, so I miss my garden and the fields. During the spring and summer I have consoled myself with a game: I have walked in St. James's Park each day, for half an hour, pretending that it is my own. I went so far as to discuss the planning and planting with the gardeners, who always seemed grateful for a little interest. I knew what was coming long before the plants appeared. Unfortunately, the game must be put away now that winter is upon us. One of the gardeners has become almost a friend: but he seems to resent my suggestion that the dahlias should be budded to give bigger blooms. "We do not grow plants to get prizes," he said. "We just like to give the people plenty of colour."

One morning he stood beside the dahlias, holding a piece of shrapnel he had found on the lawn. "Think," he said, "what would have happened if this had fallen before the mowing was finished for the year; *think* what would have happened to the blades of my lawn-mower!"

Late October. Not a word in my diary for some days. We now live in a city that is bombed almost every night: the threats have come true. I work at my desk all day, and most evenings, editing the *Royal Air Force Weekly Bulletin* which is confidential and distributed to members of aircrews, through the Intelligence officers. It was my own idea and we turned out the first ones on duplicators and flew them to France. The aim is to make the aircrews feel that they are taken into the confidence of the Air Ministry and told as much as possible about the overall pattern of the war. The *Bulletin* keeps me busy. I have little wish to write more, when the tasks of the day are over.

A few weeks ago, before the night bombing of London

began, I found a cottage in Lowndes Place, with chaste white rooms and even a patch of garden for spring cabbages. My friends lent me their spare furniture and I had just settled in when the bombing began. I had hoped that I would be braver than I am. I put up my first battle against fear by going to bed early each night when I returned from the Air Ministry. But it was not easy, lying on my back, holding a book I did not read, and watching the ceiling. I expected a little bomb to come through and, as a spider pauses when it slides down a strand of web, stop before my eyes and blow me to atoms. I think my fear was intensified by loneliness. I went through a muddled argument: I tried to say: "This will be the nightly habit of your life from now on. You will doubtless be killed in the end. So you must adapt yourself to the new danger."

I tried to fool myself with this placid reasoning, but it did not work. Three nights ago, when a bomb fell a street or so away, I jumped out of bed. The guns boomed louder and nearer. I tried to be calm as I dressed, but my fingers bustled beyond the pace of my mind. . . . I turned out the lights, banged the door, and hurried into the awful street. I have not slept in the little house since then.

I needed someone near me, physically, as I have never needed them before. I hurried along the streets, the vast night thumping with anger and destruction. . . . I stood on the corner by the Cadogan Hotel and argued against my frantic wish to run. I *made* myself walk calmly; I spoke to a policeman but he answered in a discouraging voice. I walked on to Victoria, then down Constitution Hill, towards Admiralty Arch. By the Arch I found another policeman: we talked a little and he soothed me with his friendliness.

I was conscious of the actual moment when my fear passed and I became calm again. It was outside the Whitehall Theatre where I suddenly stood still and said, "You are a weak fool." I became quiet and sensible, and walked on. The bombs were still falling.

Next morning, after sleeping at my desk, I changed the arrangement of my life. I gave up all other interests and decided

C

to live in the Air Ministry. Now I sleep in a cellar and eat at little restaurants nearby—melancholy slabs of cold meat pie—or in the canteen in the basement of the Air Ministry. We are rabbits in a vast warren, driven underground at night by the warning of the guns. The thud of the bombs is muted by the thick walls and the mass of stone above. I sleep in a low room, with twenty others. There is one blue light, a little light, that burns all night over our beds. They are bunks, rather than beds. Near me is a man who snores in great sweeps of sound. I now have a small, empty ginger-beer bottle under my pillow. He happens to sleep on his back, with his knees arched. I can creep out of bed, give him a whack on the knees, which silences him, and be back in my own bunk before he is aware of what has happened. Then comes a race: by intense concentration I try to be asleep before the snoring begins again.

The servant who makes the bed was surprised by the empty ginger-beer bottle. I said to him: "Don't throw it away; leave it beneath my pillow. It is very important to me."

November 1. Yesterday I was sent for by the Under-Secretary of State, Mr. Harold Balfour[1], and asked to write a speech for him. This Ministry is full of charming surprises. It was late in the afternoon, and I was suitably obsequious, and rather pleased. He offered me a glass of sherry, sat me down, and said that it would be 'a kindness' if I would help him. He is handsome, lively in manner, and ambitious. He no doubt has those gifts that lead to No. 10 Downing Street or thereabout, but he is also kind and I was delighted to work for him.

We sat over our sherry and planned the speech: I had an idea or two and he did not seem to think me stupid. He was a pilot in the 1914–18 war, and his warm R.A.F. heart saves him from the more horrible ravages of the political career he has chosen. I wrote the speech, took it to him, and felt like a schoolboy handing his essay to his teacher. He seemed pleased and asked me to dine, this evening.

[1] Lord Balfour of Inchrye (cr. 1945).

November 2. A pleasant friendliness comes over the Air Ministry at nightfall. Some of us cross to the Red Lion and fortify ourselves with a drink. But conscience drives one back to one's desk. So we return, to eat, and then work. Air Vice-Marshals and Air Commodores join us in the canteen or hurry, with files of papers, along the hot passages and down the acute stairs. They are mostly friendly. But I have to fight an unreasoning dislike of the civil servants, in their genteel brown suits, or black coats and pin-stripe trousers. This is quite unfair, because they try to be helpful. Wearing a uniform, even without wings or ornament, gives one dangerous self-assurance.

November 8. Sometimes, as I walk about the streets, I wonder if London will ever be the same when the war is over. Life as I have known it in my span of twenty odd years here has changed completely. Long rows of houses, each with a core of social and domestic security, are now empty and scarred by bombardment.

I remember when I first arrived in England from New Zealand, that I was disappointed by the sad façades of stone and shocked by the custom of burying servants in basement rooms. These were the first raw impressions that came to me. Then I met people and I began to know the insides of the tall London houses: the drawing-rooms on the first floor, the meals that arrived from the mystery of kitchens, the staircases that rose in one grand flight to landings and rooms the guests did not see.

I have lived in such houses since then, in Kensington and Chelsea; I know and appreciate the lives of these thousands upon thousands of Londoners, with their dinner-parties, their ritual of drawn curtains and tea on winter afternoons, when the spiky branches of the trees seem to uphold the lowering fog, like a canopy, over the street.

Now these houses are empty and forlorn. Their old ladies have hurried off to Cornwall or Wales, with their snapping pekinese and their eternal needlework. Their sons are soldiers and their daughters are bruising their hands in community kitchens or at great machines. So the houses seem to be in mourning. Some of them have lost their windows and the autumn leaves have blown in, to scurry over the parquet floors that once whispered the steps of a waltz. Torn blinds flap in the wind, and weeds come closer to the doorstep, like fingers of death.

There were faults of aloof selfishness in the old order, but it had charm and continuity. I am old enough to remember the grandeur of the squares: the warm evenings when striped canopies were raised over stretches of red carpet, because somebody was twenty-one; when cars and even carriages rolled up, and girls, like pink roses, stepped out with slim, sparkling shoes, and young men, in their first tails, played the gallant for the first time. There was something haughty about their life that will never flourish again; something shrill and proud. But there was beauty also, and one must be allowed a tear or two at such a funeral.

. . . . .

Last night I dined in what must be the last of the houses in Belgrave Square to retain its grandeur, in spite of the bombing. Almost every other host in London has hurried his pictures and his chandeliers, his vases and his books, to cellars in the country. So one eats sparse meals in rooms with bare walls and empty mantelpieces. Chips Channon's house is still beautiful. His sparkling dining-room, copied from the Amalienburg, still trembles with the beauty of rococo silver tracery and candlelight on crystal. The folded napkins float on the looking-glass table, like lilies on a pool.

We were six at dinner and the talk had been good. The candles had burned low, for we were sitting late. Outside, the guns and the bombs built up their lively crescendo. Chips had just flung some dazzling Whitehall gossip at us when a violent thump shook the walls of the room. We did not move: I did not turn, although I felt that the walls were no longer there. Chips finished his story, just as the smells of destruction oozed beneath the door. An immaculate footman entered and said, "Excuse me, sir, but the porch has gone."

Chips answered, "Oh," as if he had been told that the evening newspapers had arrived.

We rose and passed into the drawing-room, to find great swirls of flame-tinted smoke coming from the fireplace. The windows on to the street were smashed to atoms. With the dignity of relations at a funeral we went to the outer hall. It was no more: the door had been blown in and the once-stalwart pillars of the porch had been broken, like snapped sugar-sticks. The hall was pungent with the strange mushroom smell that hangs in the air after a bomb has exploded. We scrambled over the fallen pillars and the cracked marble paving, to the street. The façade of the house next door was a gaping wound. The pavement was torn and the iron railings above the area steps were twisted.

We walked across to the gardens in the middle of the square: the silence and the emptiness were unreal, after the noise and destruction. It was a harmonious and gentle evening for November; the sky had such an innocent look that one could not believe it had been so treacherous.

Chips led us back into his shattered house. We fumbled in the darkness of the hall and retrieved a noble clock from the rubble, two bronze figures and our coats and hats. The broken windows in the drawing-room were soon covered so that we could turn on the lights. Then we heard voices, outside.

Someone said, "I have come to see if Mr. Channon is safe."

"What name?" asked the footman.

"I am the Archduke Robert," he was told. Then, "I heard the bomb and I ran around to see if Mr. Channon is all right."

So the brother to the heir to the Habsburg throne came into the drawing-room, his tin hat low over his eyes and his clothes covered with dust. He had been working as an air-raid warden nearby. Some more wardens joined us and reported that no one had been hurt. There was nothing we could do, so we drank some beer and talked of other things.

November 12. A man who turns up his nose at slang is on the way to being a prig. Slang brings vitality into language, especially in the Service. Some of the R.A.F. words are twenty or more years old: *joystick*, *ace*, *hedge-hopping*, *stall and zoom*, born in the last war, are now accepted as part of our polite conversation.

One of the best-known words in the R.A.F. is *blimp*. An older officer has told me that it goes back to the winter of 1914 when Horace Short, the well-known aircraft designer, was standing on the steps of the officers' mess at Eastchurch. A violent thunderstorm was threatening, just as three small airships sailed over the aerodrome, in a hurry to avoid the storm. Rippling and rather limp, they floundered lower and lower.

Somebody standing next to Short said: "It is ridiculous to call those things airships. Why don't you coin a name for them?"

At that moment Short called the mess waiter and asked for a *blunch*, his own word, describing a drink half-way between breakfast and lunch. Hearing the word *blunch*, one of the officers looked up at the limp airships and said, "Let's call them *blimps*."

The word *crash*, to describe an accident on landing, is also old. It was first used by Paymaster Lieutenant Lidderdale in 1914. We now accept the word, seriously, but, a generation ago, it was considered witty and it even provoked laughter.

A visitor in a R.A.F. mess might think it strange to hear a pilot describing himself as *browned-off*, when he is depressed or fed-up. Nor would it be clear, when the pilot said, "I saw a *wizard job* in the village this morning", that he meant he had seen a pretty girl. There are certain distinctions of rank in using slang words: fitters and riggers will say of their aircraft, "You sort of become attached to the *kite* on which you are working, just like a groom with his horse". The officer scorns the word *kite* and insists on 'aircraft'.

I went to a R.A.F. station in East Anglia a few weeks ago and talked to a rigger who is the wag of his squadron. He said: "I was a bit *browned-off* when we were at Duxford, but when we moved here there was bags of excitement. The first day, our *kites* took off to intercept some Germans. When the raid was over we felt a bit *browned-off* because we were hungry, so we found a chicken in that farm over there and I borrowed the grid —you know, the boot-scraper from the doorstep—and four of us cooked it over a fire. It took three and a half hours to cook, but it was *wizard* when it was finished."

Many words that sailors use survive in the R.A.F., from the days when the service was under the thumb of the Navy. Even at Cranwell, in the heart of Lincolnshire, sailors would ask permission to 'go ashore' when they wished to spend the evening in Nottingham. I remember one vintage pilot telling me that when the grass before the officer's mess at Cranwell needed mowing, the N.C.O., an old sailor, came up to him and asked if "the lawn on the quarter-deck" might be cut. One good sailor's word that survives in the R.A.F. is *banger*, for sausage. I had a friend in the Service who once came to my house and cooked sausages for our supper. He called out to me, "The bangers are coming up like *nobes*." I was to understand that the sausages were swelling under the grill, like 'nobody's business'.

The survival of sailor's words in the R.A.F. is sometimes odd. I went to the balloon squadron headquarters at Harringay a few days ago, in the heart of London. They call the rectangle of concrete from which the balloon is hoisted, the *deck*, and the balloon crews go so far as to ask for the *leave tender*, when all they wish is a simple *truck*, to take them in to town.

There seems to be a second problem: to preserve the R.A.F. slang from outside corruption. When we examine the new words that are used by the pilots, spontaneously, they are mostly onomatopoeic and valid. When a man is making a fuss they say he is *getting into a flap*, or that he is *flapping*. But there is also the imaginative element: they describe the ornate gold oak leaves on the peak of an Air Commodore's cap as *scrambled eggs*.

One of the best phrases is used when the pilots believe they have mastered a problem: they say, "I have got that buttoned-up". What man thought of this, standing against a wall of porcelain and talking to his neighbour?

A few weeks ago I was on a R.A.F. station in Essex. One of the pilots said, "Oh, I'm only the can-back king."

Let us work this one out. The airman who has to carry the empty can back from a job is doing a humble task. This pilot felt that he had been exploited by his friends—forced, in theory, to carry back the empty can. Not merely this: he was forced to carry back more empty cans than anyone else and he was therefore the *can-back king*.

In the Air Ministry, we use little slang. A blight of gentility falls on the most valiant men when they are posted from the air, to an office. But they allow themselves one phrase, which is descriptive. If a young officer makes a suggestion to someone high above him, and his plan is rejected, he says, "My idea has been shot down." In the last war the phrase was, "My idea has been torpedoed."

Otherwise, the officers in the Air Ministry try to be purists. Although the war is their immediate business, there is a lively wish to write good English. Officers, recently posted to the Air Ministry from operational flying, have copies of Fowler's *English Usage* on their desks. They bother to draft their letters and minutes, in pencil, before they dictate them to the typists. There is a second war, against the clichés of Whitehall. There is one senior officer who received a document in which was the phrase, 'the orders were carried out'. I am told that he wrote, in the margin, 'Only drunks are carried out'.

A NOTE ON THE EAGLE SQUADRON. One evening, about mid-July, I was working late at my desk when Group Captain Sir Louis Greig came in and said, "I want you to write a speech for the Secretary of State, announcing the formation of the Eagle Squadron". So I went upstairs and faced the curious task of being a ghost for Sir Archibald Sinclair. I asked first for some of his own prose, so that I could absorb his vocabulary and style, then I sat at my desk and reduced an exciting story to a few hundred words.

Some months before, Mr. Charles Sweeny, an American now deep-rooted in England, offered to form a Home Guard unit of Americans in London. The authorities agreed, so he wrote quickly to his father in New York and asked for fifty tommy guns, which were landed at Liverpool a few weeks later. Guard's instructors were detailed from Wellington Barracks to train the Americans, who were attached to London Area Headquarters. They were the first United States forces to arm themselves for defence, in England.

Then Charles Sweeny had another brave idea: he imagined and inspired what became the Eagle Squadron—the first unit of American pilots to fly in battle against the enemy. He wrote to his uncle, and namesake, a West Point graduate and a romantic soldier who had fought in Mexico, Venezuela, the Honduras, Poland and Morocco, and who was rich enough to make gestures. He is one of those fearless, restless men who like the smell of war, wherever it is. And he was the man to travel about America and startle young pilots of fortune with the thought of fighting, and fulfilling his nephew's dream. He agreed to gather the squadron together and began his journey.

Charles Sweeny the younger had already described his idea to the Air Ministry and was asked to call. He was shown into Sir Archibald Sinclair's office where he expected an amiable conversation across the desk. But another door was opened and he was urged into the presence of the entire Air Council. He has since told me: "I sat down and I simply could not think. I had no ideas, or words; I was so intimidated by all those Marshals and Air Marshals, I just could not speak."

Sir Sholto Douglas whispered the first words of encouragement; he said, "We won't bite your head off." Charles Sweeny plucked up his courage and told his story.

The political implications and the publicity value of the formation of a squadron of United States combatant pilots, in Britain, were obviously vast and delicate. But everyone acted quickly, and, a few days later, Sir Louis Greig telephoned Charles Sweeny and said, "I have the first three of your boys; come and see them."

The 'three' had hurried across the Atlantic, early in the war, to fight for France—to fight anywhere, so long as they were allowed to fly, and destroy Germans. The fall of France drove

them to the coast; then they escaped to England, offered themselves to the R.A.F., and became the nucleus of the Eagles.

In the meantime, Colonel Sweeny had travelled through
America, gathering pilots on the way: parachute jumpers, crop
dusters from the cotton fields of Georgia and stunt fliers from
Hollywood. When the volunteers numbered sixty, Colonel
Sweeny flew with them across the Atlantic and delivered them
to the R.A.F.

I wrote the speech for the Secretary of State and, for some
days after, I spent my spare hours with the Eagle pilots, enjoying
the sound of their American accents in the offices of the Air
Ministry. It was a change, and a promise of what was to come,
to hear a rich Californian voice say, "Oh, that Spitfire; it's the
sweetest little ship I've ever flown," and to hear Colonel Sweeny
say, when he was asked what he thought of his new war, "Well,
it's the only one we've got, so I guess we've got to think it is a
good one." A new idiom came into the R.A.F. and it was
refreshing.[1]

November 30. I went down to see the members of the Eagle
Squadron a few days ago. They have certainly shaken the conventions of the R.A.F. to the core. One could not help smiling
as they shot craps on the old carpet—the same pattern of lurid
Turkey carpets that must have been bought in thousands. I have
seen them in Essex, Jerusalem and New Zealand. The Eagles
took possession of the mess the day they arrived. They asked
for rye whisky and ginger ale, and got it. They took the leisurely
record of 'Rose Marie' off the gramophone and put on 'The
Lady from the Astor'. They jazzed up the station beyond
recognition.

[1] When America came into the war, in December 1941, the Eagles, then
numbering three squadrons of 84 pilots, continued to fight with the R.A.F. in
R.A.F. uniform. In October 1942 they were absorbed into the American Forces
stationed in Britain, but they were allowed to wear their R.A.F. wings on the
right side of their tunics, balanced by U.S. wings on the left.

During the two years of combat the Eagles brought down 73 enemy aircraft.
Major Chesley G. Paterson, their commanding officer, decorated with both a
D.S.O. and a D.F.C., took part in 126 operational sweeps against the enemy—one
of the highest records among fighter pilots in all the allied forces.

The pilots take a merry view of the war and are out for adventure: all except Stanley Kolendorski,[1] who hates Germany with grim intensity. He was born in Jersey City but his heart and passions are with Poland. He told me that one of his Polish uncles used to travel from Warsaw to Jersey City every two years, to stay with his American cousins. When Stanley was old enough, his uncle taught him to fly. Although he has never been to Warsaw, and is, superficially, as American as could be, he said that when Warsaw fell, in September 1939, he knew that he would have to fight, for Poland. Then came news that his uncle had been killed. Kolendorski told me, "I came quickly, to avenge him." His expression as he said this was earnest and terrible.

The personality of the squadron is 'Red' Tobin,[2] from California. He walks like a wild animal and his head is a torch of red hair. His slang adds zest to everything he says: his parachutes are 'jump sacks', his petrol is 'fire-water' or 'bang-water', and when he is about to fly he says to the ground staff: "Saddle 'er up! I'm ridin'."

I travelled up to London with 'Red', in a little train that stopped at every station. He told me his story on the way.

His family call him Eugene: he was eight years old when he flew for the first time, at "a little barn-storming show at Roger's Field, on the edge of Los Angeles." He said: "My pappy gave me a dollar and I wandered off towards an airplane—an old Fairchild cabin job. I told the pilot I wanted to go for a ride and he said, 'Is it all right with your parents?'

"My father's back was turned, but a man near him swung round at that moment and looked at me, and the pilot thought the man was my pappy. We popped around that airport and I just knew that I was born to fly. I failed at school practically every year, from ditching classes and always going out to airports. Finally, when I was older, I realized my ambition; I learned to fly. I did my first solo over Hollywood, and I flew a good deal in the High Sierras. And when the war began I just felt I

---

[1] Flying Officer S. Kolendorski, killed May 17, 1941.
[2] Flying Officer E. Q. Tobin, killed September 7, 1941.

wanted to fly some of these powerful machines, so I came over here."

I asked him: "But is that all? Wasn't there any other reason for your coming to fight?"

"Well, yes," he said, "I think it was Finland. You see, I read about her in the newspapers, and she had always paid her war debts to us, so I thought she must be a pretty good little country. Then I just thought I'd go to Finland and fight."

'Red' arrived too late to fufil his duty to Finland, so he went to France: when France fell he came to England. He told me of his first air battle, over this country. "I'd never flown a warplane until I came here. When I saw that first fighter, was I excited! I said, 'Look here, boy, this is new!' I jumped in and away we went. And, you know, I found it was just another aeroplane. Absolutely no tricks. After flying twenty minutes I decided, 'I really like this thing'."

'This thing' was one of our 1,000 horse-power Spitfires.

'Red' said: "Gee, I never thought I'd fly one of those. I put in twenty hours on Spitfires before they let me take part in the blitz. The first day I met the Jerries was when we were patrolling over the Solent. I was flying at 15,000 feet and reached down to turn on my oxygen. But I couldn't. Then we went up to 25,000 feet. Flying at that height without oxygen! Well, I didn't exactly feel sick, but I didn't feel right. We came down to 19,000 feet again and saw nine Messerschmitt 110's. There were 150 Germans in the sky that day. Well, my first battle was beginning."

I asked: "Did you *think* anything about it? Did you *feel* anything?"

'Red' answered: "Not a goddarn thing. I just said, 'There we are and there we go.' I'd had no experience in fighting. I went into the attack too fast—at 370 miles an hour. The 110 I had picked out went into a turn and I gave him a quick burst, but my stuff all went behind his tail. Then I pulled the nose up quick and gave him another burst, and wrecked his fuselage. That was the last I saw of him! I didn't see him go in, so I just claimed him as a 'probable'.

"I broke away downwards and to my left: then another 110 passed practically right in front of me, so I gave him a quick burst and stopped his left motor. He swerved and I followed him down. Then I blacked out—didn't remember a darned thing. I just dreamt, I suppose. That was at 19,000 feet. I came to at 1,000 feet, flying level, at 500 miles an hour—don't put that down in what you're writing, because the boys back home would not believe it. But I was."

'Red' then swept the story aside with his hand. We were alone in the railway carriage and he drew his big body into the corner, as if to express his modesty, and said: "But I haven't done anything. I've only got one lousy victory and three probables."

I said: "It's a noble beginning. But why do you stay and fight for us now? After all, we couldn't pay *our* war debts."

"Well," he answered, looking out of the window, towards a little farmhouse, "I guess your views change once you're over here. This is a nice little country and I don't mind fighting for it a bit."

December 26. I came down to Windsor three days ago, to stay with the Dean and be quiet. As I walked up the hill to the Castle, the London guns had already begun their booming, and the searchlights rose from the distant city. It has been pleasant to be away from it all for a night or two and to sleep within the thick, ancient walls of the Castle, which has not been attacked since the time of King John.

I am in my old bedroom, where I slept for seven years when I was working with the Dean, on our Victorian books. The furniture is the same; the bedside lamp and even the turquoise-blue ash-tray. On Christmas morning I went on to the balcony quite early. The earth in the window-boxes was cold and dead. In peace-time we used to grow great festoons of petunias here. This year, the Dean grew lettuces.

It was a day for quiet thinking. There was no noise in the sky and no aircraft flew over us; our own, or the enemy. I went to a house beside the river and drank sherry with some army officers. The war seemed as distant as a chapter in an old school-book.

When I went to bed I listened to the clock in the Curfew Tower, striking, as it did for Thomas Gray, two hundred years ago.

December 27. I broadcast to the Empire every other week and I gave my third talk this morning. It is a strange experience, to slide out of the Air Ministry in the murk of half-dawn; dark, sullen London, stirring reluctantly after a night of bombardment. About seven o'clock I scramble into my clothes and walk to Whitehall, barely conscious. There is usually a taxicab creeping past the Cenotaph. I found one this morning. The driver and the taxicab were both sleepy: we moved by cautious inches into Trafalgar Square, with the fog pressing against us.

I thought I would never have enough energy to tell my story —thirteen minutes before the microphone—a ruthless test on a chilly morning. When we came to Piccadilly I stopped the taxi-cab: I went into a chemist's shop and asked for something to waken my brain and stir my sluggish will. I don't know what it was, but the effect was astonishing. I arrived at the B.B.C. and began my broadcast. After a minute, during which I was harassed, my voice dull and thick, the drug began to work. My voice grew in strength: there were tears in my eyes, so that I could barely read the script. I finished the broadcast knowing that I had done it well.

In my original script I had mentioned that I drank sherry with some army officers on Christmas Day. The B.B.C. asked me to change it to 'tea'.

December 30. Last night the fire-bombs rained on London as never before. I stood in Knightsbridge and watched the vast, spreading flames, consuming the City. I was with Katina Paxinou and I could hear her sobbing as she clung to my arm. The night was hideous and we could see the dome of St. Paul's, a serene, dark bubble, against the saffron curtain of fire. We walked to the Strand and joined some American war correspondents. The raid was almost over. One of them, who had been out, trying to drag people from burning houses, said, "I passed a stable and heard a horse crying in the fire: it is the most terrible sound I have ever heard."

1941

February 17, 1941. Poor little Shorty Keough of the Eagle Squadron has been killed. He was a tough circus parachute jumper, exactly five feet high, and full of courage, who came over here to fight for us. The first time I saw him he had just leapt out of his aircraft and he was about one hundred yards away. At that distance he looked like a boy—swinging two cushions, one in either hand, as he walked towards us. He needed the cushions to raise himself in the aircraft before he could fly.

Later, we sat by a coke-stove in the Dispersal Hut and he told me his story. "I was talked into making my first jump," he said. "I was twenty-four then. It didn't seem so good at first. I didn't like leaving a perfectly good aeroplane up there and jumping for no reason at all. Well, I did it four times, because the guy I was working for wanted me to. I was so light, you see! Then I found I liked it."

So he made his jumps in circus shows, all over the States. There would be prosperity, followed by 'a wet Sunday' when 'things wouldn't be so hot'. Then he would 'eat on the cuff' and have to put his 'airplane into hock'.

Shorty had done 480 parachute jumps by the time that war was declared. His longest delayed jump was from 10,000 feet: he waited until he was 2,500 feet from the ground before he pulled the cord.

He abandoned the circus and crossed the Atlantic, because he wanted adventure: he also wished to help the Finns, but he arrived too late. He wandered as a refugee in France, escaped from Paris as the Germans were arriving, then crossed to England and joined the Eagles.

Shorty told me that he didn't mind what air force he was with—"As long as I was flying and as long as I was against Germany," he said. He thought the English 'over-satisfied and

49

rather slow', but he admitted that the R.A.F. is 'a hell of a good outfit'.

February, 1941. *A letter from a friend in Detroit:* "If I have seemed negligent, it was not that I haven't been thinking of you and haven't been wanting to write. . . . And then too I have been so afraid—and how afraid you must have been I hate to think—that something of a more personally tragic nature might have befallen you. . . .

"We pay lip-service to the new ideology of fighting force with force, but so far it hasn't affected our lives enough to make us face facts fairly. The draft, though not slow in getting under way, has taken off so few people we know that life is not altered by it . . . we are already saying, 'Well, a couple of years and the danger will be over and most of us won't have been called up for training.'

"The implication of this is obvious. We expect you to beat Hitler. We think you can do it. But we will continue to make ourselves think this because we don't want to come into it. We don't feel we should. Yet, if there is a crisis where we are needed, not only behind you but beside you, how will you let us know in time? So much care must be taken not to cause alarm in England; so much care must be taken not to arouse the American isolationists into concerted action. And if the time comes, it will probably come quickly. . . .

"Meanwhile, in other ways, we want so much to help Britain. . . . You know that the men at one of the aircraft plants in California, which had recently been on strike, volunteered their own time and labour to make an extra aircraft for a Christmas present to England. And it is but one example—more useful than most, but no more earnest—of the spirit of the whole country. . . ."

March 1. *My reply:* "You say that it was difficult for you to write to me. It is equally difficult for me to answer your letter because of this curious gap that has sprung up between us. A year of war has simplified us and we are less intense about it than you are. Bombing, losing one's friends, seeing houses reduced to rubble, the unending sirens, anti-aircraft guns and self-discipline over food, have become the habit of our daily life. You mustn't think that the war has killed our sense of humour . . . even over the war itself. A big crop of jokes has sprung up and we are able to laugh over our disasters.

"For me, it is a little different, because I was born in a new country and I cannot feel passionately about the frontiers in Europe. But I am British enough to share the philosophical attitude of most people in this country. We have armed ourselves against invasion. We believe that this is a war against a definite force of evil—not merely a war between Britain and Germany.

"I feel that I know the United States well enough to realize that, because of its tremendous width and diversity of blood, it must react slowly to a danger that we saw in a flash.

"I object to the phrase, 'help Britain'. Anything you do is towards something greater than the fortunes of any one nation. Equally, I believe that the British people here must realize that this is not exclusively their war. . . .

"Entire squadrons of Polish pilots believe in this war enough to have faced the hazards of crossing Europe so that they could continue to fight from this island. A few days ago, a French boy of twenty came into my office at the Air Ministry. This youngster had hidden an aircraft behind a wood and had waited, because he had very little petrol, until the wind was in his favour. Then he flew across the Channel and faced the danger of being shot at, and imprisoned because, in his clear young heart, he believed that the war could still be fought from this island. Norwegians have crossed the sea in little boats, to join us, because they share the same belief.

"If you could feel the heart of this country, and see the courage with which people swallow their disasters and then go on with their work . . . clerks bicycling to their offices, down streets upon which buildings have fallen . . . and the pathetic little remnants of furniture flung out of poor people's houses and the owners standing before them, without a complaint or a tear.

"But you must remember, as I say, that we have not lost our sense of humour. Not so long ago, during an air raid, an old gentleman arrived on the steps of the War Office carrying a small package. He explained, 'I've brought this: it belonged to my grandmother and may be of some use." It was a pearl-handled revolver—the sort one might use at the gaming tables in Monte Carlo. It is this curious balance between disaster and comic incidents that keeps one on one's toes.

"Don't pity us. Send me some Lucky Strike cigarettes instead."

March 4. Katina Paxinou arrived back in London after her ship had been torpedoed, on the way across the Atlantic—to New York, where she was to play in *Electra*. She was saved from the sea by a British destroyer, and brought to the English coast. Last night, she told me her story and I wrote it down.

She began, in her lovely, surprising voice: "I am Greek. Our lives in Greece are made of tragedy. When my grandfather was fifteen years old, he saw his father's body being dragged through the streets, without his head."

Then Katina Paxinou described the attack, and the sinking of her ship.

"I was not afraid and I was not thrilled. I was angry. It was about four o'clock in the morning. I was flung from my bunk, the marble fireplace in my cabin cracked like sugar, the ship listed, the steam from the radiator hissed and beat against my face. I remember that I stood perfectly still for a moment and, violent with temper, I said: 'The beasts! They've got us.'

"I believed in the ship. It was big and strong. The torpedo had wounded it. But it was too mighty to die. It trembled and went on. The second torpedo came, and the third. Still that strong ship went on. I heard the Captain say, 'We are steaming back to the coast at full speed.'

"Of course we were not afraid. We were too busy. Towards morning I went down to make some tea. Then I opened a porthole and saw a miserable grey dawn, with a rough sea. But the other ships of the convoy were not there. They had gone on and we were alone. Perhaps a little wave of alarm went through me then. I do not know. I was making tea.

"All day we went about our little duties. Our wounded ship was hurrying towards the English coast. That seemed safe enough. But in the afternoon—the day continued to be grey and depressing—in the afternoon the great ship trembled once more and then leaned over. That was alarming. I might have then been afraid, but I heard the calm voice of the Captain, 'Everyone to lifeboats', and I obeyed.

"There was no trouble. I even looked at a watch to know the time of all this. It was ten minutes to five, exactly. The ship was so heavily listed then that the lifeboats had swung out far from the side. We had to jump. Yes, that was an alarming moment! The vast body of the ship loomed over us, and the waves beat the lifeboat against the side.

"Then the ropes were cut and we pushed off with our oars, out into the alarming space of sea; and I remember—I will remember always—the terrible and splendid tragedy of the last minutes when the ship turned over, so that her ochre-painted bottom was uppermost, a vivid colour rising from the water; and on the horizon the splendid sun and the sky borrowing its brilliance—a curtain of crimson, with that immense orb sinking into the sea. They sank together, the ship and the sun. And as she sank the ship heaved once, like an animal using its last breath, and the engines were still going so that the propellers revolved pathetically. And they departed, the sun and the ship, and darkness came and we huddled together, cold and alone.

"Our adventure was not new. I curled up my body and watched the last shreds of light leave the sky; and then, having no occupation for my hands or mind, I allowed myself to contemplate the future, for the first time. Tales one has heard of men being in lifeboats, for days. Going mad. Starvation. My body was tired enough for my mind to play with these fantasies. Then I was sick: my body was busy once more, and my mind was at rest.

"How long was that night! It was a black, cold eternity. And then, gazing into the darkness, the Captain cried, 'I think that I see the light of a ship'. Oh, in that moment, did not the years and the anxiety and the sickness pass away, and my heart leap! For life is sweet, with all its patches of darkness. We sent up a flare! And we stared into the black, and, far away, a pale green light rose through the night like a rocket, and we knew—we knew that we would be safe.

"We came upon the British destroyer suddenly. It was not there! It *was* there, and there was enough light for us to see its long zebra-painted sides. We were taken on board. It was swift and silent, for the enemy was still in the sea and might soon be in the air. With eggs and bacon and coffee, and kindness, and hot water, and smiles, and cigarettes, our spirits returned to us. And out of my dazed, tired brain there came slowly the fact that I was a Greek woman being cared for on a British destroyer. And that these bearded sailors—these sailors who had the hearts of children and the courage of lions—were the men who were keeping the Atlantic free for our ships. And then came the reward for our disaster: I saw British character in flower—or should I say in flame? I can barely speak of it because I am shy of disturbing their modesty. But I knew, oh, so certainly, as we played and sang together—as I played those crackled notes on the little old piano for the gunner to sing in his baritone voice—as I laughed with them and saw them at their duty—I knew that the war was won. Such a spirit can never be beaten!

"So they brought me to the coast of England. And as I came on shore, I forgot the torpedo and the empty night and danger. I remember only that destroyer and the will to conquer of those men.

"And I remember one thing more—right back in my child-hood. My grandmother and my mother brought me up to believe that England was a great country and that there was always the shadow of her protecting hand over the fate of our own small Greece. That story was told to me long ago. Now I know what my old grandmother meant, and I know that what she told me was true."

March 8. The blood of all the country was quickened yesterday by the news of the raid on the Lofoten Islands. I like the fine impudence of the landing: the hoisting out of the invasion barges, and the return of the ships with the three hundred Norwegians who wish to fight for their country, from this island. There was a stimulus in the air—as if we were no longer sitting on our haunches, waiting to be attacked. I lingered to see the Norwegian sailors in Trafalgar Square today, on their way to meet their King. The sight made us all feel better, incidental as it may be in the whole pattern of the war.

March (*undated*). Some cranks, and a few wise men, send in suggestions for winning the war. One correspondent has gone so far as to propose that we drop bombs 'down the throat of Vesuvius' and thus 'explode Southern Italy'. The same idea has come from educated people, in South Africa, Australia and America. The thought is painful to those of us who dream of returning some day to the enchanting coast that runs south from Naples.

Pilots who find their tasks monotonous might like the plan of another correspondent who asks for a 'fleet of fighter planes, thirty strong' which would pretend to 'run away from the enemy'. While pretending, they would 'squirt out from the rear of each aircraft a fine spray of chloroform or the strongest narcotic possible'. The trusting German pilots 'would fly into this strata and so lose control of their machines'.

There is another plan, to drop 'enormous quantities of sticky stuff, like treacle, in front of advancing German troops'. If this failed to stop them, 'coils of barbed wire could then be dropped, to trip and entangle them'. Another patriot suggests that 'you can buy a kind of open-work dishcloth with a wide mesh for washing greasy dishes'. These could be 'scattered among the enemy formations to entangle their airscrews'. A less gentleman-like suggestion is that 'long projecting knives of razor-sharpness' should be fitted to the undercarriages of obsolete and unemployed planes: thus equipped, 'they could chase the enemy airman who baled out and fly over him in such a way that the knives would cut the parachute cord, thus causing the Hun to drop to the earth with a bump'.

A correspondent from Durban proposes that 'millions of snakes' should be shipped from South Africa and released from our aircraft 'on dark nights only', over German towns. He also suggests that 'millions of cabbage leaves' should be steeped 'in a deadly poison' and dropped among the livestock in the German and Italian fields. The same man from Durban wrote, "The war will finish 2.30 p.m. 4th May, 1945, with Britain on top."[1]

April 17. We have been through London's most terrible night. It is not easy to write down anything about it because I still feel as if I have been hit on the head with a mallet . . . I was dining in the River Room of the Savoy: it was all pretty and gay, and there was music.

We took the sirens for granted when they sounded, about nine o'clock. About ten o'clock there was a nervous movement beyond the restaurant door. I went out and found a few people going down to the shelter. With calm curiosity, of which I would have been incapable a year ago, I walked on to the Embankment . . . a bomb fell, near enough to deaden the world for a moment. Then came the noise of hurrying people; little crouching ghosts, moving against the crimson glow of the river. Flares fell in the east and the gunfire grew into wilder thudding than ever before.

I went back. People were coming down from the heights of the hotel in their pyjamas and dressing-gowns. About half past ten the bombs began to fall like loosened hell. I recall the clatter of the chess-players in the bar and an old woman on a sofa, opening and shutting her bag—a nervous occupation for her crinkled hands. There was a jovial Army officer who tried to make a joke

---

[1] I am pleased I made a note of this incredible prophecy. In *Triumph and Tragedy* (p. 469) Sir Winston Churchill writes, "On the 3rd (May) we entered Hamburg without opposition. . . . Next day, having received instructions from his superiors, Freidenburg signed the surrender of all German forces in North-West Germany, Holland, the Islands, Schleswig-Holstein, and Denmark."

of it all, and a little man who simply curled himself up near the door of the ladies' lavatory and went to sleep.

It must have been about midnight when I went into the street again. The doorman, George Chamberlain, was standing there, erect and correct as ever. Soon, the night became scarlet.

"The docks!" I heard someone say.

I was told today that bombs fell at Waterloo, in Oxford Street and King's Cross; in Victoria and Piccadilly. I suppose that I remember them. . . . About 1.30 a.m. the bombs came nearer. I went back into the hotel, up the stairs and into the hall. The Army officer was sitting there, erect and silent. The waiters smiled faintly. Then I returned to the Embankment. While I was away two bombs had fallen across the river. The smell was strange; like the smell of steel against a grindstone; like stale mushrooms. I do not know. Flames curled up from the opposite bank: then I realized a danger that involved myself. There was fire, to the right and the left, and I knew that if the flames came nearer there would be no way of escape except by jumping into the river.

Three more hours passed before the most terrible bomb of all fell, within a few yards of the hotel. . . . The building staggered. I imagined that the vast stone structure was cracking, like biscuits, and that I was living in the last second before death. Glass was flung at us, like hail through an open door. Then I smelled falling masonry. I do not remember a cry or a movement from anybody. We stood still, in the hall, waiting. The silence yielded nothing for a moment. Then I realized that the hotel was still above us. We walked over rubble and glass; then there seemed to be nurses, and people bleeding, and George Chamberlain being carried in. There was complete orderliness: injured people in a line, their faces cut, their hands cut—one with her face slashed, carrying a bottle of brandy in one hand and a powder-puff in the other. "We were blown out of bed in our flat," she said. There was only one noisy person; a warden who had been wounded, while he was on duty beside the river. They carried him in. He cried out: "I must go back to my post! I must go back to my post!"

The nurses held him down, for he was badly wounded. I

remember Mrs. Hofflin's calm voice, and Mrs. Pleydell-Bouverie, with bandages, and a Polish doctor who came forward and said, "Can I 'elp?" But they could not hold the warden: he kicked the nurses until he was free and then ran up the stairs towards the street. They cried, "Stop him!"

I was nearest so I simply had to follow: I ran after him and touched his arm. I spoke to him and he came back like a child.

I tell all this because I was pleased not to be afraid. It is the conquest of a year. I recall the early bombs, that drove me out, to the street, in the summer of last year: then my palms would sweat with fear.

There are curious gaps in my memory: I recall nothing between the moment when I spoke to the warden, and five o'clock, when I stood with some people, looking into the Strand. Two of us walked into the roadway which we had seen yesterday, busy with vehicles, cluttered with people. It looked amazed and broken in the morning light. Buildings I have known for twenty years were no more than cracked walls, with all their life collapsed into rubble. Little tongues of violet flame still licked the edges of big advertisements and the air was heavy with dust. We walked to the Adelphi, edging our way past deep holes that had been torn in the pavement. The placid Adam fronts of the houses looked afraid: I do not remember inanimate objects seeming so physical and conscious of what they had endured. Even the trees were wounded; there were scars where the bark had been torn.

We crossed the Strand. London was coming to work; message boys on bicycles had to cut half-circles to avoid the places where the rubble had tumbled into the road. I remember coils of broken wire, and those strange, little old men who haunt the London streets early in the morning; homeless, secretive, dirty old men, mumbling words that come from their clotted brains.

We walked up towards Covent Garden. There was a little pub open and we went in. It is strange that conventions could survive such a night; the barmaid said: "I am sorry, sir, but officers in uniform cannot be served here. If you'll go beyond that curtain, I'll bring you a couple of glasses of beer, certainly, sir."

Behind the curtain we found a market porter and his wife. The porter said: "We were along seeing our daughter, because her husband is in the army and she was alone. My missus had said to me, 'We'd better go and see if Elsie is all right,' so we went out. My, they were falling like hailstones then. It was about the worst time of all then, sir. We went along Gray's Inn Road to see Elsie: it's no more than a stone's throw from where we live. And we stayed with her until it was all over. When we went back to our house, it was no more. Nothing. No, nothing left!"

The woman could not speak: her face had no expression. They stood close together as if misfortune had fused them into one being. The little man went on: "Elsie will have to go to work so I brought the missus along with me to have a Guinness before I go to the market. I thought she'd be better waiting here for me until I finish." She sipped her Guinness through crinkled lips. "Well, I'll be going now, sir," said the man. He patted his wife's hand and hurried off. We followed him; we stood by the corner and saw the pageant of spring flowers; trays of cinerarias and daffodils, bright green palms with their bowing fronds, and trucks of vegetables, arriving at the market. The country feeding the town; the life of London going on. I went back to my room, took a cold shower and stumbled off to the Air Ministry.

April 18. Last night I met a Dutchman who has just arrived after spending six months on the journey from the Dutch East Indies to London. He came by way of the United States. He told me that the people in the Dutch East Indies are of one mind about the war: they work and pray for the destruction of Nazi Europe —that there were faint murmurs against us in India, but less anger than two years ago. He says that the English are more friendly than they used to be. "They are all so kind," he said. "I have not felt as a foreigner for one moment since I arrived."

April 20. *A letter from John Nesbitt Sellers*[1]*:* "The clouds have now become my neighbours. Great solid white cumulus monsters lolling in a brilliant blue sky, five, six or seven thousand feet above the patchwork of England. A short time ago, for the first time, my instructor and I climbed to 6,000 feet. I was 'under the hood', flying by instruments. I saw the altimeter slowly ticking up the feet. I had never been so high. I felt gay and at ease. I could hear my instructor whistling in the telephones.

" 'Right, I've got her. Hood back,' he said. I pulled back the hood and blinked in the white sunlight. All around were enormous white clouds. We were in a dark blue lane between two of them. And, as far as I could see, they lay like colossal lumps of snow in blue sauce. Far below, England was green and red and black.

" 'Look—that lane on your right; go on, turn down there. Don't touch the clouds.' We turned into a crevasse. It reminded me of crevasses in the Franz Josef glacier—except for the great size of the towering white walls on either side.

" 'Turn round that corner. Keep left. Don't touch the cloud.'

" We skirted the cloud. 'Hope no one's coming the other way, keeping right.' We laughed.

" Then we hit a small cloud. 'Oh, smash,' cried my instructor. And next, 'See that little cloud down there! Shoot it up.' Down we dived. Then, whish, up and we took off the top of the cloud. 'Oh, poor little cloud,' came the voice from the front cockpit.

" Full of life, we settled down to more serious work. Loops, spins, etc. Since that day I have climbed up above the clouds, alone, choosing a nice big gap to climb through, to practice loops and spins. I like the clouds, and I like to see the clumps of balloons lying above them—provided they are miles away from me, of course!

" Have you ever looked at England from 5,000 feet, upside down? Don't. It looks terrible! Especially if your straps give a little, and your posterior moves a couple of inches away from the solid seat. The first time we flew upside down, my straps

---

[1] John Nesbitt Sellers, a New Zealand friend. Staff of *The Times*, 1939-1940, killed while flying, on November 19, 1941.

clicked and I dropped down an inch. I thought one of them had burst. I brought the plane round 'topside' in a roaring dive. My instructor said, 'That's not much good. What's the matter?'

"I told him that I thought my straps had gone wrong, and it had disturbed me.

"'Yes,' he said. 'I heard a click, but I saw that you were still there all right.'

"Consoling, no doubt, but I *still* felt very suspicious about those straps! It's extraordinary, you know, but the chief impression I get from flying upside down is the smell of petrol. It seems so strangely 'of the earth, earthy' to smell petrol 5,000 feet up. Incidentally, how damned funny we must look, sailing along with the undercarriage sticking up in the sky.

"'Upside down' reminds me of a charming incident a few days ago. A new pupil said he felt he was going to be ill. So his instructor said, 'Well, you're not going to make a mess in *this* machine,' and promptly flew upside down until the worst was over.

"Everybody is doing solo aerobatics now. It is an amusing sight, sometimes on a cloudy day, to watch the inside of a break in the clouds. It will soon seem to be filled with crazy flies, all looping and rolling in the blue gap.

"Personally, I prefer my very own piece of sky, on a fine day, for my aerobatics. One's friends are so familiar and inclined to be matey in the air! Alone, you only have passing Wellingtons, Hampdens, or Hurricanes, etc., to watch for. Sometimes I daringly chase a Hampden, and then an awful doubt comes over me. What if it should be a Dornier? It makes you feel very silly when you think such thoughts!

"My cross-country test is a pathetic tale. I had to fly solo to another station, 60 miles away . . . far from being a wildly exciting tussle with maps, pinpoints and compass, it was very tame. Simply, I put myself on course and, in general, just sat there while the clouds rolled by overhead and the earth rolled smoothly by underfoot. Each pinpoint popped up in the right spot and it was all rather dull.

"At last the strange aerodrome came in sight. Here was the climax! I circled twice, then down. A 3-pointer. Doubtless an admiring crowd would be on the tarmac to see my monoplane. (Those Moths look such kites!)

"Not a soul! Just a solitary airman who was annoyed because I wanted petrol when he wanted lunch. Was I mortified!

"With 60 hours in my logbook I feel quite confident now. It's got to the stage when our instructor looks at the weather, notes where it is thickest, and then sends his three pupils off solo, to find tiny pinpoints, like windmills, pubs and churches, from 2,000 feet. When we turn up after the usual 45 minutes, he says, 'Good God! You back again! What a nuisance you are! Why don't you get lost?'

"It's grand to feel your confidence growing, and grander still to be able to show your instructor that his time and care have not been wasted. Grandest to hear him say it."

April 24. *A letter from John Simpson,*[1] *Aldergrove, N. Ireland:* "Many months have passed since I brought down my last enemy, in daylight . . . so many things have happened in between . . . that the combats of the summer and autumn of 1940 seem to be a complete and distant chapter of my life. I brought down German aircraft over France, Scotland, Southern England and the North Sea. That story is dead and done with. My combat at night, over Northern Ireland, when I brought down a Heinkel III, demanded tactics and method of attack so completely new that my past experience was of very little help to me.

"I was in the Mess when news came that the Germans were dropping bombs on Belfast. It seemed rather strange. The war had not come so close to Ulster before. Incendiaries had been dropped, and high explosives were on the way.

"I was next to patrol. It was about 1.15 in the morning, dark, with a sickly moon shining through a mist. I took off and climbed to about 9,000 feet, passing above the clouds, into another world, where the moon, in its second quarter, shone out of a

[1] Group Captain J. W. C. Simpson, D.F.C. and bar. Died, August 12, 1949.

"We have been through London's most terrible night" (see p. 56)

Sergeant James Allen Ward, V.C., R.N.Z.A.F. (see p. 79)

blue-black sky, peppered with stars. Below was the floor of clouds like silver-grey snow.

"I was told that there were aircraft near me. My eyes searched the blackness. There was no horizon; no object upon which to fix one's eyes. And one had the illusion, travelling at two hundred miles an hour, that every one of those brilliant stars was the tail light of an aircraft.

"I searched among the moving pattern of lights and my eyes rested on two black objects. I could see them because, as they moved, they obliterated the stars. They were quite near when I recognized them as aircraft . . . whether enemy or not, I was unable to tell. So I flew nearer and learned soon enough. The rear gunners of both aircraft fired a shower of bullets at me, some glowing red . . . perhaps incendiaries. They missed me and, for a minute, I lost them. Then I saw them again, farther apart, moving against the white floor of the clouds below me: black, and quite clear. The advantage was now mine: they were perfectly placed as targets. I crept down to attack the rearmost of them. They were flying slowly and it was difficult for me to withhold my speed so that I would not overtake them. At a distance of about two hundred yards I opened fire from slightly below.

"Then came my next surprise . . . the blinding flash of my guns, in the darkness. In daytime, one does not see it. At night it is terrific: I was so blinded that I lost sight of my enemy. I broke away and lost him for a few seconds. I next saw him going into a gentle dive towards the clouds. The increase in his speed made it easier for me to attack, and I closed in to eighty yards. I opened fire once more. This time I was prepared for the flash and kept my eyes on the enemy. His rear gunner returned my fire, but only for a second. I had apparently got him, for he was silent after that. I continued my fire, closing in to about fifty yards: then I saw a comforting red glow in his belly. I was still firing when the Heinkel blew up, with a terrific explosion which blew me upwards and sideways. When I righted myself, I was delighted to see showers of flaming pieces, like confetti on fire, falling towards the sea which was now below me. I had travelled forty to fifty miles during the combat. When my mind was quiet again, I was

E

able to enjoy the satisfaction of knowing that I had brought him down *before* he had released his bombs.

"The second Heinkel had disappeared. I asked for homing instructions over the wireless. The beacon which guided me was, unfortunately, the glow of fire on the clouds; the fire which the incendiaries had made in Belfast.

"There is one note I should like to make before I end. People are a little too apt to give all the credit for these victories to the pilot, forgetting the keenness and pride of the ground crew. I felt this very much when I went to my aircraft next morning, after a few hours' sleep. On the side of the fuselage are ten swastikas. I landed soon after two o'clock in the morning, after bringing this fresh Heinkel down. The crew were waiting for me, to rearm and refuel, in case I had to go up again. They did this quicker than ever before, and I went off to the crew-room. When they finished their work, they painted a new swastika on the fuselage, by the cockpit, so that it would be there for me in the morning."

April 26. Another letter from John Sellers: "I assume you know why I am here. It all seems a little unreal to me. Who am *I*, to presume to hope to instruct? Think of it; three new pupils to know; to study, to help fly, to stop crashing you, every few weeks. I am flying *Moths* here—just retribution for my sneers in the past.

"I am twenty-seven and a half today! And one hundred hours. I mean 4 days and 4 hours. What? Why, one hundred hours flying, of course. I thought my first solo would be the most memorable of all things. That is wrong. One hundred hours is more exciting.

"In my last flight this morning I had half an hour more to do to reach my century. What a half-hour! I did loops, and stall turns and slow rolls. I sang, and I sideslipped almost to the ground before straightening out to land. Talk about the Emperor of Abyssinia arriving back in Addis Ababa! His feelings couldn't have touched mine. One hundred hours and still alive! A journalist! Imagine it! Applying my case to the international scene . . . well, I just don't see how we can lose this war.

"Since last I wrote I have moved from . . . the smutty, smoky Midlands, to an E.F.T.S. in Scotland. . . . Here, amid banks and braes and ghillies and White Label, I am training as an instructor. I can't believe it. . . . How marvellous to be able to do the job for others that our instructors did and are doing, for us!

"My instructor before was, as you know, a Canadian. He is my model. My instructor now is an Englishman who has just come off Hurricanes. He is calm, cynical and charming—just the type to round off my flying. And simply a mass of practical tips. My God, what grand luck I have had in the R.A.F.! If civil life ever comes again it's my ambition to be a 'Flying Reporter'.

"I must tell you the devastating results of a further development. Over a pint I told my new instructor how I now watch birds; how we all watch a crow or a gull and say, 'What a superb stall turn!' 'Look at that glide!' 'Wow! Look at its landing attitude—magnificent two-pointer.' And he told me about flies. Flies have given him a hell of a lot of trouble. How the devil do they land upside on a ceiling?

"Well, I went into a pub a week or two ago and brought the subject up to the landlord—ex-R.F.C. 'How do flies land on the ceiling?'

"'Oh,' he said. 'That's easy. They hit it at the top of a loop.'

"Then a local inhabitant piped up. 'You're wrong. That would break their legs. Obviously they do a slow roll and then grab the ceiling at stalling speed.'

"Profound silence. Then a young man in the corner, aged about 18, came up to the bar. 'If I may intrude,' he said, 'what about this idea? Perhaps they just climb, lose speed, switch off, and then, just before spinning down, they touch up?'

"That settled it. Or started it. Two hours later people in the bar were behaving like an acrobatic troupe. Mine host hit his head while demonstrating a loop. In one corner, two Polish soldiers were almost fighting. In another, an old Scot was silently and concentratedly swooping his hand over his Scotch ale (very strong) trying to make his palm land on the bottom of the mantelpiece! Chaos!

"A week later I dared to return. Said mine host: 'Your flies! Young Angus has gone to join up in the R.A.F.' (He was the young man in the corner.) 'And look!' With the concentration of a scientist, the old Scot was silently swooping his hand over his drink, still trying to make it land upside down on the mantelpiece!

"'And the bother of it all,' said mine host, 'is that not one bloody fly has been in this bar from that day to this!' "

May 20. The scene was a little restaurant in Chelsea. A young officer walked in, with his respirator and tin hat over his shoulder. But the drab tin hat had no badge painted on it.

At another table sat an old gentleman with a magnificent beard.

"What is he? Is he an artist?" asked the officer.

"Yes," said the waiter, "a very clever artist."

The young officer went over and said: "Excuse me, but I hear that you paint. Would you please paint my badge on my tin hat for me?"

"Certainly," said the artist. He was Mr. Augustus John.

May 24. In the early days of the war, when Mr. Winston Churchill was still waiting for his conquest, I lunched at Holland House which has since been bombed. After lunch, I was sitting next to Mr. Churchill: the talk moved to the King and Queen, then at the beginning of their war work and influencing the country with their quiet example. Somebody at the table tried to define this influence and Mr. Churchill, with his genius for quickening the occasion with the right phrase, said, "Yes, they have the rare talent of being able to make a mass of people realize, in a flash, that they are good."

I have been wondering about this quality of 'goodness'. How important is it in relation to the war?

There emerges one truth, in regard to the leaders on both sides. It is significant that none of the rulers of the Axis powers is a 'good' man, in the sense that Mr. Churchill spoke of the King and Queen. The only one with an ideal family life was Hess who, for reasons that remain his own secret, chose to imperil his wife and children to save himself.

Hitler is, of course, a pathological case: a subject for Freud, or even Havelock Ellis. Mussolini, who might have been a great man, had he remained a domestic reformer and not hankered after extravagances of power, has sacrificed his domestic happiness in untidy morals.

One summer day, ten years ago, I spent an hour with Mussolini, in his room at the Palazzo Venezia, in Rome. I thought him charming and I believed in his greatness. I wonder now what poison there was, behind his friendly talk of England: what weakness turned him from the achievements of a solid domestic reformer, to play such a humiliating role at the heels of such a master?

The way that both enemy leaders throw aside their associates and generals is some guide to the low degree of confidence that exists between them. They are men without friends: their relationships are laced with suspicion, fear and treachery. They are ungenerous and pompous.

It is exhilarating to turn from the gloomy concept of human nature that Hitler and Mussolini represent, to the leaders of our own cause; to the manners and code of behaviour shared between Mr. Roosevelt and Mr. Wendell Wilkie, and Mr. Churchill and Mr. Neville Chamberlain. Last November, when Mr. Roosevelt was re-elected President, Mr. Wilkie—his opponent—said of him: "We have elected Franklin Roosevelt President. He's your President. He's my President. We all owe him the respect due to the high office. We give that respect. We will support him with our best efforts for our country."

In the afternoon of Tuesday, in the same week, Mr. Churchill said that it had fallen to Mr. Neville Chamberlain "In one of the supreme crises of the world, to be contradicted by events, to be disappointed by his hopes, and to be deceived and cheated by a wicked man. These hopes, these wishes were surely among the most noble and benevolent instincts of the human heart."

What a difference lies between the manners and ethics within these two stories, and the jealousy and suspicion that hamper the leadership of our enemies!

June 2. I have been in Cornwall for three days, with John Simpson. Last evening we walked down to St. Ives. The gulls had deserted the beach and the black-out lay on the coast. A careless fisherman on the far side of the bay struck a match and, against the enforced darkness, it was quite a dangerous blaze, had there been an enemy aircraft about.

The bar-room of the little pub was so full of smoke that the twenty odd sailors peered at each other through a haze. They reminded me of fish in an aquarium, swimming up to the glass and gliding back into mistiness again. The barmaid was hot and tired, and her hair fell in wisps over her eyes when she bent down to draw more and more pints from the barrel.

Here is the last tongue of English land that stretches into the Atlantic—a brave piece of land, extended towards America. The Cornish are born with the smell of the sea in their nostrils: in peace-time they are fishermen, but now they defend their island with the same grim pride that compelled their ancestors into battle, a thousand years ago.

We were sipping our beer, and gossiping. The talk moved to the subject of *fear*, and the effect of bombing, on our nerves and courage. A stout little man in the corner, with his sailor's cap pushed back on his head, said: "Well, I don't mind admitting that I have never been so scared in my life as when the first bomb fell. But I've got rather used to them now."

Then the police-sergeant's son, who knows every rock on this coast for a hundred miles or more, leaned over the table and answered: "It's funny. We can talk about fear quite sensibly nowadays. One doesn't seem to be ashamed of it. From what I've seen, it's the man who is capable of fear who is best in an emergency. He has more imagination to work on. There's a lot of rot talked about fear."

We tried to dig into this mystery of human courage and someone told the well-known tale of the early days of bombing. Some men were working on an unexploded bomb that had plunged into the earth. It was their job to dig it out and they worked, face to face with death, for several hours. Then an air-raid warning sounded and they dropped their spades, deserted the bomb, and ran to a shelter.

One of the sailors in the bar has been with convoys since the beginning of the war. (I have seen few lovelier sights than a convoy of merchantmen cruising slowly down the coast: some-times fifty mighty ships, bow to stern, coming safely home, heavy-laden with food.) He is home for a rest, filling an already comfortable stomach with Cornish pasties, and pilchards, the favourite food here, when lobsters are out of season. The sailor's views on fear were brutally final. He said: "Well, what's the use of fear, anyway? I think that if your number's up, it's up." He went on: "It's funny, the thoughts that pass through your head when you're in the water. Now I was in a ship when we were proceeding down the coast, as they say, and we were attacked by a Jerry bomber that came down on us out of a cloud, like a flash. I was looking after the Lewis gun but I hadn't time to do much about it before a bomb struck the ship. The 'old man' tried some evasive tactics, but it was no good. Two more of those ruddy bombs came, and it was all up with us. Well, to make a long story short, the ship was done in, and she went down so quickly that some of us hadn't time to get into the boats.

"I jumped—that's all. I was in the water for about ten minutes. It was quite warm and I thought I'd better swim. I don't know why I did it, but I started to take off my clothes, thinking that if I had to swim, I'd do it better that way. And do you know what I suddenly thought of? The half-dollar in the pocket of my belt!

"And there I was in the water, and all I thought was, 'If I take off that ruddy belt, the half-dollar'll be gone, and I won't have any money to buy a pint when I get on shore—*two* pints, to be more exact. You can bet your bottom dollar I kept on that belt until somebody hauled me into a boat.

"It was Spitfires that saved us from being fired on while we were in that lifeboat. Those ruddy Jerries hadn't the guts of a louse. They'd have flown over us and machine-gunned us into mincemeat, if it wasn't for those Spitfires that arrived. Do I love Spitfires? I'll say I do.

"Do you know what I did when I landed? I went home to my missus and ate everything she had in the house, along with a couple of pints. Then I took out my motor-bike, which isn't much use to me at sea, anyway, and I took it round to a garage and sold it for seven pounds ten, and gave the seven pounds ten to the Spitfire fund. I've got a soft spot in my heart for Spitfires."

The police-sergeant's son said: "Speaking of that half-dollar, I've got a friend who was blown out of his ship, and he landed in the water safe as a daisy. A bit shaken, he was, but not a mark anywhere. *He* took off his clothes to make it easier to swim. Then he was picked up by a boat, just as it was getting dark. There were some others picked up too and, just as they were going off in the boat, he saw a dark shape floating in the water. He thought it was one of his mates and he fished it out. And do you know what it was? It was his own trousers, with five ruddy pound notes in the pocket. That puts your half-dollar in the shade."

Then the old sailor spoke. He said: "The only thing that's ever frightened me was fire. I don't like fire. It puts the wind up me. I was in the *Valorous* in the spring—April it was, I think. We were escorting a fairly big convoy, bringing food, when an Me. 110 came down much closer than was good for us. But we got the bastard. Yes, we got him all right. He just crashed down, missed us and fell into the masts of one of the ships we was convoying. Astern of us, it was. The Me. 110 broke up and pieces of it fell on the deck. The most part of it fell into the sea. I saw it topple over, like a sort of big dead bird, but the petrol had leaked out and it ran all over the deck and it caught fire. God Almighty, it wasn't too cheerful, seeing those flames leaping up. They were so high one minute that you'd have said the ship was a goner.

Then they got them in hand and there wasn't a sign of anything. And, do you know, I heard afterwards that the men in the galley just went on making the tea, which they were making anyhow, when the Jerry crashed. And the officers sat down to their tea, punctual to the minute, as though nothing had happened."

Then we fell to talking of prisoners of war; of how frightened some of them are when they are picked up in the water. The old sailor told us of a German who had been entangled with his parachute. When one of our sailors took out his knife to cut the cord, the German screamed. He thought that he was about to have his throat slit.

A corporal on leave, proud of his new stripes, told us the next story. His brother is a gunner's mate and his ship had been sunk by a German aircraft. He jumped clear and kept himself afloat on a piece of wreckage. The soldier said: "He was clinging to the plank of wood when he saw a raft—at least, he thought it was a raft. So he let go the piece of wood and swam over to the raft and, believe it or not, it was a rubber dinghy—a German one, with three Jerries inside. They were from the aircraft that had sunk his ship; it had been hit and it had crashed into the water. And, believe it or not, those Jerries were so windy that they handed their revolvers over to my brother and gave themselves up as prisoners. So he just sat there with them until they were picked up."

At ten o'clock the barmaid was already washing the glasses: the host gave us a hint by turning out one of the lights, so we left the pub and walked to the silent shore. The sailors left us and went home to their cottages, that clung together, in groups, near the sea. I walked up the hill with John, who has brought down twelve German aircraft since the war began. We came to the height of the cliff, with the great spaces of the night about us and he said, "That was interesting; they are great people." Then, slowly: "You were all trying to say something that is true of people who live on an island like this. The reason why the English have never become decadent is because they *are* islanders. We have had generations of fishermen, and sailors going out into the world and their healthiness has corrected the usual diseases of civilization. That is why the British are able to fight the Battle of the Atlantic."

When we came to the last headland, before turning from the sea, we saw a group of men, in uniform, silhouetted against the sky. We were challenged: one of them spoke to us and flashed his torch upon our identification cards. But there was one who did not turn his head: he looked over the Atlantic, searching for any sign of the enemy.

June 8. Last evening I went to the first night of *The Gondoliers*, at the Savoy Theatre. Rupert D'Oyly Carte is rather brave, bringing the company to Town during the blitz. Some of the theatres are bombed and useless; most of them are empty.

It was all so quick and pretty, one forgot the war for two hours or more. Almost every man in the theatre was in uniform. In the interval I talked to a friend who is with the Navy. He was torpedoed on his last voyage. He arrived at Plymouth yesterday morning and, hearing that the theatre was opening last night, he jumped on a train because, he said, he 'felt like some music'.

June 12. I talked with Mr. Hofflin, manager of the Savoy, for a long time last night, about the early days of bombing. At the beginning of the summer blitz in 1940, he went into every one of the five hundred rooms each time bombs fell nearby. It took him almost two hours to open every door and examine each room with his torch. He did not dare switch on the lights in case the black-out had been blown away.

The first bombs that hit the hotel were two of a stick that fell in November of 1940. One struck the parapet in front of the hotel and exploded in mid-air. The second bomb was a direct hit: two people were killed in one room, which was destroyed. There are scars on the façade. . . . The Savoy suffered a little from bombing in the last war, so it is now a veteran.

The effects from the mid-air explosion are interesting. Nobody was hurt, but shrapnel and broken glass were blown into the bedrooms, so fiercely that furniture was pierced in many places. The minute pieces, that went through wardrobe doors, tore the garments inside to ribbons. Two weeks later, people were discovering rents in their clothes from small chips of shrapnel that had made almost indistinguishable holes in the wardrobe doors. Sixty rooms were put out of action, but life in the hotel went on.

Mr. Hofflin said that he was so disturbed by his responsibility to people in the hotel—sometimes nine hundred of them— that he could not rest. There were deaf, dumb and blind people among the nine hundred and his anxiety drove him into a restless parade of the passages, hour after hour.

The effect of the bombing on people's nerves varied. One night, during a violent raid, Mr. Hofflin opened a bedroom door and found a Dutch banker, sound asleep, although a bomb had fallen outside and blown all his windows in. There was a similar episode with one of the American war correspondents whose windows were blown all over his bed. Fortunately, the shower of glass missed his head: he got out, emptied the glass from the eiderdown, went back to bed and was asleep again in a few minutes.

One of the most valiant is Larry Rue, who represents the *Chicago Tribune*. There must be an odd streak in Colonel MacCormick's stubborn insensitiveness, for him to choose Larry Rue, for he is the least prejudiced, most authentic correspondent of them all. On the night of the worst blitz he was playing a three-handed game of chess with Hiley Bathurst and Fred Neumann in the bar. Even when the nearest bomb came, with a thunderous whack that made the building tremble, while glass fell in clattering showers and people were blown on to the floor, each of the three clung to the chess-board with one hand and to his drink with the other. Then they went on with the game: Hiley Bathurst swears that one pawn fell off the board and that, in the fuss, he was able to put it back in an improved position.

June 13. *Another letter from John Sellers:* ". . . By June 15 I shall be an instructor *and have my wings*, or else be a failure. Those wings never seemed more desirable than now, when they are actually in the shop window! How doubly desirable too, when one knows some of the people who wear them; for they are the incentive and spur to the greatest of any efforts. At the moment I feel so tired and stale that I am almost despondent about my chances in the C.F.S. test. My gliding approaches have cracked up, my judgment gone, and I—who used to be known as a 'hog for hours'—find myself actually relieved when I am told, 'No more flying today for you.' It's probably what psychologists call a 'plateau period'.

"If it were hot, Scotland would be a dream now. We hired a car last week. We left here at 11 a.m. and returned at 11 p.m. We travelled 120 miles through lochs, glens, woods, shoots, mountains and little towns; through all the greens in the colour system; among birds; among lambs that dashed to us and bit our hands. The change was tremendous: to be away from routine; to have the company of one's choice.

"Now I know why Scots and New Zealanders mix so well. Their countries are to the same design, although the scale differs. The people are similar; forthright, community-minded, solid, and generous to visitors. And we met a woman typical of Britain—only produced by Britain, and a fast-fading type. Aged about 50–60, dressed in tartan. Fishing all day. Excellent shot. Knows all Scotland and all in it. Contemptuous of what others think of her. Civilized, eccentric, alive."

June (*later*). I was on leave in Essex when news came of the attack on Russia and the spreading of the war, to the east. John Simpson was with me. He said, "Well, with the Russians in as well, we'll be less alone." Then, "It should give our boys a rest: the Huns will have to lay off us for a while." This seemed such a pale comment, on an event that will no doubt change the tides of the war.

We went down to the village pub and listened to the drinkers, wondering what 'the Russians' were like. But there was no excitement, or realization that such a mighty ally will engage much of Germany's air power and allow us a lull in the long horror. I was irritated by the casualness: yet, when we returned to the house and worked in the garden, weeding and hosing, we never mentioned what was turning over and over in our own minds.

July 8. After my leave was over I drove up to London with John Simpson. He wears his D.F.C. as a reward for his 'confident and offensive spirit'. As we were passing through Stansted, a bee flew into the car and settled on his leg. He stopped the car; then he lifted the bee carefully, between the thumb and first finger of his glove, and threw it out of the window. He turned and, with a serious, strained look, he said, "You know, I have been terrified of bees ever since I was a child."

July 29. I went to Buckingham Palace today, to see John receive a bar to his D.F.C. The ceremony was simple and personal. The King's smile, most engaging to watch—he never seemed to tire or show the slightest anxiety as he shook all those hands, and pinned on the medals.

In the long line was Miss Victoria Drummond whom I met at Windsor, many years ago. She is a god-daughter of Queen Victoria. The span of time seems wide when one realizes that four sovereigns have lived at Windsor since she was smiled on by her godmother in the last year of the Queen's reign.

At the age of seventeen, Victoria Drummond startled her Scottish family—the Drummonds of Megginch—by saying that she wished to be an engineer. Every morning she travelled from the lovely old castle of Megginch, into Dundee, for her training. Then she went to sea; she sailed to the Antipodes many times, as third engineer. She is the only woman engineer afloat with the mercantile navy. Her story is best told by a sailor who was on her ship.

"She's a bundle of character—that's all you can say. Not a pretty woman, mind you—big hands, no fear, no nerves. I remember someone saying that her inside must be made of copper wire and catgut. She has what you might call a 'way' with engines. She coaxes them; she has an uncanny way with them: she'd get as much as three-quarters of a knot more out of them than any of the others. She once said that she 'just talked nicely to them'. Well, we were glad she did.

"One day we were bombed. A Jerry with four engines attacked us when we were 470 miles from land. He was a big devil, and he bombed us for thirty minutes, until he hadn't the sign of a bomb left.

"It was a hot thirty minutes. All that was breakable in the ship was broken. We had to eat everything off one plate after the battle was over. Phones and speaking-tubes were put out of action—clocks, everything. But we were still floating, thanks to God, the Captain, and Miss Victoria Drummond. You see, she had been below all the time, coaxing those engines, and she'd got twelve and a half knots out of them, which they hadn't done in all their eighteen years.

"Miss Drummond was talking to the Chief Engineer on deck when the Jerry came over. It was as lovely a day as you could wish. She just went below and took over, cool as a cucumber. Not a bit of fuss! Down there, in that engine-room, she did her stuff. The first salvo flung her against the levers and nearly stunned her. I suppose she realized then that all was up. At least she must have thought so, because she called the engine-room staff and the stoke-hole staff together and, so they told me, she just pointed to the ladder and said, 'Get out!' You see, she gave them a chance for their lives and, as it was her job, she stayed down there, with scalding steam coming from the main injection pipe, just above her head. That pipe should have burst by rights. But she 'just coaxed it', as she said, each time there was an explosion from those bloody bombs. She just eased down when one of them was coming. I suppose she could tell by the noise. Then she opened up the steam again, when the blast was over, and went hell for leather for speed.

"One of the officers saw her during the action, when he looked down a skylight. He said that she was standing there, calm as you like, on the platform. Her arm was stretched above her head and her hand was holding down the spoke of the throttle control. She was urging every pound of steam through the straining pipes. He said that her face was as white as a sheet, and a long streak of fuel oil ran down her face, blinding one eye. It must have been hell for her. He said that she had jammed her ears at first, with oily waste, to deaden the noise: but then she tore the waste out, in case she missed some orders from the bridge."

The sailor ended his story. "I saw Miss Drummond when the bombs finished and we were quiet again. She was a bloody marvel. She just forgot all about it and was full of beans again. I saw her picking up spent bullets and splinters as if—as if they were acorns."

Miss Drummond would have delighted her god-mother who once said, "Strange, but I have never known what it was to be afraid."

July 18. I have just returned from an R.A.F. station in the north of England—a dull, flat aerodrome, within a mile or so of the sea. There are not many trees, and no hills; and there is no town in which the aircrews might find diversion when their tasks are over. So they have to invent their own amusements. They were contented, amiable and kind. But what I liked seeing was the mixture of blood and race among the men working there. I saw an alert little airman from Barbados, darting about under a bomber that had just landed. There were Irishmen, Scotsmen and Englishmen from our own islands, a South African commanding the station, an Australian sergeant-pilot, and twenty or more Canadians. A Pole arrived for lunch, and a Czech pilot landed and joined us during the afternoon.

While the war goes on, with hazard and conquest, these men are meeting together all over the British Isles. I like to think that they are forming an international army of the mind that will fortify us when peace comes. As an older man, trying to see the war in terms of history, I believe this meeting of pilots from all over the world is an important and good aspect of the war.

I spoke with the Canadians; one of them said, "We need the experience you can give us." Another said, of the mixing of nationalities in the squadrons on the station, "It will make us less insular, all of us. It is good for a pilot from Warsaw and one from Saskatoon to eat side by side. They learn a lot from each other."

August 13. I was in the bar last evening when I was called to the telephone, by name. I had not noticed a group of New Zealand pilots, drinking their sundowners. When I left the telephone one of them walked over to me. He comes from Eketehuna and his name is Page. His friends called him 'Babe' because he is as high as the average shoulder. He said, "Look here, you are Hector Bolitho, aren't you?"

I said, "Yes."

He challenged me, "You were born in New Zealand, weren't you?"

I said, "Yes."

Then, "Are you ashamed of it?"

"Of course not—why?"

"Well," he answered, "why haven't you got *New Zealand* flashes on the shoulders of your uniform?"

I explained that as I have not lived in New Zealand for almost a quarter of a century I did not believe I could, or should, wear them.

This morning, 'Babe' arrived early with two *New Zealand* flashes for my shoulders. "Have those sewn on, Squaddy," he said, "or we'll have you laid on the floor."

Meekly, I sent my tunic to the tailor and within an hour I was a New Zealander again.

I dined with the New Zealand pilots. It was a great occasion for me. They are not all pleased with England. They think the English cold and aloof, and not very efficient. The moment they cross into Scotland they are happy.

Marshal of the R.A.F., Sir John Slessor, G.C.B., D.S.O., M.C.

From a photograph by Karsh of Ottawa

A U-boat, attacked and destroyed by a Liberator, in the Atlantic, April 23, 1943

August 17. I dined with some Americans and did not realize for some time that my neighbour, Sam Spewack, was the author of *Mr. Deeds*. He was very depressed because there were no bombs: the sight of our old London wounds is not enough for him. I smiled with veteran superiority. He is very good company; no Hollywood nonsense and no airs. And the most warming smile. He told me that the aircraft factories in California are turning out machines, day and night. The noise of testing them, over Hollywood, is so great that the studios can no longer take outdoor shots. The recording devices pick up the sound of the aircraft so the film directors must now do all their work inside the studios.

September 20. On the night of July 7, a Wellington bomber was returning to the English coast, having dropped bombs on Münster. One of the crew was Sergeant James Allen Ward of the 75th (New Zealand) Squadron. He was already an old hand at bombing the enemy: in his own words, he had done "two Kiels, one Düsseldorf, one Cologne, one Brest, one Münster and a Mannheim".

The Wellington was passing over the Zuider Zee at 13,000 feet when a Messerschmitt 110 rose out of the darkness beneath and hit the bomber with cannon shell and incendiary bullets which set the starboard engine on fire. The flames were fed by petrol from a split pipe and it seemed that they might spread over the entire wing. As the bomber flew on and the fire increased, the crew broke a hole in the fuselage so that they might turn the extinguishers on to the flames. In desperation, they even used the coffee from their flasks. But the fire was too strong and it continued to spread.

Jimmy Ward then volunteered to climb out, along the wing, and smother the flames with an engine cover: he said he would go without his parachute, to reduce the wind resistance, but his companions induced him to take it. A rope was tied to him as he climbed out of the fuselage: but this precaution was also a danger —had he been blown off the wing. He broke footholds into the

F

fabric, with his boots, then he descended, three feet, on to the wing. He said, afterwards: "It was just a matter of getting something to hang on to. It was like being in a terrific gale, only much worse than any gale I've ever known. As I got along the wing I was behind the airscrew, so I was in the slipstream as well. Once or twice I thought I was going."

He hung on to the wing and smothered the flames in the fabric with the canvas engine cover: then he tried to push the canvas into the hole and on to the leaking pipe. Each time he withdrew his hand, the cover was blown away. In the end, it was dragged out of his hands by the violence of the wind and lost in the night, but the flames had been subdued. Jimmy Ward began his cautious return, along the wing and into the aircraft. He said: "Getting back was worse than going out; by this time I was pretty well all in. The hardest of the lot was getting my right leg in. In the end the navigator reached out and pulled it in."

In the official report that came to the Air Ministry I read, "The flight home had been made possible by the gallant action of Sergeant Ward in extinguishing the fire on the wing in circumstances of the greatest difficulty and at the risk of his life."

A few days later I read that Jimmy Ward had been given the Victoria Cross.

As a New Zealander, of an older generation, I wondered what he would be like. New Zealanders are no longer English: their skulls are a different shape and they are tall, broad-shouldered and loose-limbed. When I first met Jimmy Ward, I was surprised, for he was short, and timid at first. He was sitting on the edge of the Savoy Hotel bar, swinging his legs, like a schoolboy sitting on a desk. His voice was neither deep nor sonorous. He did not talk of bombers and I was too shy to speak of the quiet maroon ribbon—his V.C.—on his tunic. But he became less shy and talked of New Zealand, for England had not yet touched him. He talked of the Maoris and, because he had been a school teacher, in a Maori school, he sang us some of their songs.

On the third day of his leave he seemed a little tired. I suspected that the limelight was bothering him, for the autograph hunters gave him little peace, so I said, "Let's lunch quietly by ourselves. We won't talk of the R.A.F. or of bombers. Just let us gossip about New Zealand."

His enthusiasms were curiously chosen, and personal. The school in which he had been a teacher was near a forest, so he loved trees. He said, of the old tree-trunks that had been buried in the Wanganui River, for thirty or forty years: "They make beautiful panelling. The graining in some of those panels I have seen is simply exquisite."

Jimmy Ward was to return to his squadron next day, so a few of us gave him a farewell dinner. At the end, when he took out a cigarette, Eric Baume, who was sitting next to him, handed him his lighter. It had been over-filled and some petrol ran on to Jimmy's finger. It suddenly burst into a flame—a tendril of flame that lasted for only a moment. Jimmy fainted: the memory of fire near his hand, 13,000 feet over the Zuider Zee, was too much for him. We took him up to his room and the doctor bandaged the little burn on his finger and wrote out a note for him to take back to the medical officer on his station. It was obvious that he was not fit to fly.

I saw Jimmy before he left next morning. He said that he had loved his leave, loved the hotel, the people and the kindness. Then he said, "But, between ourselves, I want to get back to the boys."

I have learned since that he did not give the doctor's note to his medical officer, when he returned. In two days he was sent on a bombing raid over Brest and he did not come back. We do not known into what darkness he fell.

This morning I received a letter from Jimmy's mother, in New Zealand. She wrote:

I shall always be glad, whatever happens, that Allen had the desire of his heart. He wanted to be in plane work from a child. At a very early age he was always asking us to draw a plane for him, and once he said to a friend who often made him all the drawings he wanted, "Now draw an aeroplane out of sight."

How this has come into my mind now! For a long time the lad wanted to be a designer of planes, and we did our best to get him placed, but it was not possible. He has been iust thrilled through his training and flying.

For all these things I am thankful. Also, for all the kindness shown to him. Now we just hope we shall see him again. If it must be otherwise, we leave our dear lad with our Heavenly Father, who knows best.

September 22. Last evening I was asked if I would go to Southwark to speak to a squadron of Air Cadets. They were eager youngsters, from a sad, bombed part of London, and they were giving up their Sunday morning to pay a tribute to the pilots of the Battle of Britain which was raging a year ago. I was told that there was no officer to inspect them, or speak to them. I pointed out that as I had neither wings nor decorations, I would mean nothing, so I asked John Simpson, who has his D.F.C. and bar. He was shy at first, but he said "Yes, if you will do the talking."

So we got up early this morning and drove to Southwark with a tidy little officer who looks after the cadets. We came to melancholy streets of gaps between broken houses and crashed masonry—the honourable scars which seem to have fallen to the poor more than to the rich. Then to the playground of a grim, tall school. There were about one hundred boys, mostly in uniform, some bombed from their houses, standing with their tumbled world about them. But they were proud youngsters, with bright, clean cheeks, and they stood like guardsmen.

I told them that I was old enough to remember being forced on my knees to thank God that the South African war was over. And that I could remember the last war. And that men of my age were sometimes a little despondent—wondering if life held any hope of tranquillity in the future. And that I found the answer in them. I meant it. They were healthy, and valiant, rising out of the dust of their broken houses.

Before John inspected them, I told them that he had brought down thirteen German aircraft. It was the only time their eyes moved, slightly, towards him, for he had been standing apart while I spoke. Then he went from one to the other, saying a few words. I came away with a curious sense of humility, because they had listened to me so patie⋯ They seemed to hold the inherent valour of the Cockney in their hands.

September 24. The Poles have a nice word for people who cannot stop writing—they call it *graphomania*. It becomes an epidemic in Whitehall. During the day, in the Air Ministry, the files and documents pile up in the IN tray and, with weary eyes, one reads them and passes them across to either the PENDING tray, or, better still, into the one marked OUT. (One young pilot recently posted from the air to a desk job, introduced a fourth tray on his desk, marked TOO DIFFICULT.)

I become so tired of files that I look out of the window, where the pigeons eat the remains of the typists' sandwiches, on the parapet, and envy them their freedom. I dream of lying on a beach, in the sun, for the rest of my life—never writing or reading another word.

Last night, when I should have been in bed, I went with Viorel Tilea to the Berkeley, to see the cabaret. The star was a brilliant juggler. I was encouraged in my dalliance: at the next table sat Air Chief Marshal Sir Charles Portal,[1] master of all the war in the air. I cannot help remembering that I am a biographer by trade, merely dressed up in uniform. I watch these lords of war with a biographer's eye. My pick as subjects would be Air Vice-Marshal Slessor,[2] who is clear and uncomplicated as an arrow, swift in the air, and Sir Charles Portal. When he was a boy at school, Sir Charles became interested in falconry. I believe it is still his dearest relaxation. He looks and moves like a bird. I saw him one day, walking up the stairs into the Air Ministry: he extended his hand towards the brass rail, with the caution of a bird. Only once have I been summoned into his presence: when he put out his hand towards a document, in a tray, he moved with the same slow, careful motion. And he looks like a falcon, with his beak-like nose, and his intelligent, cautious eyes.

He was back at school tonight, as he watched the juggler. He gurgled with joy: for a few minutes the falcon was dozing and the dove of peace was taking wing.

---

[1] Marshal of the Royal Air Force Viscount Portal of Hungerford, K.G., G.C.B., O.M., D.S.O., M.C.

[2] Marshal of the Royal Air Force Sir John Slessor, G.C.B., D.S.O., M.C.

September 28 (*Wales*). The war is a cramping experience for an ardent traveller when his horizon has suddenly become the edges of a desk in the Air Ministry. I have never stayed upon this island for two and a half continuous years, during all my life in England. Now, even a journey from London to Wales breaks the monotony, for it means that one takes out a suitcase, buys a ticket, and enjoys the illusion of travel.

The house in which I am staying is on the edge of an industrial town. Beyond my bedroom window, eight portly silver balloons ornament the sky. The park is vast, but the faint purr of industry comes through the trees. Yesterday, we heard gunfire, out to sea, and in the afternoon, as we walked beside the lake, my host showed me where incendiaries had fallen, a month ago. The flank of a noble elm showed a scar, where it had been burned by a bomb.

This house stands for the continuity of English life. In the hall is a beam of oak from which one of my host's ancestors was 'hung, drawn and quartered on Kennington Common in 1746', for 'joining the rebellion in favour of the Young Pretender'. In the garden is the grave of the horse upon which another ancestor rode in the Charge of the Light Brigade. In the smoking-room is a painting of the big yacht commanded by my host's father, in the Battle of Jutland. It is a house of great beauty, with a Michelangelo figure catching the sunlight in the hall, and room upon room of treasures.

I wonder what all this will mean when the war is over. Will this kind of security and elegance be doomed and rejected? Will the purr of industry come nearer and nearer, so that the lovely shell of the house will tremble with machinery; and the oaks and cedars fall, to make space for some of the crowded world?

I was thinking yesterday, as I played an amiable game of croquet beside the rose garden, "How far has the Royal Air Force changed the tempo and the habits, and the conversation, of a house like this?"

I remember the early days of the R.A.F., and the old gentlemen who wrote angry letters to *The Times* whenever new aerodromes were being built. The Service was not popular then: old ladies rattled their tea-cups in nervous protest when aircraft dived over their lawns. They were antagonized and they did not comprehend the young pilots, with their fast motor-cars, their lively slang and jovial tippling. The R.A.F. was developing a new type of warrior who saw service life, not over a parade ground or a quarter-deck, but in the heavens. "His pathway was a canyon between the clouds; his companions were the sun, and the stars."

The first pilots seemed impatient when they were on land: they had found a new and exciting battlefield, in the air, and they openly said, "Please God, send us a nice war." They had to wait until the war came before they were comprehended by the men anchored to the land. Now they are the heirs of Drake and Hawkins, in the public heart.

In a great house such as this the R.A.F. was a stranger until two years ago. Even flying had little place in its story. In the garden is a rare rhododendron that was brought from the Himalayas by an aircraft, but the milky-white petals, with touches of cerise, pleased my host more than the achievement of a pilot making his lonely flight in the precincts of Everest.

Now the house is air-minded. The men who mother the local balloons are quartered over the stables in which the gallant horse from Balaclava spent the autumn of its days. A Wing Commander from a nearby aerodrome came to lunch on Saturday: yesterday, we entertained an Air Commodore who told us stories of the war in France. My host, who is all intelligence, said to me afterwards: "You know, I have never met a man in the Air Force who is a bore. It is their mental honesty that one finds so refreshing."

On the table in the library are books about flying. My host is a rich man and proud of his early manuscripts and fine bindings. He said, last evening: "I shall have to make a collection of books about the war in the air. It is a duty to one's descendants."

October 2. I returned to London last night and met a man who has been inspecting London children, evacuated to the countryside. In one village he was told of a Cockney boy, aged ten, who was surprised when he saw two country children kneel down to say their prayers.

"What are they doing?" he asked.

When he was told, he said: "Prayers! What is that?"

October 7. For some days we have watched the plans for an exchange of wounded prisoners: a lane was to be cleared across the Channel, guns were to be silent and no bombs were to fall, as hospital ships brought our own wounded across from Dieppe. In return, wounded German prisoners in England were to be taken home. I wished to see the ships depart from Newhaven, so I went there, and reached the little port after sundown. There was a big moon, hidden now and then by passing clouds. The hospital ships, vast and white, were alongside. Newhaven was to be the English end of the lane of temporary peace, so there were dazzling lights on the wharves: dazzling, and delightful, after the long habit of darkness. The German prisoners, some with broken legs, bandages, and sticks, hobbled on to their ship.

Then news came that the mercy ships were not to sail: the Germans had cancelled their gesture, so our wounded are to remain, and the Germans in Newhaven, already prepared to sail, were brought ashore again. To me, it is the most terrible act of mental cruelty since the war began. We might expect the Nazi mind to take some dark pleasure from seeing our men on to the ships at Dieppe, and then taking them back to the prison camps from which they were so recently freed. But to know that their own wounded were ready, to sail from Newhaven, down the lane of lights, and then sweep *their* hope away, is horribly cruel.

Two incidents in the unhappy venture reveal the gap there is between the nature of the ordinary Englishman and the man that Nazi-ism has bred. While I was at Newhaven I had to climb down a long and very steep gangway, from the hospital ship to the shore. Since an accident when I was young, I have been afraid of heights, and have to fight the old and familiar wish to jump.

When I was leaving the ship and saw the long, steep slope of gangway, I paused, to pull myself together. There was a soldier on guard and, in my bewilderment, I explained to him: "I am sorry, but I must wait a second. My stomach always turns a somersault when I look down like this."

The quiet, sensitive British Tommy said, "Then I'll go first, so that if you do slip I'll catch you." He preceded me down the gangway and, summoning my courage, I followed him without hesitation. It was a pleasant gesture of gallantry, within a few yards of the German prisoners who were waiting to be taken home.

Compare this with the effrontery of the German soldier walking on to the hospital ship, after being cared for in an English hospital. He was photographed, waving his stick at us, as he shouted *"Schwein"*!

November 1. A good day for me. Two years have passed since I ran off the first copies of the R.A.F. *Weekly Bulletin*, shabby and badly printed. I have edited it ever since; it is my constant and rather exciting task. Today, the *Bulletin* appears as the *Royal Air Force Journal*, thirty-six pages, illustrated and well printed, and in so many thousands that there will be one copy for every two hundred men in the R.A.F. It will be distributed from Iceland to Singapore.

I have fought my way through all the barbed wire of White-hall to achieve this. I have walked on air all day and I have allowed myself the comfort of pride.

November 18. About ten o'clock last evening I was sitting in the hall of the Savoy Hotel with Lady Oxford, looking at a drawing by Mr. Augustus John that he gave her during the afternoon. Her son, Anthony Asquith, and Arthur Macrae, were with us. After we had looked at the drawing I placed it on a chair beside us and we talked of other things. There were many people, flowing between the pillars and up the stairs: two of them, an officer and a woman on his arm, tottered towards us and paused before the John drawing. Lady Oxford did not realize how well they had dined: she smiled amiably and said, "Are you interested in drawings?"

The officer swayed and said, "Yeees, and thaat's a fake."

Lady Oxford sat up straight and answered: "Nonsense. Augustus John gave it to me today."

The officer moved towards me and said, "And you're a fake too." I stood up and whispered to the woman, "If I get a taxi will you please take him away?" She was belligerent also; she looked at the *New Zealand* flashes on my shoulders and said, "I hate you bloody colonials." Then she turned to Arthur Macrae and said, "And there is something of the fake about you."

War was declared and we were all rude, except Lady Oxford. Her spine was straighter than ever, but she was silent. The officer pointed to the John drawing again and said: "It's a fake. You are all fakes." Then the woman led him away.

Some minutes passed. Lady Oxford suddenly darted across the hall, whirled through the swing doors of the hotel into the black-out. The tipsy officer had grabbed the Augustus John drawing from the chair and disappeared, with Lady Oxford at his heels. Two of us followed and found her outside: she had grabbed the officer, and the drawing, and was saying: "You cannot do this sort of thing in England. We do not steal in this country."

With lovely speed of thought she turned to me, still hanging on to the officer, and whispered, "I've no idea what country he *could* do it in, but that doesn't matter."

The officer and the woman disappeared into the darkness and we returned to the hall of the hotel with the drawing. This morning a note arrived with my breakfast:

I can't sleep as I am so hot. In any case I could not go to sleep before thanking you for standing by me in our very curious drama of tonight. Even if that insolent man had struck me I would not have allowed you to report him.

War makes strange beasts of even the nicest men. He was not a nice man. In any case, I would not like any human being, even in peace-time, to suffer through me.

Yours affectionately,
Margot Oxford.

December 4. The doctor tapped me and frowned. "Nerves," he said. "You must have a few days in bed." Sergeant-Pilot Andy Kronfeld came to cheer me up. He is a New Zealander, so we had much to talk about. His father was a trader in the South Seas and his mother was a Samoan princess; a serene, beautiful woman whom I knew when I was a little boy. She had known Robert Louis Stevenson.

Andy is virile, unpredictable and charming. He tells modest stories when pressed. He was trained in Canada: for a boy used to roaming the South Seas, the discipline was oppressive. He has since done fourteen sweeps over enemy country. He said: "The first time I saw a Jerry was over Rouen. Two appeared beneath us. My pal went down and got his. I got on to the tail of mine and I was so excited that I put the safety-catch back to *Safe*. I pushed like hell and nothing happened. I put the catch back, but Jerry had seen me by then. He dived and I could not follow him down. Four others were on my tail, but I shot off his right wing-tip. Was I sore about the safety-catch when I got back! I just threw the cannon-magazine through the wing of my aircraft I was in such a temper."

I looked surprised.

"Yes," he said, "I got it in the neck all right when I went up before the C.O. I deserved it. I've got a lousy temper. But I have learned a lesson since then."

His Samoan blood and his New Zealand frankness blend well in him. He said, "We must do something about those nerves of yours." So he sang me a Samoan lullaby to send me to sleep.

December 9. Andy Kronfeld came to see me again and told some more stories. Last night, with three or four other pilots from New Zealand, he was drinking in an innocent-looking pub in the Strand when some smart Alecs sidled up to them. "Would they like to go to a nice club? Nice girls and very nice music."

The New Zealanders went: they climbed some dim stairs where there was no music and, as Andy said, "Girls old enough to be my grandmother." The smart Alecs suggested a game of cards.

In New Zealand we are brought up on poker; we learn to cut the pack when very young. The pilots and the smart boys sat down at the card-table and there was much winking, turning of rings and straightening of ties, by the sharpers. But New Zealanders can also wink, turn the rings on their fingers, and straighten their ties. Andy and his friends left the nice little club with fifty pounds between them.

Andy told me of the first enemy aircraft he shot down. "I felt bloody scared . . . there was a lump in my throat. I had lost my squadron and I was alone. Then I looked up and saw another plane, doing crazy things. I felt lonely so I went up to keep him company. I swung in and nearly collided, so I flew alongside, to signal. Then I saw that he was leaning forward, his head on the reflector sight, his helmet in his dead hand. It shook me. Then some Jerries appeared; I was out of ammunition, so I just stuck my nose down and headed for home."

Andy added savagely, "That was the end of that blighter."

I asked him why he had come to England to fight. His quick answer surprised me; he said, "To keep the war out of the Pacific." I asked then if he felt anything about fighting for England and he said: "No, nothing when I came. But that has changed since I have been here. The way the working class have done their job has made me want to go harder than before. They are worth fighting for, after what I have seen."

December 16. I love England and I know it has given me chances I could never have found in my own country. But I remain a New Zealander at heart. I often worry over the attitude of many English people to the men from the new countries. Australians and New Zealanders continue to complain that they are not happy in England. This feeling of difference must be broken down; it is bad for both of us.

About eight months ago, before I wore my *New Zealand* flashes on my uniform, I was travelling to Newcastle on a train. The restaurant car was crowded and some civilians were lingering over their coffee. At the end of the car stood some ten Canadian soldiers, waiting to eat. One of them walked up to the waiter and said, calmly: "We have been travelling since last night and we are pretty hungry. You promised us a table an hour ago."

The waiter ignored him and gave me my coffee. He said, believing that I was an English officer, "Really, sir, these colonials seem to think they are going to run the country." I told him that I was a New Zealander and gave him a piece of my mind.

Unfortunately, waiters are the easiest people for visitors to meet and the harm done by such remarks is alarming.

This protest is inspired by a letter I have just received from an old lady in New Zealand. She wrote:

I am now almost seventy and I can remember being in London for the last war, quite well. We still have our cottage on the coast, but we do not go there every week-end now as we feel that we should save the petrol for our boys who are fighting so bravely in the air.

December 20. Since the early days of the war I have carried a small newspaper cutting in my cigarette-case—from an article by Dean Inge, in the *Evening Standard*. He wrote, "Bismarck, when he was asked what was the most important fact in modern history, replied, 'The fact that North America speaks English'."

When news of Pearl Harbour came, I took out the newspaper cutting and read it again. One felt less alone, when Russia joined the war, in June, but they are vague and distant people, alienated by a different tongue. For those of us who know America, the pattern of alliance now seems complete.

The effect of the news, on the American war correspondents, is heartening to watch. Journalists write history day by day, but their own part in it is seldom recorded. I wish to say something of the American correspondents, most of whom are my friends. I have seen them during the nights of bombing, hurrying to the scene of destruction, not merely to gather news, but to help and be kind. For them, America coming into the war is a stimulus to their pride.

But I cannot forget that, in spirit, they have put up their own kind of fight on our behalf, ever since they came to London. Some day a writer should analyse the effect of the thousands of war reports sent from London during the past two years, and measure what the correspondents have done to awaken America's conscience. Jamie MacDonald of *The New York Times* wept when the news came that his country was at war.

December 21. I am at St. Mawes, in Cornwall, beside a window from which I can see the Atlantic Ocean. Immense fans of sea-spray rise over the rocks and increase the splendid sensation of being on an island. In the misty distance is the point of land that the captains of the grain ships used to see, as their first piece of Britain, after their long journey around the Horn. At the top of the hill is a fortress built in the time of Henry VIII. It was used as a stronghold by Royalists when they fled to Cornwall, from Cromwell's soldiers. It is a stronghold still: when I walked up there yesterday a sentry saluted me.

Every hour there is some sign of the war, even in this slumbering little village. During the night I heard the throb of an aircraft, and distant gunfire. Soldiers stamp past the window, their hob-nailed boots striking sparks from the pavement. Two submarines appeared during the morning, returning from the outer sea: in the afternoon I saw a convoy of eight or ten ships, their protecting balloons still sailing overhead, catching the meagre winter sun. Safe at home, with American food for England.

December 22. We went for a long walk over the hills; myself and my host, who is home on leave from the Navy. For an hour or so we were out of sight of every sign of war. We talked of "What will you do when the war is over?" which is a pleasant form of escape. But the peaceful theme did not last very long. We turned a corner and came on a belligerent scene: a sturdy sergeant instilling bayonet drill into a bunch of recruits. One, a small frog of a man, was using his bayonet as if it were a feather duster. "No!" said the sergeant. "Aim at ees throat—at ees *throat*."

December 23. We have found the local pub. There was a sturdy old Cornishman with his nose over his beer who told me that he is a signalman doing a 'very secret' job. He had a suitable hush in his voice, but he spoke with delight, of his son. "He's a pilot with your lot. From a boy, he wanted to fly. He was working in the butcher's shop here, as a lad, and whenever one of those five-shillings-a-time aeroplanes flew over he'd just leave the joint he was cutting and run out and watch it. Now he's flying a Spitfire."

Christmas Day. I walked up the hill to the fortress this morning. The sentry was looking over the grey water towards the harbour, where the ships are resting, in a Christmas Day hush—as his ancestors may have watched, with arrows in their quivers, hundreds of years ago.

The cynicism and independence we may have collected during our lives is never strong enough to resist the appeal of Christmas. There lingers an instinctive, comfortable wish, to listen to old voices from the past. A pleasant benevolence has settled on the fishing village below. I found a place, above the barbed-wire entanglements, and sat down to enjoy my Christmas thinking. I remembered a sentence, I think from Plato, "We set the claim of duty above the desire for happiness." For those of us who sit on the ground and serve in a negative, dependent way, I suppose this is the lesson we must learn—to set the claim of our duty above our happiness. To subdue one's selfishness and egocentricity to such an order is not easy.

December 26. I left the coast of England today for the first time in two and a half years. The little rust-bucket, once a 'pleasure steamer', smelled of fish, oil and old paint. It carried us to Falmouth: then we crossed to the Helford River from which we climbed to the isolated farm country where one finds Cornishmen in the raw. We came to a farmhouse, sheltered from the outside world by mud and loneliness. There we ate with a family of old brothers and sisters, unmarried, who have farmed together all their lives. One sister, who hugged the fire, was bent up, static and silent. She did not even turn her head, when we moved or spoke: she stared into spaces we could not see. The others were cheerful, but remote, and they shuffled over the old earth floor, beaten hard as tiles, in slovenly slippers. One of them said: "My name is Philadelphia. There's a town in the Americas by the same name, I'm told."

One of the brothers was a spry old fellow. While we were there a woman ran in from a neighbouring cottage and said that someone had stolen her frying-pan. He snapped at her, "You can't buy anything to cook in it anyway, so it is no use making a fuss." He told us that he had fought in the last war, in France. He said: "I'd sooner fight in a trench than in one of those aeroplanes. If you get wounded in a trench, you fall over and someone comes along and looks after you. But if you fell out from up there it would be a bit awkward."

Then the eldest of the sisters told an extraordinary story. "Our nephew, he's with the Flying Corps. He's brave, is our nephew. When they was going to make he a pilot they tested he first. They made he walk along a dark lane, alone, and a man jumped out at he from a hedge, and our nephew knocked he down. Then another jumped out and he knocked he down too. And there was a third one, but he ran away. And when our nephew got to the Flying Corps a very fine officer sent for he and said it was a test they had made for hees nerves."

1942

January 13, 1942. The Dean of Windsor, whose mind remains refreshingly young, said that he wished to meet some American war correspondents staying at the Savoy Hotel. My immediate choice was Larry Rue. I added Charles Collingwood of Columbia Broadcasting, Richard Collet, John Simpson and Roger Machell. We had a round table in the Princess Ida Room, and Santarelli was able to produce our weekly ration of lamb. It was my first attempt at a party for two years: the talk was really good, without clinging to the war all the time. The Dean, who can remember the Franco-Prussian war, who preached one of his first sermons to Queen Victoria, and who can remember meeting Dizzy, lent a certain dignity and age to our younger opinions. He startled us all by saying: "You see, I am older than Germany. Anthony Eden said something the other day about modern Germany being a hundred years old. His history is all wrong. When I was a boy, Germany did not exist." Then he went on to describe how he visited an Air Force station a few weeks ago and flew in a bomber. The span between the Franco-Prussian war and a bomber in 1942 seemed very wide.

Larry talked of his childhood; of his Lutheran father, of home-made bread with molasses and of his very devout upbringing. He clutched his wine glass with fierce zest and poured talk on us all: the flow was certainly rich and unstinted. I saw the Dean sitting back with a tolerant smile, benevolent and patient. Then Larry said, "But I am afraid this is a monologue."

The Dean answered, "I am reminded of what they said of Macaulay's conversation: that it was a monologue, with flashes of brilliant silence."

February 7. A small paragraph, no more than two inches long, in the morning newspaper, announces that the Pacific Council is meeting in Washington. So the affairs of the Pacific, of Australia and New Zealand seek their own centre, in the New World.

Disraeli anticipated something of this when he said:

"Remember always that England, though she is bound to Europe by tradition, by affection, by great similarity of habits and all those ties which time alone can create and consecrate, is not a mere Power of the Old World. Her geographical position, her laws, her language, and her religion connect her as much with the New World as with the Old. Still, if ever Europe by her shortsightedness falls into an inferior and exhausted state, for England there will remain an illustrious future. We are bound to the communities of the New World, and those great States which our own planting and colonizing energies have created, by ties and interests which will sustain our power and enable us to play as great a part in the times yet to come as we do in these days, and as we have done in the past. And therefore, I say it is for Europe, not for England, that my heart sinks."

February 10. I now work at Adastral House, in Kingsway, and all the pattern of my Service life has changed, although my task is the same. I have a big staff, including David Langdon and James Hadley Chase, and we produce our *Journal* with the competence of a professional magazine. But I have one new, frightening responsibility: I have been told that, in the event of invasion, I shall have to defend part of the Air Ministry staircase. Early in January I had to lead my staff to revolver practice, in a curious cellar, somewhere below Baker Street railway station. I had not fired a revolver for thirty years and then only in an idle fashion at a nearby tree.

The presence of James Hadley Chase was enough to intimidate me: when I saw the sergeant in charge of the range, and the revolvers, I withered with fear. The sergeant was big and contemptuous, and, in a voice that might have made all Sandhurst shiver, he told us that we would fire so many shots, in the aim, and then so many shots 'in rough alignment from the waist'. James Hadley Chase and David Langdon fired and did well. Then I took the revolver: it shook like a feather between my fingers. I prayed for wisdom and skill to flow into my hand, and —quite astonishing—I beat them all. The sergeant called me 'Sir' with warm approval in his voice.[1]

I felt less of a penguin and more like a bird of prey.

Yesterday I was duty defence officer for the first time. When the duty corporal reported to me in the morning he gave me a cracking salute, but I could see by his cold, aloof eye that he considered me to be a silly old duffer sitting at a desk.

I was not to be intimidated again by these seasoned warriors. When I joined him to 'do the rounds' last evening I said, "Well, Corporal, tonight we will inspect every outside lock in the Air Ministry." He demurred, "It is not usual, sir."

I cleared my throat, lowered my voice and said: "Element of surprise, Corporal! Element of surprise! Very important!"

I scrambled at his heels, up and down exterior wrought-iron staircases, and along subterranean passages. We tested every door that led to the streets. I found one unlocked and the chain of a safety-catch on another door useless and broken. I was delighted. The corporal also called me 'sir', with a hint of respect in his voice.

James H. C. and David Langdon were amused when I told them this morning. David is the least belligerent of warriors; when he did 'fire guard' on the roof recently, incendiaries and bombs fell about him. There was one comfort: he could see what he thought to be the tin hat of another officer, a few yards away. He said: "I felt less lonely as I looked towards him. Then an incendiary fell quite near and, in the flash of light, I saw that the tin hat was only a sort of cowl on top of a drain pipe."

We have been given cryptic passes, and codes, for the destina-

---

[1] Recalling the episode thirteen years later, James Hadley Chase wrote to me, "I remember most distinctly that why you shot so much better than any of us was that you had the intelligence—and the audacity—to use your left arm, bent across your chest, on which to rest the barrel of the pistol. Although strictly against the rules, the sergeant in charge was too astonished to admonish you— hence your beautiful bulls. You may have forgotten this, but I haven't."

tion to which we must hurry, with our secret papers, if the Germans arrive in Kingsway. I am horrified when I think of myself, revolver in hand, defending the stairs; but I feel that courage is a strange force, and that an emergency will inspire the valour it requires.

.   .   .   .   .

This afternoon I went to the balloon squadron site at Harringay Stadium. It is a curious and demoralizing arrangement; although the R.A.F. occupy part of the stadium, as offices, the greyhound races are still held in the adjoining arena. There is a big glass screen through which the officers can watch the races, by taking a few steps from their desks.

We are inclined to think that the balloons are amiable silver monsters, hoisted up by equally amiable old gentlemen turning a handle. The commanding officer, Wing Commander Aste, told me that early in the war one of the balloons was lost in a gale. About half-past one in the afternoon, while the crew were working on a new balloon, bombs were dropped on the site. One of them made a crater twenty yards away: another fell only ten yards from the balloon, but did not explode. The site could no longer be used and the crew had to move to another, 250 yards away. In the evening, while this was being done, there was another raid, and more unexploded bombs fell nearby. The crew had to move again, across a railway line, and make a new balloon bed, at dawn next day. The balloon was flying by three o'clock in the afternoon.

Next day the balloon was shot down, and a 500-lb. bomb fell within twenty yards of the crew. They had no proper shelter during the raid: three went to a house near by and two hid behind a tree, ten yards from where the bomb had dropped. The lorry carrying the enormous bottles of gas was thrown into the air: fortunately, they did not explode. When this third raid was over, the crew salvaged as much as possible of the cable, obtained another balloon, and had it flying that evening.

When the commanding officer proposed that the crew should rest, they said, "No, sir; we are quite all right and able to carry on."

There was one nice, lighter story. One evening a new, young sentry was guarding the balloon site, for the first time. The corporal went up to him and said, "What would you do if you saw a stranger walking near you in the dark?"

The sentry answered, "I would ask, 'Who am I?'"

The corporal said, "Oh no, you would ask *him* who *he* was."

"Oh no," answered the sentry. "If he didn't know who I was, he would have no right on the bloody site."

February 13. When I lived in Essex I was near enough to an inn of peculiar charm. There was nothing grasping about the owner, or his wife: when bores, chatterboxes or the flagrantly rich arrived on the doorstep, the owner would join the few permanent guests in being so rude to the intruders that they drove away.

One of the permanent guests was a landscape painter of considerable talent, but she drank too many dry Martinis and the November of her talent had set in. She would go to the river bank with her easel, canvas and stool; also a small folding table to which her drinks were brought. She would begin to paint the scene of bulrushes and water-fowl, reasonably; but as the empty glasses multiplied beside her, a wild, surrealist quality came into her work.

The second was a scholarly man whose gifts, habits and looks reminded one of the Prince Regent. He had spent six years writing the biography of a half-remembered Bavarian prince, and was still teasing the chapter, 'Childhood and Early Influences'.

The third was an extraordinary lawyer, with an enduring love for claret. His doctor had ordered him salt-water baths, but he hated the sea: so he brought, in the back of his car, some twenty bottles of Brighton water which were emptied into a footbath and set out for him, on the lawn.

The fourth permanent guest was incongruous in this setting. He was about twenty-one, slim, conventional in manner, carefully dressed, and devoted to cricket, which he had played for Harrow. He listened to our jokes with a delayed, patronizing chuckle, as if he were improving them in his own mind. He was like a bird-watcher beside the river, patiently observing the scene rather than becoming part of it.

Sometimes the owner of the inn would say "Sssh" to us; and then, "Mr. Rattigan is upstairs working on his play." One day he told us that it was to be called *French Without Tears*.

All this was some ten years ago. Today, Terence Rattigan arrived back in London after two spells of service with the R.A.F. in West Africa—as a rear-gunner in a Sunderland. When he went on his long, weary patrols, some lasting thirteen hours, he took a portable typewriter with him, in the rear turret: as he flew over the grey nothingness of the ocean, he began to write another play. He came on leave with it half-finished and then flew back to duty, by way of Gibraltar. He was told that the danger area was around Brest, so he stayed in the gun turret for three hours. Then his place was taken by a sergeant air-gunner, while Terence Rattigan went to one of the midship gun positions to stretch his legs. After twenty-five minutes he looked out and saw a Heinkel 115 coming towards them: the alarm was given. He wrote the story for me.

"It was the moment towards which all my training had been directed; the one in which I saw the enemy for the first time.

"The Heinkel made its first attack dead astern of us, firing with two cannon and one machine-gun. The inter-com. broke down and the pilot received no orders to change course. So we kept dead ahead and took no avoiding action at all. We were an absolute sitter to the Jerry, yet he missed us. He had cannon, but we had not. He came in from 800 yards, breaking away at 450. He came in again from the stern, evidently thinking it was too good to be true. By this time we had the inter-com. going again and the pilot was able to take avoiding action as the Heinkel came in. The Jerry made five attacks in all, but he never had the chance he lost the first time. He broke away out of range of us each time. We fired every gun we had at him. In one attack he put four bullets in our tail plane. Otherwise we were untouched. He obviously ran out of ammunition, for he circled round us twice and then went home. This was about midday—in the Bay of Biscay."

The Sunderland put into Gibraltar for repairs and then began the last lap of her journey—fourteen hours. After flying six and a half hours, one of the engines cut and finally seized altogether, breaking the reduction gear. There was danger of the propeller coming off and damaging another engine.

Terence wrote, "We were unable to jettison the useless tank as the Captain did not dare risk sacrificing the petrol that was in it. Then he decided to force-land. Night had fallen, but there was a good moon. We were then about half-way to our destination.

"When the Captain decided to come down, he told me to be ready with the landing flares. The alarm was sounded and the rubber dinghy was got ready. Then we sent out an S O S, which was picked up by Malta, and then lost.

"The moon was still with us—we made for shore, losing height all the time. We came down low enough to see the ocean. There was a swell—and we could see the high cliffs— with no possible landing place. It was the coast of the Sahara and to have been stranded there would have meant internment. The engine had sheared off by this time, and we could not have taken off with only three engines—and we could not have repaired it. We opened up the page of *African Pilot* and noted that we were near a Moorish settlement. According- ing to the *Pilot* the natives were 'reported unfriendly to strangers'.

"The swell made it unlikely that we could come down in safety. The moon was sinking, so the Captain decided to go on with three engines. Our misfortunes piled up in grand style. The fitter reported that there was not enough petrol in the usable tanks to carry us to Bathurst. To keep going at all, the remaining engines had to be driven at considerable boost.

The navigator estimated that we would be forced to come down eighty miles short of Bathurst.

"To gain height it was necessary to jettison every possible object. We began with our own personal kit, which was noble of us.

"My suit-case was going out—it was poised at the galley hatch—when I remembered the manuscript of the two acts of my play. I pulled the suit-case back, dived into it and found the note-book. I tore off the cardboard cover and kept only the pages.

"One bitter blow was when we had to throw away a dozen bottles of sherry and a dozen bottles of whisky which were to fortify us in West Africa. Everything went; instruments and freight. Then we took axes and chopped away every piece of the aircraft that was not actually necessary to keep us in the air. It was just wholesale destruction—'We don't need this!' Bang!

"Messages came down from the bridge to say that we were not jettisoning enough, so we changed into shorts and shirts and threw our uniforms overboard. The last sacrifice of all was the mail for the airmen in Bathurst and Freetown.

"The moon had gone in by this time and it was inky black.

"If another engine had failed we would have gone straight into the drink. We were flying at 800 feet and there was not another object that could be thrown overboard. We flew on through the thick night for four hours, calmly, with our Mae Wests on and the dinghy at our feet.

"There was nothing for the crew to do but sit, and wait, and listen to the engines. Then God was kind: a tail wind of thirty knots blew us into port, at dawn, with a few minutes of petrol to spare."

So Terence Rattigan walked ashore, with two acts of his play, saved. During the weeks that followed, in between three hundred hours of flying—with baboons as neighbours, crocodiles as enemies and little monkeys as pets—he finished the play.

This evening, with a dance band, chandeliers and champagne

for company, he showed me the typescript. I saw the title, *Flare Path*; then Terry opened the pages. There was some dust between them and he blew it away—not cigarette ash, but light red sand, from the Sahara.

February 15. At nine o'clock last night we listened to Mr. Churchill, consoling us for the escape of the battle-cruisers, *Scharnhorst* and *Gneisenau*, on their way from Brest and up the English Channel, to seek haven in the German ports. But the terrible news was of the surrender of Singapore.

For the English, this is perhaps the most humiliating capitulation in their history. But for Australians and New Zealanders, the fall of Singapore and the knowledge that thousands of our fellow-countrymen are in the hands of the Japanese, is most terrible, near, and personal. It is the realization of a horror that we learned about when we were very young. Just as English children grew up to believe that the devil hides in Potsdam, so we in Australia and New Zealand were brought up to believe in the sins, and the perfidy, of the Japanese. There was a book, *The Yellow Peril*, that sold among us, in thousands. On the cover was a black rising sun and, in the centre, the head of a Japanese, with a knife in his mouth. I can remember my early lessons in geography, in a school in Auckland: our eyes measured the nearness of Japan, and we felt as a man must feel when he sees a burglar's hand on the edge of his bedroom door.

I sat before the radio with an Australian and we were drawn together in our grief. The military significance of the defeat is vague to me, compared with the haunting knowledge that thousands of New Zealanders are at the mercy of those un-Christian hands. I waited up till three o'clock in the morning and read an ominous statement made in New York by Mr. Henry Luce. "Much of the burden of the protection of the Dominions is to move from London to Washington. . . . Australia and Canada are more and more to look to America for leadership and strength."

For us, coming from the Antipodes, these words have more meaning than for the English—they give a new spaciousness to our thinking.

March 11. Last evening, I sat with a solemn, introspective Australian pilot, and wrote down what he said to me:

"When England got into the war, I just went to my boss and said, 'I am going to join up.' By a hell of a lot of wangling, my brother and I managed to get into the same fighter squadron. We came over here a year ago—a year before Australia was really in danger. Now that we are here, we have lots of time to think but no opportunity to speak. We just wonder. But we know that the only thing to do is what we have been trained to do—shut up—just shut up. *Theirs not to reason why, Theirs but to do and die.*

"I am in love with a girl in Australia. She is pretty as poetry to watch. We are crazy about the same things. She is everything I love. And, by Christ, I have a capacity for love. If the Japs get into my country and if anything happened to her, I would give myself up entirely to war.

"Don't worry about the young being killed off. There are thousands more to take their place. Jimmy Jones can be produced in a mould, thousands upon thousands of times. It doesn't matter what his reactions are to James Joyce and Steinbeck.

"I am certain of three things: my love for my girl in Australia, of my own concern for my brother and my family, and that it would be a lot of fun to kill a lot of Germans.

"I joined the Royal Australian Air Force because I was scared of hand-to-hand fighting. I can shoot down an aircraft because I do not think of it personally. If someone put a bayonet in my hand I could not fight."

April 22. Two and a half years have passed since I first walked into the Air Ministry. It is a strange and astringent experience for a civilian, used to the perils of individualism. My friends used to say to me, "You know so clearly what you want, and you always get it." The task here has been to subdue this independence and fit into a pattern, with subordinates below and betters above. For a long time I was spoiled: my master was Air Vice-Marshal Douglas Colyer, who sympathized with penguins trying to hold their own in an eyrie. But there have been changes, and my new master bristles with dislike.

Since the beginning, I have fought the word, *personnel*, and have tried to keep it out of the *Journal*. Our antagonism began over this trifle. Then he used the minor punishment of keeping me standing at attention before his desk, for as long as twenty minutes—most galling after two Chiefs of the Air Staff and the Secretary of State have always offered me a chair. David Langdon says, "Don't be silly; you are too sensitive." This does not help. My savage pride is unsubdued. But I may have learned something during the two and a half years, because, like Vesuvius, I present the sunny slope of a smile and keep my savage forces within. But, after my acrid encounters with my master, I think of some lively answers as I walk home, along the Strand.

I spent the evening with a young officer in the Commandos, back from fighting at Dakar. He talked of music and pictures, and the book he is writing, and there was not a hint of self-pity or complaint. Perhaps the young are more adaptable to misfortune; perhaps, at my age, I am too set in my habits to fit into the elaborate mechanism of an impersonal service.

April 23. Mr. Somerset Maugham's book, *Strictly Personal*, was published a few weeks ago, by Heinemann. I enjoyed the speed of his story, but paused over pages 136–137, to read, several times, what he says of the pilots in the R.A.F. He pays tribute to their 'daring, their coolness and presence of mind, their indifference to odds' and 'their endurance'. In 'their presence' he is filled 'with a great humility'.

Then he describes, but does not name, a pilot he has known 'somewhat more intimately'. He was "a little older than the others, twenty-four, and quite a little chap, not more than five-feet-four . . . jaunty, with a care-free look in his impudent blue eyes. He had crashed early in the war and had nearly broken his neck, but after a few weeks in hospital and a niggardly leave, had gone to work again. He came to see me soon after his return from France. . . . Shortly before, he had had a scrap with two German planes, one of which he had brought down; a lucky shot pierced the oil tank, and so close were they that the oil splashed over his own plane, with the result that he could not see through his windscreen, but had to guide himself home by looking backwards over his shoulder."

Mr. Maugham asked if he wasn't 'scared', and the pilot answered, "Not then. I've never been scared in a scrap—it's too damned exciting."

Then, "But I'll tell you when I have been scared. When I was on a reconnaissance by myself. When you're up there all alone, hour after hour—— Gosh, my knees shook. You feel there's no one in the world but you, and the sky looks so damned big. There's nothing to be afraid of really, I don't know why it should make you feel funny."

"Infinity," Mr. Maugham suggested.

The episode ended with Mr. Maugham's description of the last time he saw the pilot:

> "He was in tearing spirits because he had two days' leave and was determined to have the time of his life. He was full of plans for the future. After the war was won, he was going to buy a sailing-boat, forty foot long, and sail with a friend to the South Seas."

The pilot is Wing Commander Ian Gleed, D.S.O., D.F.C.[1] He has brought down thirteen enemy aircraft and is now O.C. Flying at Middle Wallop, in Wiltshire—which means that he controls the daylight attacks by Spitfires on enemy aircraft assailing our coast.

Soon after he joined the R.A.F., in peace-time, he used to

[1] Death presumed, on active service, April 16, 1943.

come and see me at my house in Essex. The picture I suddenly
recall is of myself at a desk, before the window, looking out at
Ian playing with my Dalmatian on the lawn. They were both
at the puppy-dog stage and had much in common. His enthusiasms were enchanting: his escape from flying was a little
sailing-boat, the modest forbear of the forty-foot sailing boat
in which he will seek freedom in the South Seas, when the war
is over.

I closed Mr. Maugham's book at page 137 and telephoned
Ian Gleed, at Middle Wallop. "Yes", he would be delighted to
see me. If I arrived by the afternoon train, he would meet me
and we could dine at the Haunch of Venison, in Salisbury, that
night.

So I travelled down from London to see what had happened
to the boy who had played on my lawn. We dined at the Haunch
of Venison, off legs of chicken that seemed as old as the oak
beams above us, and we talked. Ian's merriment made it hard
for me to believe in the thirteen combats with German aircraft.
When we relaxed into seriousness, over our pallid coffee, I
realized, in the depth of his voice and the quiet of his mind, that
there was wisdom behind his laughter.

After dinner we strolled along the bank of the Avon, to
Harnham, and we did not speak of war all the way.

Next morning, I walked with Ian to the aerodrome, to see
his new Spitfire; past the bombed skeleton of a hangar—a great
dinosaur of steel bones, with birds flying in and out. The Spitfire
was fresh from the factory and ready for battle: Ian stroked its
fuselage with the palm of his hand. Five airmen were working
on the aircraft, tinkering and screwing and painting, poking
their heads into its mysteries so that their behinds and legs hung
in mid-air. We went again in the evening: the five were still
working and one of them was painting Ian's mascot on the
body—the cat from *Pinocchio*, smashing a swastika with its
paw.

We walked back to the mess—a calm, lovely Wiltshire
evening; great shafts of light from the setting sun, stillness
and peace.

Another old friend, John Tharp,[1] came into the mess, before taking off on night operations. I knew him also in Essex—he lived at Chippenham, near Newmarket, and was younger than Ian. I remember him when he made houses in trees, in the park that is now an aerodrome, with three miles of beeches all felled to make for safe flying.

Next morning I slept late, and Ian was already flying over the French coast when I was shaving. A lovely clear morning. I went to the telephone box and was sitting there when John Tharp came in, after his night flight. I had heard that his squadron had brought down a German aircraft during the night and I asked him, "Who got it?"

He shifted from one foot to the other, as if he had been caught stealing the jam, and said, "Well, as a matter of fact, I did. I have drawn my first blood."

Then we realized the miserable blight of the secrecy in which we have to live. I sat, with the telephone in my hand: nothing would have pleased me more than to put a call through to his mother, also an old friend, and tell her the gallant news. But it was not possible, so we went to the Pheasant[2] and drank a glass of sherry, to celebrate John's victory.

John and I lunched there, with John Cunningham,[3] who commands 604 Squadron. He has done as much as any pilot in the R.A.F. to develop the technique of night fighting—'Cat's Eyes Cunningham', they call him. He is annoyed because the newspapers explain his unique vision by saying that he feeds almost entirely on carrots.

I tried to induce him to put the story of his night-flying experience on paper, for an article in the *Journal*. He half-promised, but I could see that for the moment, he was less interested in night flying than in what was happening outside the window. An airman was mowing the lawn as if all his life depended on it. The poor little mower, two hand-spans wide,

[1] Flying Officer J. D. A. Tharp. Death presumed, on active service, April 14, 1943.
[2] A requisitioned inn, used by 604 Squadron as a mess, some eight miles from Salisbury.
[3] Group Captain John Cunningham, D.S.O., O.B.E., D.F.C.

leapt over the rough grass like a rabbit. John Cunningham suddenly said, "Come and see the raspberries." We went into the garden where the aircrews grow their own fruit and vege-tables, with a farmer's pride.

On the third day at Middle Wallop I listened while Ian briefed the Spitfire pilots before he led them on their task for the day. I realized the incredible authority that has developed in his little frame: he sat on the edge of a table while he gave his orders and his shoes did not touch the floor, yet he seemed to be expanded by his own will. His quiet, still-young voice never hesitated as he told his men exactly what they were to do, what they might expect from the enemy, and where. The pilots looked up at him, tense, leaning forward to absorb every word that might increase their chance of survival and return. Then Ian swung his feet, jumped from the table and walked over to me. I went to see him take off in his new Spitfire; then I spent the hours of his absence watching a tough football match, and writing at a desk.

When Ian returned, he washed and changed, then said, in a quick, rather harsh voice, "Come for a walk." We went, but he was mostly silent. After about an hour he said, "I lost two of my boys this morning: the Messerschmitts came down on them out of the sun."

We dined, and afterwards we sat in his room, drinking and talking—of his wish to be a writer,[1] of his dream of the forty-foot boat and the South Seas. Then he said, "I've grown up too fast. Forget all that you saw today. I want to be treated as if I were a boy again: it is something I have lost, and I want it back."

May 23. I was asked—yet ordered—to give a 'pep talk' to 'some recruits' at Swiss Cottage. I imagined a hut, with perhaps fitfy boys listening amiably to my story, but found as my audience more than two thousand recruits in training, packed into the Odeon Cinema. I have faced enormous audiences, in American arenas, but there is a pattern in such a crowd, of varying colours,

[1] Ian Gleed had already written his first book, *Arise to Conquer*, which was published by Gollancz, May 18, 1942.

H

faces and ages. Today I looked down, and up, at 2,000 youths, all about the same age, all in uniform, all sitting erect and drilled —a vast bowl of taut, disciplined faces and blue tunics, with their brass badges like flecks of sunlight.

Five minutes passed before I could even make them relax and realize that I was not merely drilling them. Then I held them as best I could, with my stories of the New Elizabethans—the Drakes of the air. I wrested applause from them towards the end, when I reminded them that King George VI is the first qualified pilot to be crowned king of England.

When I told them stories of his training at old Waddon aerodrome, they leaned forward, at last, and the end was very touching. But I was physically so tired that I went to Regent's Park and sat beside the lake, to recover my strength; before returning to my desk, with its trays, IN, OUT and PENDING.

June 14. Richard Hillary came to my office this morning, with a copy of his book, *The Last Enemy*, published by Macmillans. He wrote in it, "For Hector, whose studied imbecility among the bouncing brasshats is so refreshing. Affectionately, Richard."

The affection has not come without tribulation.

Some six months have passed since I first met him; when Air Vice-Marshal Colyer summoned me to his office one morning, early in January, and said, "In the next room is a young pilot you can help. He has been badly burned and you may get a shock when you see him and shake his hand." Then —"He wishes to write and his first book has already been accepted in America."

Richard Hillary came into the room and, for a moment, I held his parched, burned fingers in mine. He had been shot down in September 1940 and, for the better part of a year, he had endured continuous skin grafting, and operations, in the hospital at East Grinstead. But his exceptional good looks still shone out, from the mask of grafted skin. When the Air Vice-Marshal told me what to expect, I had steeled myself not to show any sign of surprise and to be all sympathy. But I have never known a mutilated man less in search of pity. All the stimulus and valour came from him—and the will that gave shape to our conversation. He was aggressive and certain of himself, as a writer rather than a warrior.

Richard was justified in protecting himself with all the defences he could muster. From the long months of operations at East Grinstead, he had been sent to Washington, in June 1941, to lecture to the Americans. It had been a sad blunder, for the sight of his wounds and burned skin was not likely to encourage mothers and wives to send their men into the perils of battle. His valour during this time must have been incredible: out of his inward alarm grew the pride that shows now, in his defiant blue eyes. Only another writer can appreciate the fortitude with which he sat at a desk, during this unhappy venture, to finish the book he had begun in his bed at East Grinstead.

I am fond of him, and we have become friends, but we argue frequently, and his frankness is sometimes startling. The second time he came to Adastral House he brought me two articles. "You can have one of these for the *R.A.F. Journal*," he said. Then—"But I want to sell the other one."

I sent the article to Mr. Edward Hulton, by hand, hoping to have good news for Richard as soon as possible. I had described the circumstances to Edward Hulton in a letter, to hasten his decision. Within three hours he telephoned me: he said that he would be delighted to use the article in *World Review*, and pay twelve guineas.

I called Richard immediately, with the encouraging news. All he said was, "Good! Couldn't you push him up to fifteen?"

As compensation for his long pain, he began to enjoy the first glow of literary success. It was delightful to watch him with a copy of the American edition of his book, or the proofs of the English edition, which was being nursed through Maxmillans by Lovat Dickson, who became his Maecenas from then on.

Richard Hillary has told his story in *The Last Enemy* with

such sensitiveness and talent that it would be silly for me to add any more. But I must write of an episode that followed a bristling argument one morning, when he tried to hustle me into an opinion I would not accept. We became quite angry, over our glasses of sherry, and then silent. After a minute or two he said, "Oh, by the way, I think you ought to dine and meet my publisher. He may be of some help to you."

The victory was his. When I said, "Of course," he answered, "All right, Claridges tomorrow, at seven-thirty."[1]

August. Feeding the R.A.F. is a constant task, organized by a department that works modestly, among horrible problems. It is some comfort to discover that one of the officers who tries to reconcile the physical needs of the aircrews with the stingy supplies that are available, is named Squadron Leader Turtle.

I use the columns of the *R.A.F. Journal* to introduce wholesome ideas into the minds of the men who fly; who prefer the food that fills to the food that sustains. They do not eat enough green vegetables, and as they sit cooped up for hours—especially in Coastal Command aircraft, making their thirteen-hour vigils over the ocean—it is important that their physical plumbing should work as well as possible.

A few days ago, I realized that the arch-vegetarian, Mr. Bernard Shaw, might write something that would seduce the aircrews from their doughy puddings and slices of swiss roll, and make them enjoy their cabbages and brussels sprouts. I wrote to him and, with a gracious note attached, he sent the following reply to my question:

"I am not a sky pilot; and at my present age (86) am not likely to qualify for that accomplishment. But, as the R.A.F. carefully teaches its novices everything except how to feed themselves, and most aces devoutly believe that a heavy job

[1] Richard Hillary returned to active service in the R.A.F. and was killed on January 7, 1942. His biography was written by Lovat Dickson and published by Macmillans, in 1950.

needs a heavy meal, it may surprise them to learn that it is more than 60 years since I last ate flesh, fish or fowl. I have given up eating eggs, though I eat butter and drink buttermilk sometimes when I can get them. I am a six footer, and am told that my weight should be at least twelve stone ten. As a matter of unromantic fact it is nine stone, and stood at ten stone eight during the most active part of my life. Yet I find myself working as hard as ever, a bit deafish and dotty, as becomes my second childhood, but still in fairly good form as author, playwright, biologist, philosopher and political pilot, not to mention journalism as a side line.

"You will say, perhaps, that if ever a man needed a plentiful and stimulating diet I am that man. But on such gluttony I should have gone stale or died years ago. Dickens, who ate and drank generously, died before he was 60. So did Shakespeare. I have lived longer than they did by about 30 years, and written my most famous books and plays during those 30 years.

"Or perhaps you will say that inkslinging is not work, and that a raid on Danzig and back would show me up. Well, I grant you I am no athlete; and I am certainly, like most literary geniuses, a born coward; but it is a hard fact that an emergency rush of literary work can tear a man's nerves to rags, and that my remedy for this was to get on a motor bicycle and blind round the crooked lanes of Hertfordshire for an hour or so, at the end of which I was again as steady as a rock. And for 30 years I spent my holidays driving my car all over these islands and beyond them as far as Eastern Europe and North Africa, when flying was easier and in peace-time less dangerous. In the last century, when the push bike was a new invention, I had plenty of opportunities of learning how to feed myself on a long day's ride.

"Consequently it may interest you to know that if I were sent off to bomb, say Tokyo, I should take with me a packet of thinnish slices of brown bread—not dirty bread made of shop-sweepings but real stoneground bread with a layer of red currant jam between each pair of slices. I should eat one of these sandwiches every two or three hours. For drink I should take a flask of buttermilk. I should know that though flak is dangerous, a square meal would be certain death; for within 15 minutes after it I should fall asleep over my controls and nose dive to destruction.

"That is what will happen to you if you eat a between-rib beefsteak and drink a bottle of Guinness on a serious job.

"I should have mentioned that I have never smoked, never drunk intoxicants, and never shaved. That is a better record than even that of the famous centenarian who was asked to what he attributed his longevity. He replied, 'I attribute it to the fact that I never drank, never smoked, nor ever had any relations with women until I was 14 years of age.' "

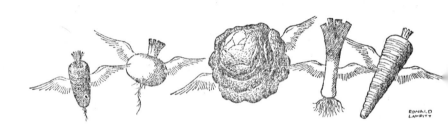

I published Shaw's letter in the *R.A.F. Journal*, with the title, *To Tokyo on Buttermilk*. Ronald Lampitt drew a tail piece for it, which is reproduced on this page. Within a few days, H. E. Bates sent me a reply to Shaw's letter, which he called *Back to Methuselah on a Beefsteak*.

"Like Mr. Shaw I am no pilot, though I belong to the R.A.F. Like Mr. Shaw again, I am a writer. But unlike Mr. Shaw I am not a vegetarian and at my present age, 37, I am not likely to qualify for that accomplishment, though you never can tell. The fact is that I don't want to be either a pilot or a vegetarian. I don't even want to be Mr. Shaw. I want to be a writer.

"Now Time will decide, eventually, what places in literature Mr. Shaw and I will occupy: not whether Mr. Shaw will go forward to Tokyo, by which of course he means immortality, on buttermilk, or whether I shall go back to Methuselah, by which of course I mean posterity, on a beefsteak; but whether or not we were, in fact, good writers. To achieve our ends both of us need, as Mr. Shaw so well points out, a plentiful and stimulating diet, and Mr. Shaw's idea of a plentiful and stimulating diet, it seems, is red currant jam. It isn't a pilot's idea and it isn't mine. But then, of course, Mr. Shaw is extremely crafty. He doesn't really care two hoots about red currant jam. What he really wants, as he has wanted it for the past 86 years, is a revolution. And what better chance of that, you English dumb-clucks, than if you were to put R.A.F. pilots on red currant jam tomorrow? The red currents, you see, in the scheme of things.

"We meat-eating writers, in Mr. Shaw's view, do not seem to live for a very long time. Dickens, it is true, died at sixty; but he managed to write *Pickwick Papers* before he was twenty-five, at which age Mr. Shaw was, in a literary way, in short pants. Keats died before he was thirty; but managed to write *Adonais* before he died. Chekhov was just over forty when he died; but he succeeded in writing half a dozen plays which Mr. Shaw, on his own confession, would have given his beard to write. Chaucer died at sixty; but wrote the *Canterbury Tales*. Shakespeare, too, died young, but before doing so—but then, everybody by this time knows that Mr. Shaw himself wrote Shakespeare.

"It is in fact not when you die, or what you eat and drink before you die, but what you do before you die that matters. Some men eat beef and write *Hamlet*; some eat sturgeon and write *The Cherry Orchard*. Some eat red currant jam and write, if it doesn't surprise you, *The Doctor's Dilemma*.

"Mr. Shaw, in fact, wants jam on it. He not only wants to be an Irishman and the author of *Saint Joan*, which ought to be enough for any man, but he wants to teach pilots the best stomach on which to fly Stirlings. To Tokyo, he says, on red currants; or to Germany, if you prefer it, on gooseberries. I should know, he says, that flak is dangerous. And so, he should know, is belly-ache at altitudes.

"Now I am a beefsteak writer myself and am fond of the gravy and onions of life, and almost the only thing I regret about that life and about myself as a writer is the fact that I have never met Mr. Shaw. I should in fact very much like to meet Mr. Shaw. And what I would like to do if I did meet him is to take him to see pilots eating. We would go to a south-coast station, and Mr. Shaw could have lunch in the Mess there. We would lunch with pilots who fought at Dieppe and who might, indeed, be fighting over France again that same afternoon. Mr. Shaw could choose his lunch from four or five salads, stewed fruits, melba toast, cheese and, if he really liked, red currant jam.

"And while we were eating I should tell a story. It could be one of the many stories about Mrs. Patrick Campbell and Mr. Shaw. For it seems that Mr. Shaw was once rehearsing a play of his, with Mrs. Patrick Campbell and Sir Herbert Tree in the cast. Said Tree to Mrs. Campbell, referring to Shaw, 'Let's take him to lunch and give him a beefsteak.'

"Said Mrs. Campbell to Tree, 'No, for Heaven's sake! He is bad enough as it is; but give him a beefsteak and no woman in England will be safe.'"

September 28. I lunched today with H. E. Bates. Thirteen years have passed since I first knew him—a shy beginner as a novelist. We walked in a garden at Windsor: I remember his surprising knowledge of all the trees and flowers—and I liked his modesty and eagerness. There have been other meetings—once, lunch with Edward Garnett in a Soho restaurant; and talks in Jonathan Cape's office. In 1941 he wrote to me, "Do you think I should join the R.A.F. and write for them?" I answered, "Yes, they are the greatest people in the world." Today he handed me his little book of R.A.F. stories. He has called it *The Greatest People in the World*, and has written a charming note of acknowledgement in the copy he gave me.

He has absorbed the R.A.F.—or the R.A.F. has absorbed him—in a way that I envy. He ascends, while I seem to be kicking the ashes of failure. I fear I shall lose my *R.A.F. Journal* because of the continuous conflict with my commanding officer.

Notes on a new task. In the late summer of 1942, I ended my work as editor of the *Royal Air Force Journal*, which had become the popular magazine for all the Service. Three years had passed since I ran off the first copies on a duplicator: since then, writers as eminent as George Bernard Shaw, J. B. Priestley, Eric Linklater, Robert Graves, Clemence Dane, David Garnett and H. E. Bates had written for me. Eric Kennington, David Langdon and Cecil Beaton had provided illustrations.

There comes a time when an editor and his magazine must part company, so I sought fresh fields, and found them, in secrecy and hard research. I was appointed editor of the *Coastal Command Intelligence Review*, which was produced so furtively that each copy had to be signed for and kept in a locked safe. The two hundred or so copies, of each issue, were printed by H. M. Stationery Office, at Harrow. We worked together, as editor and printer, as carefully as if we were producing a rare folio. It was a perfect, selfless pattern of co-operation, in which the individual was always second to the task. I mention this because I wish to record my appreciation of the kindness and talents of the small group of craftsmen who were chosen for these secret jobs. The head printer would work with me 'on the stone', allowing me to suggest and experiment with the make-up: the blockmakers met my wishes and were as excited as I was in trying to present the illustrations in the way that would best help the aircrews. I was able to enjoy the full pleasure of being a writer; of nursing my words from when they were wet under my pen, until they emerged, printed, illustrated and bound.

This association between writer and printer is one of the nice rewards of my trade, and I never appreciated it more than when I worked with the Stationery Office at Harrow.

For my new duty I was posted to Coastal Command Headquarters, a requisitioned Victorian mansion of horrific design, at

Northwood in Middlesex. The house had once been an hotel, where the 'lamps shone over fair women and brave men', in their pink dresses and dinner jackets, every Saturday night. But the sounds of revelry were over: the dancers had departed to more serious employment and the R.A.F. ensign flew from the useless tower. In the surrounding park, girded by genteel villas, there were perhaps fifty sly 'hutments' hiding beneath the trees. Within the mansion was the office of the Commander-in-Chief, aloof with his secrets and his power. Here the war against the U-boats, and the air attacks on enemy shipping, were planned. It was a separate battle, this hunting of German submarines to the death—'to absolute destruction'. I was nearer to the naked swords of war than I had been in the Air Ministry, and the warriors who fought it became my friends.

I was billeted with Mrs. Albert Ball, in her pretty, spick-and-span house, within three minutes' walk of the guardroom. She gave me a tray of tea each morning; and her daughter, Patricia, aged five, cleaned the brass buttons on my uniform. She used to say, "This is my war work." When there were air raids we sat together in the shelter and Patricia held my hand. I hope that the lamps have learned to shine on her, and that she has now joined the company of 'fair women and brave men' on the dance floor: at the tender age of five, she polished her way to my heart.

Thus established, in comfort and kindness, I began the most formidable mental exercise of my life. I had to comprehend the history and technique of attack on U-boats by aircraft, and attacks on shipping. The heroic generalizations of the *R.A.F. Journal* were no longer enough: I had to seek accuracy in every word, and know what was happening in terms of mathematics and perfection. I had to study the significance of oil streaks from wrecks, and oil bubbles from U-boats after they had been attacked; to understand the laws and whims of dinghy drift, because they concerned the fate of ditched aircrews. I had to recognize the difference between wakes and swirls, in photographs, and the abracadabra of radio aids to navigation. I was forced into terrifying new exercises of the mind. The experts were there to control and guide me, but I had to interpret their judgments into print, and simplify their essays so that the aircrews could read and absorb them. I dared not continue as a fool too long, so my brain had to pretend that it was back at school again. The brain was older and less resilient, but it revealed a new, higher ceiling, to contain most of what was required.

I recall one night, sitting up when all else were asleep, trying to comprehend something of the distribution and migration of whales. I began in a state of mouldy boredom, with a chart, and a long article written by an expert. But, as I studied I became aware, and astonished, by the importance of whales in our corner of the war. Pilots sometimes mistook them for U-boats and squandered time and their depth charges on them. I began to see the war through the eyes of the pilots; not merely along an avenue of files and papers. What I wrote, or edited, and nursed through the press, was directly related to the fortunes of battle. So the difference between U-boats and the forms of Finner, Blue and Humpback whales became exciting knowledge, because it could be planted into the vision of the pilots and save them from error.

I remember that in August 1943, one of our aircraft dropped four depth charges on what he was convinced was a U-boat. The target did all that a U-boat should: it disappeared and, after the attack, the pilot saw 'a possible patch of oil 40 yards in diameter'. But the target was a whale, and the oil was its death blood. Such episodes gave a solemn meaning to the work at my desk.

The accuracy of my use of words could affect the success, and even the survival, of aircrews during their missions. Some time later, I met a navigator who had been shot down in the cold northern sea. He was one of the few survivors and had to cling to a piece of wreckage for two hours before he was saved. He said to me, "I was going to kick off my boots, to be more free, but I suddenly remembered reading in the *Coastal Command Review* that, in cold water, this would probably end in freezing my feet and losing the use of them. So I kept my boots on."

It was like a boyhood story come true, to read of immense turtles, paddling amiably in mid-ocean, being mistaken for dinghies; like reading *Moby Dick* again to spread maps on the table, with photographs beside them, and build up my visual knowledge of the oceans and coasts of the world. Iceland was no longer a mere outline in the Arctic seas. I knew the wharves of Reykjavik and Akereyri by sight, the shape of the runways, and the heights and features of landfalls.

In the Air Ministry, I had allowed myself the pleasure of being sorry for myself. This was no longer a temptation, and the chore of learning soon became romantic and a delight. I was in a new world of knowledge, and as happy as I have ever been. It was so true that being useful bred a contented mind.

Retrospect and Achievement. The history of Coastal Command falls into three periods. The first was under the command of that splendid sailor with wings, Air Chief Marshal Sir Frederick Bowhill, who began to fly in 1912. He was Commander-in-Chief of Coastal at the beginning of the war and until June 1941. But his valour and imagination had little chance during those perilous days when we were so poor in aircraft that we could put up little or no defence against the German submarines. During the first two and a half years of the war, the Command killed only three U-boats, sharing a fourth with the Navy.

In the summer of 1941, the time of preparation began, under Air Chief Marshal Sir Philip Joubert. From then, during what was left of 1941, and in 1942, we turned from timid defence, to offence and challenge.

When Air Chief Marshal Sir John Slessor was appointed to direct Coastal, the Command was so strong in aircrews and aircraft, that we were able to attack and kill, ruthlessly. These were the months when I was settling into my task, and they were, for me, a time of lively inspiration.

There is a boy scout quality in most of us that urges us to regard a great soldier with awe. We easily return to the spell that Marlborough and Wellington cast over us when we were young. Somewhere, early in my diary, I wrote of the wish to write two biographies of R.A.F. officers—Lord Portal, and Sir

John Slessor. The wish was based merely on a distant view of both of them, within the impersonal pattern of the Air Ministry. The near view of Sir John Slessor, controlling the fortunes of Coastal Command, during the months of achievement and victory, deepened my wish to become his Boswell.

The first time I was summoned to his office I was intimidated: after being asked to sit down, my right hand, unseen by him, played nervously with my cigarette lighter, in my pocket. The wretched lighter suddenly opened and burned my fingers. My face must have shown my alarm, but somehow I closed the lighter, withdrew my hand, and tried not to look like an idiot. I said "Yes, sir" to all I was told. I went back to my duties and, during the months that followed I enjoyed a remarkable experience.

Sir John Slessor disliked dictating even his briefest memorandum. In the archives of the Air Ministry, and of Coastal Command, there must be thousands of his notes, of order or suggestion, written in pencil: scholarly, slow writing, with the vowels nice and round. This was his way of holding his forces together and of commanding us all. Sometimes one heard a murmur of protest, "My God, another note from the Old Man!" But the protests were superficial: the notes made us all feel that we were in friendly touch with our general.

In his manner, Sir John was seldom warmly personal, and he wasted little time on jokes or small talk. But he compensated for this with his refreshing memoranda: *they* were always personal, and their literary touches, and nice sense of what a sentence should be, gave his orders the grace of requests.

Sir Philip Joubert had controlled the Command *Review* at a distance: he sent for one and announced decisions, often making one feel like the sergeant of the guard being given his orders for the day. Sir Sholto Douglas, who followed Sir John Slessor at Coastal, also believed in remote control, and he had a genius for delegating tasks to other people. But Sir John Slessor seemed to catch us up in the net of his written words and, through them, to inspire devotion and obedience.

Sir John wrote the summary of the month's operations for the *Review* himself, which neither his predecessor nor his successor cared to do. The manuscript arrived in my office, or I was summoned to receive it, never a moment late. (I may say, as an editor, that he was the perfect contributor.) His personal assistant told me that the Chief sometimes sat at his desk until two o'clock in the morning, to keep faith with me, and with the printer. While making history, he still cared about the writing of it.

I recall the morning when I read what he had written, as the great victories began. "April 1943 was a bumper month for Coastal Command." Then he described the 150 sightings of U-boats and the 86 attacks. There had been 4 certain kills and 3 more 'reasonably certain'. Then came one of the sentences with which he spoke so personally, to every member of the aircrews. "That hard-hearted and unimaginative body, the Admiralty Assessment Committee, may ultimately credit us with as many as 8."

At the end of May he wrote, "It is very satisfactory to be able to look back on another record month . . . all previous records against the U-boats have been put in the shade." From May, to the first week in August 1943, aircraft of the Command sank 53 U-boats, 18 of them in May alone.[1] At the end of the month came another stimulating report, from the Chief, "August has seen a new turn in the critical and hard-fought Battle of the Bay." The victories mounted, towards the summing-up at the end of December. I remember the foolscap pages in their clip, the sober narrative in pencil, beginning, "The year 1943 will have many claims on history; high among them will be that it saw the defeat of the U-boat menace in the Atlantic which, at the beginning of the year, bade fair to strangle our strategy in Europe and held out to the Axis their last remaining hope of avoiding defeat."

The statistics of success—compared with the miserable total for the first two and a half years of the war—were remarkable, and satisfying. Of German, Italian, and Japanese submarines, some 250 had been destroyed during 1943. Surface ships got about 80 of these and our own submarines killed another 14.

[1] The victory was announced to the House of Commons by the Prime Minister: he said, "In May, for the first time, our killings of U-boats substantially outnumbered the U-boat output. That may be a fateful milestone. . . ."

Aircraft operating from carriers accounted for 24, and shore-based aircraft were proved to have sunk more than 120, of which 81 fell to the squadrons of Coastal Command.

Of the thousands of ships crossing the Atlantic, in the ceaseless convoys, only 83 were sunk by U-boats.

This was the heartening story that Sir John Slessor was able to announce, in his last tally for the year.

.   .   .   .   .   .

These victories for Coastal Command had been made possible by two important developments in the art of hunting U-boats. During the first three and a half years of the war, our short-range aircraft could not cover the vast, central area of the Atlantic, where the U-boats were free to stay on the surface and attack the convoys bringing armaments and food to Britain. The vessels had to depend on their Naval escorts and their own guns for defence, and had to cross the Atlantic 'Gap' without air cover.

Then came the Liberators, stripped of some of their armament to make room for extra fuel tanks. Squadrons of these long-range aircraft were based in Newfoundland, Iceland, and Britain: at last, Coastal Command was able to keep its vigil over all the Atlantic and the 'Gap' was closed.

The second development was the creation of what was called the 'Unclimbable Fence'. As our aircraft strength increased, we were able to hunt and attack U-boats before they could leave their hiding-places in the Bay of Biscay. They were forced to add several days to their passage out of the Bay, to avoid being seen. Their hunting patrols were cut down accordingly. By the spring of 1943 the air power of the Command was such that an area 100 miles deep could be patrolled continuously, right across the Bay. U-boats, at that time, had to surface every 100 miles to recharge their batteries, so they were almost certain to be located and attacked. Even when they surfaced at night, they were vulnerable, because of our use of Radar, and the Leigh light—the fierce searchlights fitted to the aircraft that could be switched on, like immense torches, to catch the sitting U-boats by surprise.

By May 1943, Dönitz realized that his submarines could not evade the 'Unclimbable Fence', so he ordered them to sail across the Bay on the surface, and fight back. He increased their defences with 20 mm. guns and machine-guns, and he posted Junkers 88 heavy fighters to aerodromes south of the Brest Peninsula, to engage our aircraft and divert them from the U-boats. There was one more change: the U-boats made out from the Bay in packs of three, to achieve concentrated gun-fire against our aircraft. But every one that was sighted was attacked and there were weeks of most successful killing.

In October 1943, in spite of all the enemy's new tactics, twelve U-boats were destroyed by Coastal and Canada's Eastern Air Command, each operating nearly 1,000 miles into the Atlantic. A further kill was shared with surface craft. The U-boats were forced, temporarily, to give up the battle, until the German inventors could devise some new trick with which to outwit us.

But we also suffered our losses. They had been heavy and tragic in September, after we had introduced intensive anti-aircraft patrols, with Mosquitoes and Beaufighters. At first, the patrols were successful: so many German aircraft were destroyed that they were no longer a considerable menace to our heavy aircraft patrols and attacks on the U-boats. But the Germans then tried a new plan: they sent formations of Focker-Wolff 190's, single-engine fighters, to beat our Mosquitoes and Beaufighters back. We lost many men and many aircraft. During one task, three of six Beaufighters were shot down, and in a later operation four out of six were lost. But our fortunes ascended again: this new opposition was broken down and, some months ago, the Germans admitted failure by withdrawing their fighters by day—allowing them to fly only at night.

Coastal Command is perhaps less romantic than Fighter Command, with the glory it enjoyed during the Battle of Britain; or Bomber Command, raining death and destruction on the cities and towns of the enemy. The long, lonely vigils over the

Atlantic lack the drama and sudden flashes of battle that please public imagination. Also, there is a deeper darkness of secrecy on our tasks, because continuity of surprise is a good friend to Coastal Command. The circumstances of flying in the three commands are different. If a pilot in a formation of bombers meets enemy aircraft, he has a chance of survival: if he is hit over land he may be able to bale out and be picked up. In the heavy aircraft of Coastal Command there is less risk of attack by enemy aircraft, but when the Junkers do appear, they are usually in packs of twelve, and even sixteen. The Junkers can use cloud cover: it takes a very big cloud to conceal a hefty Liberator. The chances then, of being shot down into the sea, are miserably high. The cloudless days of last summer were a harsh test for the determination of our pilots, when as many as twelve swift Junkers would fly out from Brest, every day, to turn the Liberators back from their attacks on the U-boats.

Also the chances of rescue from the sea are slight, in spite of the vigilance of the aircraft of Air-Sea Rescue. Our heavy aircraft fly four and five hundred miles from land, and aircrews shot down in these lonely stretches of sea endure days, and even weeks, of hunger and faint hope, sitting in their rubber dinghies, often wounded, watching the sky for the heartening sight of a friendly aircraft, or the horizon for the sight of a ship.

At the end of last summer, it was obvious that the Battle of the Bay had been won. U-boats were attacked, day and night, and they were forced to travel under water at reduced speed: it was in this healthy state that the last battle against the U-boats was to be fought, during the first weeks of the invasion of Europe.

October 1943. When I had been at Coastal Command Head-quarters for some months, I suggested to my Commander-in-Chief that pilots who had been through some terrible experiences, in battle, or drifting in dinghies during long periods of anxiety and privation, might half-rid themselves of their memories by writing them down—narratives into which they could release their pent-up feelings.

Some of the pilots, rescued after being shot down and drifting in their rubber dinghies, develop a fear—a hatred of the sea—and they become temperamentally unsuited for further flying and combat.

I began my experiment on a twenty-one-year-old pilot, Jack Foss, who had been adrift for seven days, off the coast of Portugal. He is a direct, kind boy, but the horrors of death and madness among his crew, during the almost hopeless journey, had soured his heart. He came to Coastal Command Headquarters and we put him into a comfortable room, with a tumbler full of sharpened pencils and a pile of foolscap paper. He was reluctant to begin his story: he was not used to writing more than letters home. Then came an astonishing change: during two days, he wrote a narrative of almost 6,000 words.

Now and then I went in with a cup of coffee, or to ask him how he was getting on. Every time, his head was low over his paper and he was writing, in a fever of energy, as if—as I had hoped—pouring his terrible privations into the form of words helped to rid him of their poison.

This is the essence of Jack Foss's story:

"We took off from Gibraltar on a September morning on an anti-submarine patrol. The weather was just the type that Coastal Command boys hope for; a steady wind, a warm and pleasant atmosphere, with enough cloud to protect us in case enemy fighters attacked us over the Bay of Biscay.

"Everyone was in high spirits. We wished to find and destroy a U-boat, which our crew hadn't done up to then. This, coupled with the ideal weather, was the reason for our feeling joyful and pleased.

"At one o'clock in the afternoon everything was going fine. We were travelling fairly close to the Spanish coast. It looked peaceful.

"Later, as we flew westwards, the wind gained in strength until there was no cloud to be seen. At ten minutes past three we had just levelled off at about 3,000 feet, everything shipshape, when we saw what was to prove a very fatal, solitary cumulus cloud. As we approached, one of our gunners shouted, 'Aircraft dead ahead just entered cloud.' The skipper immediately altered course to starboard: then, out of the corner of his eye, he sighted another aircraft attacking us in a dive from the port bow. He immediately shouted over the intercom., 'Look out, boys! Junkers! Jettison bombs.' While he shouted that, he was turning into the attack, hoping to get out of the enemy's sights. We both looked up and were just thanking God that we had foiled the attack when I saw flames spitting from the leading edges of the Junkers' wings. A second later the skipper turned to me and said, 'They've got me,' then seemed to go stiff.

"I took over the controls. A very upsetting feeling came over me because I could see the hole in his chest where the cannon shell had passed through. I shouted over the intercom. that the skipper was hit but got no reply. It was several minutes later that I realized that the intercom. was unserviceable. Then a horrifying dryness came into my throat. I couldn't swallow or part my tongue from the roof of my mouth because I realized that without fighter control from one of the gunners it was really a matter of time, unless clouds came along, before we were shot down.

"At twenty past three we knew beyond all doubt that there were four of them attacking us. And we knew that we would be very lucky indeed if we got away. The little cloud the Junkers had been dodging in and out of was far too small to conceal our Liberator.

"For the next two or three minutes the four Junkers circled around us while I was busy keeping the aircraft doing everything that they teach one not to at training school. Five minutes after, the second attack began, from the same Junkers as before.

"This time it was a starboard frontal attack. I immediately turned in, undulating fiercely. But this time he really had us fair and square in his sights. I had just pushed the aircraft over into an almost vertical bank when I looked up and saw flames coming from his wings again. My heart almost stopped beating, because this attack was identical to the first attack when the skipper had got his cannon shell. But I was lucky again as regards to myself, but poor Jimmy in the mid-upper was hit badly. He had bullets in his foot, leg and in his rear, and scratches all over his face and neck. He fell more than climbed out of the turret.

"I shouted for someone else to get in quickly as that turret has 0·5 guns, and Jerry doesn't like those. Jack was just about to get in when Jimmy called, 'It's no use. The turret feeder block is busted.' It was well and truly busted.

"While I had been throwing the aircraft about I noticed that the controls were getting difficult to move. I glanced around at the skipper's seat and found out why. His body had somehow got jammed in the controls. I would have got him out earlier had I been able to. I shouted to F/O Thornton behind me, who was a passenger, to get him out of the seat and sit there himself. After a bit of hard struggling he did. I was still throwing the aircraft about the sky as if it was a fighter: it is no easy job to keep one's balance when an aircraft is being flown like that.

"F/O Thornton had no sooner sat in the seat behind the armour plating when a hail of cannon shells came screaming through the aircraft, smashing every instrument on the panel except the air-speed indicator, and thudding into the armour plating at our backs. It was a good job that he moved into that seat otherwise he would have been smashed to pieces later. It was in this third attack that our tail turret was smashed, and the tail gunner got a cannon shell through his backbone. He was fatally wounded, but he crawled out of the tail turret, just in time to get to one of the side guns. Then he got a good burst in, at one of them, just as he died. Although none of us saw, we believe that Junkers crashed into the sea, because from that moment there were only three attacking us.

"Suddenly the engineer came rushing out of the bomb bay. He knocked my hand off the throttles and shouted, as he was feathering the prop, that our No. 2 engine was on fire. Luckily, the fire went out when the engine stopped turning. But by that time our No. 3 engine was set on fire and throwing a 30-ft.

flame alongside the aircraft. It was in that attack that I think everyone in the aircraft got wounded as the bullets and cannon shells absolutely raked the aircraft from tip to tail. I got wounded in the arms and legs.

"I went to feather No. 3 engine, but there were no levers there to pull. When I tried to get the engine fire extinguisher alongside me I found that it was covered with twisted bars of metal, done by the cannon shells. From that time on they just did attack after attack. As I was getting weak I told F/O Thornton to push or pull the control column with me, so that I could keep the action fierce.

"The controls were getting fairly mushy and the aileron control was almost unserviceable. The flames were beginning to cook the petrol, the port wheel was hanging limply down, the flaps were unserviceable, two engines had gone and the outer two were beginning to seize up. So I decided to ditch. I shouted to the boys, 'Emergency hatch open, ditching.' It wasn't easy for them to move because every one of them was wounded.

"When the boys were in their places, I started the aircraft into a shallow dive from a thousand feet and levelled out just above the tops of the waves. We had to go along the swells of the sea, until the aircraft was down near stalling speed. Then I sat her down before a wave could knock us down—more by good luck than judgment.

"The aircraft immediately sank and we went down with it —twenty feet under water—completely dark. The terrific impact with the water had broken its back and almost ours as well: like hitting a brick wall at a hundred miles an hour. It was far too dark to see anything. I just breathed in water and thought, 'Here it is'. We must have been under there nearly two minutes before any of us struggled free. No one can realize the horrible feeling it gives one, to be jammed in an aircraft under water and slowly drowning. But we did struggle free.

"When we finally got to the surface, all except the skipper and Pat, I suddenly saw daylight and took a deep breath of air. We were appalled to see only one dinghy: the rest had gone down with the aircraft. It wasn't easy getting seven of us into the two-man dinghy. Our Mae Wests had been riddled and didn't keep us up. Some could not swim and their wounds made it difficult to hoist them aboard. The sea was rough and we were sick over the side, from swallowing so much salt water.

"We hadn't been in the dinghy more than an hour when we sighted smoke on the horizon. Somebody said, 'Surely we're not saved already,' and started to wave the telescopic flag. The smoke came nearer and we saw the shape of a vessel, altering course towards us. We all started talking and cheering like wildfire as we thought we were going to be picked up and saved. As the craft got nearer we saw it was a 517-ton U-boat with a modified conning-tower. It was dirty yellowish in colour. The navigator gave the order not to answer any questions; just to say 'water'.

"The U-boat came within twenty yards and we saw the Germans quite clearly. They were clean-shaven. One of them called, 'You British? You Allies?'

"We did not answer: we just shouted 'Water!'

"When the commander of the U-boat gathered that we didn't intend saying anything, he gave orders to his men to carry on, which they did, roughly in a westerly direction. Ben said, 'Would you sooner be taken prisoner, rather than risk your chance of being picked up?' We all said, 'No, we'd sooner take the chance.'

"We were all highly thankful as none of us wished to be taken prisoner, especially on board a U-boat. We were thankful also because we were all expecting to be raked with machine-gun bullets at any moment so we were ready to dive into the water as soon as any of the Germans got behind a gun. Although some of us were badly wounded and dying, there still remained the thought that life is sweet, and we were determined to live as long as possible. Had they fired on us, I don't doubt that we would all have been killed, even if we had dived under the water. We couldn't have stayed there for ever and they would be certain to have got us when we came up.

"When the U-boat had passed on, we really gave vent to our feelings: a very lurid description of what we thought about

U-boats and Germans in general. The description certainly isn't
befitting to write on paper. There were some really choice words;
among them, 'The bastards have gone.'

"Later on in the evening, we took stock of what we had and
the results were not very encouraging. We only had two small
cans of water, one small tin of orange juice, a green lemon and
the usual Horlicks tablets and chocolate. As you can see, this
was not going to last long between seven of us. And there was
no knowing when we might be picked up—if ever. Ben said,
'Well, boys, there isn't much chance of shipping being this far
down the Bay.'

"Our morale was very low for a short while, but in true
English fashion we soon got over our low feelings and started
seeing how badly wounded each of us was. Ben had wounds
everywhere; a lot of them being caused by the ditching and the
rest by bullets and shrapnel. Jimmy had bullet wounds in his
face and leg and also his rear. We had to lay him down in the
bottom of the dinghy, as he was in so much pain. Then there
was Jack: he had the front part of his leg blown off by a cannon
shell. He said, 'Even if we are saved I suppose I shall have to
have my leg off when we get back.' Dick had a bullet right
between the shoulder blades. Mike, Jerry and myself were the
most fortunate of all. Mike had only a cannon shell blow a piece
out of the side of his knee. F/O Thornton had a scratch on one
of his fingers, and myself a bullet in the wrist and shrapnel in
the knees.

"When we had finished bandaging ourselves with odd bits
of torn shirt and handkerchiefs, we settled down as best as
possible along the walls of the dinghy, bracing ourselves so that
we wouldn't fall back into the water. It was terribly cramped.
Had any of us fallen out I doubt if the rest of us could have
got him back again because we were beginning to feel the
reaction from the attack and the ditching; also from the experience
of being jammed in the aircraft under water.

"That night was hell to us. The biting wind went right
through us, like a knife. We were soaked through and through
again. There was no covering to protect us in any way whatso-

ever. Our wounds were paining us horribly, because our circulation was still fairly good. As the night went on each of us wanted to turn around or move our legs because of a cramped feeling we kept getting. This in the dead of night, with the sea throwing us around was no easy matter. We didn't talk much. Just mumbled, 'Bloody cold,' or 'For heaven's sake keep still,' when someone moved. Never before were any of us so thankful as when the dawn came.

"All that day we kept a watchful eye out for aircraft or ships, but we were all getting lower and lower in ourselves. We just looked at each other. We were chilled to the marrow of our bones. We had not even seen so much as a bird or a piece of driftwood. After we had had our meals of Horlicks tablets and a suck of the lemon all round, the lemon being finished after this, we began to settle down for another night. We were just about to give up hope when Mike sighted a Sunderland a few miles away. We said, 'Good boy, Mike, nice work.' Everyone cheered and began waving frantically. But it was to no avail as the Sunderland didn't see us at all. One could read the thoughts of everyone quite easily, as it was so plain to be seen.

"I thought of my wife and the little baby she is going to have. And of my people, who are not in very good health. I wondered how they would be now as they were sure to have been told I was missing. That thought was more horrible to me than anything I was suffering in the dinghy.

"That night was just one long nightmare. We had had no food or anything warm to drink that would help to keep out the bitter cold, and when dawn came we were so cold that the pain from our wounds had ceased. But another pain was coming, to our feet and legs, caused by the continual soaking from the sea. This meant that to bend or unbend our legs was sheer agony and torture. But we had to move every now and then because of cramp in our bodies. We had plenty of pain and agony.

"All that day we kept watch for aircraft until we felt our eyes would drop out from staring. About six o'clock in the evening we sighted an aircraft in the distance. But it was too far away for us to recognize what it was, let alone signal to it. So

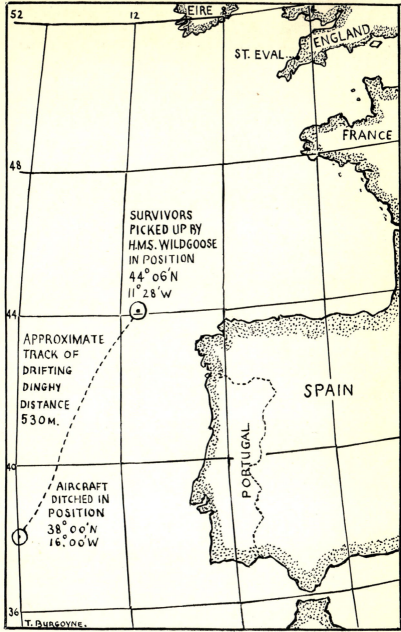

52 12 EIRE 8

ENGLAND

ST. EVAL.

48

FRANCE

SURVIVORS
PICKED UP BY
H.M.S. WILDGOOSE
IN POSITION
44° 06′N
11° 28′W

44

APPROXIMATE
TRACK OF
DRIFTING
DINGHY
DISTANCE
530 M.

SPAIN

PORTUGAL

40

AIRCRAFT
DITCHED IN
POSITION
38° 00′N
16.° 00′W

36

T. BURGOYNE.

Chart showing distance and direction of drift of Flying Officer J. Foss's dinghy from the day he ditched to the time of his rescue, seven days later (see p. 128)

Marshal of the R.A.F. Lord Douglas of Kirtleside, G.C.B., M.C., D.F.C., D.L.

From a portrait by Eric Kennington

U-boat, sunk by a Sunderland of the R.C.A.F. in the Atlantic, on March 3, 1944

The crew of the same U-boat in their dinghies

"The officers' mess . . . is a stark, requisitioned hotel by the sea" (see p. 150)

we just gave that one up as a bad job. We had our meal, which was the usual Horlicks tablets, and the tin of orange juice this time. Then we settled down as best we could to wait for the night of horror that was to come. That night the sea was very rough. The ones that could, took it in turns to keep the dinghy headed into the sea with an oar which we had found under the rubber seat. This was torture anew for us, because we had to sit upright in the dinghy and face the full blast of the weather. By the time the next one's turn came, the one who had been guiding the dinghy was frozen stiff.

"The following morning, when it was light enough to see, we took stock of ourselves. Everyone was blue with cold and it was almost impossible for any of us to move our legs. Poor Jimmy and Jack. Their wounds were beginning to go gangrenous. They could see it and it turned them slightly hysterical. We managed to quieten them down though, with such things as, 'We are bound to be seen today,' and giving everyone a piece of chocolate, which is part of the small emergency pack.

"I can say, with the deepest of sincerity, that a piece of chocolate to us in our condition was thought greater of and treasured more than a home-cooked dinner would be to people who had plenty. The mere thought of a home-cooked meal was nearly enough to send us mad. Our condition was so low by this time, and our nerves so frayed, that we began to be snappy towards one another. We barked, 'Watch my foot,' or 'Look out for my arm.' I think if it hadn't been for the fact that two aircraft passed nearby, four or five miles away, we would probably have started fighting. They missed us, of course, but they gave us hope. The slightest thing anyone did or said that didn't quite suit the other person near by, then an argument started straight away. All that day it was just one argument after another, and by the time nightfall came we each and every one of us were utterly exhausted.

"That night again was the same as the other nights, just one long torture. The wind was getting colder than ever, for we had been drifting in a northerly direction all the time. In one way this helped us, because of the greater possibility of seeing ships.

But the water was getting colder. As I have said before, the wind, coupled with the fact that our resistance was now very low, had rather drastic effects on our will to live. . . .

"Early next morning one of the boys started muttering to himself and flinging his arms about. Jack and I gave him some morphia. Then Jack cuddled into him to keep him warm, and I think that was one of the main reasons why he kept going that day, as he was able to get some warmth back into his body. But it also meant that Jack was getting worse, as he had nothing with which he could replace the heat.

"In the afternoon of that day we had luck at last. Dick sighted a Sunderland. We all waved our hands and the flag as best we could. When it saw us and altered course towards us, none of us could speak. We all had a lump in our throat as we were so happy to think at last that we were going to be saved, that we were almost crying. We signalled frantically for the aircraft to land as the sea was smooth. The captain realized what we needed for he dived over us and dropped Horlicks tablets and water in some Mae Wests to which we frantically paddled. When we got the water in the dinghy we all went crazy for a while, because instead of trying to save it for as long as possible, we just drank tin after tin until the whole dozen tins had gone.

"Soon after dropping the water the Sunderland made off for base, as his fuel was probably getting low by this time. That night Catalinas came over with searchlights to keep in touch with us. But we had nothing to signal back. One of the flame floats they dropped fell near to us. The flame was five or six feet high and we had to paddle away or it would set us on fire. Although the searchlights swept across us several times, they didn't seem somehow to see us, and just before midnight they gave it up and went away.

"The next day never seemed to be coming as we were all so eager to have another aircraft around us to show that they were still in touch with us. Though we strained our eyes continually that day, we never saw an aircraft anywhere. It wasn't until late in the afternoon that we gave up hope and resigned ourselves to our fate. Late that evening we decided to try fishing with bent hairpins and a piece of string. We bought the hairpins in Gib., for our wives. We used chewing gum for bait. We tried for over two hours but we had no luck and gave it up as a bad job. We tried a piece of rag as bait and the fish came up to the surface. But they would not bite. If we had caught any fish, it wouldn't have been fried either, as by this time we were hungry enough to eat it raw and really enjoy it. In any case, there wasn't likely to be any frying-pan in the dinghy with which to fry the fish, so fried fish and raw fish were to us just a thought.

"After we had given up fishing, we tried knocking down seagulls which were flying around us, fully determined to eat them raw and suck their blood. There were about twelve of them, crying and swooping.

"We beckoned them with our fingers and said, 'Come near my beauty.' But they were far too quick for us to hit with the oar and so we had to go hungry again, having only one Horlicks tablet each that day.

"As the night came we began to get very thirsty and, try as we could to resist it, in the end we were drinking sea water like ordinary water. When the first one drank it, we said, 'Stop, you'll go mad.' But he did not stop. We all drank it in the end. I think that was one of the main things that hastened his death, because just around midnight he died. We stripped him and took his personal effects, and then buried him at sea. Jack said a little prayer for him, the rest of us closing our eyes and placing our hands together. Early the following morning Dick died, and we did the same again, and I think those two prayers were the sincerest I have ever heard, as every word was meant, and it came from the bottom of all our hearts.

"Early the following morning two Sunderlands arrived, but we were far too gloomy to shout or cheer. We just acknowledged them, and when they dropped their supplies we picked some of it up, being far too weak to get it all. They dropped a first-aid kit on a parachute, but although we tried hard, the remaining five of us, we just could not get it aboard. We were too weak. So we cut the parachute away and used it to break the wind.

In one of the packs we picked up there were some distress signals, and our eyes glistened when we saw these, as it meant we could keep in touch with the aircraft that night.

"The dinghy by this time was leaking badly at the valve, and we had to pump it up about every hour. This was using up all our remaining strength, but we managed to keep going somehow. That night Catalinas came over again with searchlights. This time we were prepared and we let off distress signals every now and then and kept in touch with them until they left for their base.

"Early the following morning one of us went delirious and, after trying to bite everyone for about half an hour, he collapsed in the bottom of the dinghy. He tried to bite at Bill's jugular vein, to suck his blood.

"After this little bit of trouble we settled down in a more or less dopey condition. About an hour later two Sunderlands came along, one of them circling us, and the other going off in one direction and returning again. We knew what this meant, but by this time we were too far gone to even trouble about being saved. We agreed to pump the dinghy up once more and if we weren't picked up by the time it deflated, we would go down with it, as our will to live had long been extinguished.

"Luckily, about twelve minutes after we had made this decision, H.M.S. *Wildgoose* appeared on the horizon. Instead of cheering or shouting with joy, we all just sat there with tears in our eyes, for at last we were saved. They picked us up at about a quarter to ten that morning. They took us below into the marvellous warmth and gave us boiling coffee, which we drank as if it were only lukewarm. All our feelings had gone out of our bodies. The doctor took charge of us then, and as there wasn't room for all of us in his ward, I was taken aft to a cabin.

"Later that night another died, and sometime later Bill died as well. The doctor did not tell me until about a week later, as he wanted me strong enough to be able to take it, in case it had a fatal effect on me. All that day I lay in bed, thinking of them, what they had gone through, how they had suffered, and when they were safe aboard ship to suddenly pass away and to have suffered in vain.

"The Navy gave them a ceremonial burial at sea, and there they lay at rest; two men who gave their lives for their country, so that it may be free and beautiful to live in for years to come.

"So out of the nine of us who started from Gibraltar that fateful day, only three of us are now living to tell the tale of an experience which makes us have a hardened outlook on life; not smiling or laughing like we used to, but remembering those seven horrible days as if it had only just happened."

Note.—The chart showing the drift of the dinghy, during seven days, is reproduced opposite page 142.

1944

IN mid-January 1944, Air Chief Marshal Sir Sholto Douglas[1] took over command of Coastal and, during the next four and a half months, he directed the war against the U-boats and prepared for the final battle. Although the rough seas of winter hampered the patrols at the turn of the year, 36 U-boats were attacked during January, and there were 5 attacks on shipping off the Norwegian coast. But there was punishment: an equal number of our aircraft were lost in these northern waters.

The assessors of our victories, in the Admiralty, were always cautious, and we had to wait until they had made their slow, honest reckonings over their desks before they would announce the balance-sheet of conquest. It interested me, as a New Zealander, to watch their English unwillingness to boast, or claim the slightest victory, until they were certain. Late in January the statistics of attacks on enemy shipping were given to me for the *Review*: they made good reading. From March 1, 1941, to the end of December 1943, 339 enemy ships—representing more than a million tons—had been sunk, seriously damaged, or damaged, by aircraft of the Command. It was a solace to realize that even a damaged ship was a useless ship, until it could totter back to be repaired and sail again.

During these months before 'D' day I remember that there was less idle pleasure in our lives at Headquarters. Although we worked in a London suburb, aircrews arrived almost every morning to describe their attacks: we were thus constantly aware of the battle, not merely as a succession of reports arriving on our desks.

I recall one day when two Liberator crews arrived—one American, the other British—to describe a fatal attack they had shared, on a U-boat. The Americans, big-limbed as bears, and at ease, sat on one side of the room: opposite sat the British crew, shorter men, compact, and more taut in their movements.

[1] Marshal of the R.A.F. Lord Douglas of Kirtleside, G.C.B., M.C., D.F.C., D.L.

At the table between sat Captain Peyton-Ward[1] and the other
assessors, to listen to the evidence of attack. The pilots spoke in
turn; each described the part his crew, and his aircraft had
played, one flying in after the other, to drop the depth-charges.
It was touching to listen to their slow, modest statements,
neither of them wishing to detract from the valour and success
of the other. The Americans were willing to give all the victory
to the British: the British were equally anxious to concede that
the Americans had dropped the charge that sent the U-boat to
its doom. They seemed old and wise, although none of them
was out of his twenties: their nobleness and modesty were
moving to watch.

I am recalling all this, after eleven years, but I do not think
that I imagine the increasing seriousness that came into our lives.
There was less triviality in our evening diversions in the mess—
less singing of 'The Ball at Kirriemuir' and splashing of beer
into the grand piano. We already smelled the final battle that was
to come, so soon. After dinner, instead of playing 'liar-dice'
and pouring our strained jocularity over the bar, we would go
into the Operations Room and watch the ominous score on the
gigantic map, the symbols of aircraft, U-boats and ships being
moved—all that was happening in that moment over the seas,
from Iceland to the Azores, patrolled by Coastal Command—all,
in miniature, within the area of a wall.

During these months I had as my helper a young pilot who
had crashed into the sea, after long months of action against
the enemy. My older mind was sharpened by what he explained
to me: on this eve of invasion, he made the coming conflict
real and terrible. I remember sitting beside him as we read the
report of the explosion of a depth-charge, so close to the hull
of a U-boat that the aircrew saw chunks of metal flying past
them. Sammy,[2] with his experience, was able to describe to me
what this meant: the aircraft flying at fifty feet, the vicious
attack, almost body to body, of aircraft and U-boat, the hull
split into smithereens, and the fragments flying up 'like birds'.

[1] Captain D. V. Peyton-Ward, C.B.E., R.N., Senior Naval Staff Officer with
Coastal Command.
[2] Flight-Lieutenant A. C. I. Samuel.

We studied the combat reports and I became gruesomely aware of what it meant for a U-boat, with forty men in it, to be destroyed and sent into oblivion. He made the task of meteorological reconnaisance flights real to me, and—not always patiently, but wisely—he would force me to comprehend more of the speed of ships, dinghy drift, the history of torpedoes, and the oneness of mind necessary among the crew of an aircraft during an attack. It was all alarming, but adventurous, after my years of editing old letters and Victorian journals.

There was a subdued, yet strong influence in Coastal Command that impressed my civilian mind: the absolute co-ordination and sympathy between the Naval officers and the R.A.F. officers working at Headquarters. It is folly for a civilian, used to his untidy freedoms, to suppose that he really becomes service-minded. I like to think that I was at home in my uniform and badges, but I was never truly absorbed into the R.A.F., and I remained a writer, seeing the battle, and the play of characters, through a writer's eyes. I was always astonished by the high example in human behaviour, within that incredible Victorian mansion—whether it was in the Operations Room, the mess, or on the clock-golf course, which was the best we could do for exercise, with so many villas pressing in about us.

The considerable Naval staff, under Captain Peyton-Ward, worked in the same offices with the R.A.F. Captain Peyton-Ward's selfless devotion to his task made pettiness or inter-service jealousy quite impossible. My own work benefited from his willingness to help. I began by knowing nothing of what the bombing of a U-boat meant, and I had to go to him, several times each month, for reports of attacks. He was busy, with great problems of policy, but he would always spare me time in the evening to go over the details of an attack, so that I could, in turn, write of it with every fact in its place. I have known few men who combined a strong will and perfect manners in such nice balance. As Captain Peyton-Ward spent his leisure hours in the mess, and slept within a few yards of his office, he was never off duty, and his influence on us was constant, salutary, and delightful.

During February, March, and April 1944, the tactics of the enemy showed that they were nursing their U-boat strength for the last round. Their fleet at sea, in the Bay area, nearest to the probable route of the 'D' day invasion, numbered about sixty. To conserve his forces, Dönitz ordered them to risk meeting our aircraft only during daylight, and to submerge at sundown. In May, our Intelligence brought the pleasing news that many of these sixty U-boat commanders were inexperienced men, some on their maiden patrols.

Our state of quiet confidence led to the morning when a sentry with a bayonet was posted outside Captain Peyton-Ward's office. We suspected that the plans for 'D' day had come and that they were in his safe. I learned afterwards that his W.A.A.F. officers, Phil Davies and Sue Cull, who knew the secret, had been ordered to share the same bedroom in case either of them talked in her sleep.

Late in May. The A.O.C.-in-C. sent for me and said I was to fly with him on an interesting journey. We took off in his sumptuous white Hudson and made for the coast of Kent, flying at 1,000 feet. I could see the London road—no longer a rolling English road, for it was thick with American jeeps, like beetles crawling along a yellow ribbon. We passed over an airfield with Old Glory flying: then we came so low that I could see American sailors sitting on a gate. About eleven o'clock we flew over Gravesend, where Pocahontas is buried. I had the curious illusion of no longer being in England.

Then we left the coast and were over the ocean. To starboard were the white buttresses of England: across the water, in the mist, lay the enemy coast. We flew on and came to a gentle stretch of sand and surf, where children paddled in the old days. The beach was a labyrinth of barbed wire; the surf was bitter with almost five years of war.

From Dover we looked across to Dunkirk. The story of Mr. Churchill, in France, in 1940, seemed like an episode far away in history. "We will go on fighting," he told them. "What with?" they asked. "I don't know," he answered, "I haven't had time to think about that yet."

Dunkirk retired into the mist. I thought of our poverty, four years ago, and of our allied riches now. The coast is thick with the engines of war: the pontoons that cross the rivers are low in the water, laden with tanks and gun-carriages; and thousands of aircraft are waiting on the aerodromes. In the shelter of benevolent old trees, planted in the reign of Queen Anne, there are Nissen huts packed close with soldiers. Within the enclosures of the hedgerows, where the early honeysuckle is in flower, the harvest is of bayonets. The sounds of England have changed: the rattle of farm carts on the cobbles, and the noise of birds, are overwhelmed by a symphony of clanging steel. We are on the eve of invasion: the island, crowded with Britons, Americans, Australians, Canadians, New Zealanders, and South Africans, Belgians, Frenchmen, Dutchmen, Poles, and Czechoslovakians, has one entity. England is like a single armed warrior going into combat.

I thought over the four years since May 1940, when I saw Mr. Neville Chamberlain walking with his wife in St. James's Park, raising his hat to soldiers and sailors as he made his way to Downing Street and his desk. The silver balloons over London seemed complacent: the barbed wire entanglements along the grass verges of the parks were already beginning to rust. We imagined that our soldiers and pilots were safely entrenched in France. Then came May 10, when the Germans invaded Holland; then Belgium and Luxembourg. A new leader walked into Downing Street, and when he was asked to state his policy he answered, "To wage war."

Then came Dunkirk: our soldiers stood shoulder to shoulder in the surf, with the ghosts of Agincourt, Blenheim, and Ypres to encourage them in their tragic withdrawal. Three hundred and thirty-five thousand of them were brought back during the 'miracle of deliverance', but there was a considerable army left in France. Two thousand four hundred British guns were in the hands of the enemy, and all the transport and tanks that had been with the army in the north—seven hundred tanks and fifty thousand vehicles in all.

Our forces at home were less than a score of divisions, against Germany's two hundred. The Secretary of State for War admitted a year later, that of tanks there was 'virtually none'. In 1942, more figures were admitted: Lord Beaverbrook said, "Forty-seven warships were sunk in the operations off Norway and Dunkirk. When the evacuation was over, half the destroyer fleet lay awaiting repairs in the dockyards." The R.A.F. had lost forty-five per cent of its bomber strength during forty-two days fighting in the Battle of France. While the soldiers were waiting to be brought home from Dunkirk, we were so short of aircraft that a pilot, attacked over the beach, returned to England, plugged the bullet holes in his aircraft with chewing-gum, and returned to fight again over the terrible water.

It was not easy to realize this weakness of four years ago as one soared over Kent—above roads choked by the traffic of invasion.

We flew inland again, to an aerodrome from which British and American pilots will go into combat together, when 'D' day comes. Old Glory waved at one end of the aerodrome: at the other end was the blue flag of the R.A.F. Sir Sholto Douglas spoke to the allied company, telling them a little of the coming tasks and exciting their valour with a short but moving speech.

Then we flew back to London, over miles of farm land, and occasional clusters—of church steeple and cottages, nestling into its protection—and the 'big house', the park, and consoling acres of corn. The farms beneath us, like all the farms of England, have increased their produce by seventy-five per cent since the dreadful warning of May 1940.

The statistics are romantic. From the poverty in air power, after Dunkirk, the factories worked night and day until, during the year ended March 1944, they produced 27,273 aircraft. Then one recalls the park railings of London, salvaged, to help to build more destroyers. We became excited by little sacrifices: a postcard, forgotten in a writing-desk, made fifty cartridge wads. Gramophone records of old dance tunes were made into accumulator tops for aircraft: forty-two useless door keys became a steel helmet.

It was not until two and a half years later that we were told, in the House of Commons, that we had been on the brink of famine and that we had been saved by the food sent from America. She had made up her heart, while she was waiting to make up her mind.

The old fears and misfortunes seemed to lose their meaning as I flew over southern England today, in the May sunshine. I returned with the sensation of having seen something formidable and frightening—an army, and an air force, waiting for the dawn of battle: an island prepared to invade a continent.

We landed at Northolt. As we drove back to Coastal Command Headquarters, Sir Sholto Douglas said, "There was a purpose in our jaunt this morning. I have a job for you to do: you will know about it in a few days' time."

May 28. Three days ago I was summoned by Air Vice-Marshal Ellwood[1] to be briefed on a high level regarding the plans for the Command on 'D' day. (On a table in the corner of his office was his violin, which he played for me one evening when the day's tasks were over.)

The Air Vice-Marshal opened a safe and brought out a map of the Channel, and the dreadful documents. It was like being initiated into a religious mystery, watching his finger outline the area of water, and the coast, where the invasion of Europe will begin.

When he had explained the dark secret, the Air Vice-Marshal described my task. I am to go to a Coastal Command station in Cornwall, to stay with 224 Squadron which flies Liberators that will help to shield our invasion forces from the U-boats now lurking in the Bay of Biscay. My headquarters will be with this one squadron, but I must also travel to all the aerodromes in

[1] Air Marshal Sir Aubrey Ellwood, K.C.B., D.S.C.

South-West England and describe the combats between heavy aircraft and U-boats; also the attacks by our lighter aircraft on German fighters and enemy shipping, off the French coast. These combats will constitute The Battle of the South-Western Approaches. What I write each week is to be sent to the Commander-in-Chief.

I hope to weave a second purpose into my diary; to leave some record of the character and spirit of the Command which I serve. This spirit is not insular, because the Command is not insular. Its bases extend from Iceland to the Azores; from Norway to the Mediterranean. The aircrews of the heavy aircraft are unlike the men who fly fighters: their long vigils, sometimes thirteen hours, over immense spaces of sea, give them some of the tranquillity of sailors, with occasional, unpredictable flashes of temper or exuberance. They, also, are companions of the sea.

The aircrews of 224 Squadron are an astonishing company. Forty-four are Canadians, thirty-three are Australians and New Zealanders and one is an American. There is also a Swiss pilot, who has helped to build up the illustrious reputation of the Squadron, a Chilian and a Brazilian. Among the N.C.O.s is a Chinese who was born in Australia. One hundred and thirty-seven are Britons.

The officers' mess where I am to live is a stark, requisitioned hotel by the sea, where old ladies and clergymen on holiday drank their daring glasses of sherry, in the days of peace. It is called Watergate and is as ugly an arrangement of stone, bricks and glass as I have ever seen.

June 2. A dismal bus carried us from the quiet beach, over the Cornish hills, to the aerodrome at St. Eval. Trees cannot survive the ruthless storms on this coast: we look out over barren earth and thirsty fields. There are clumps of stingy tamarisk, a few yellow irises in the stream, and dusty purple veronica on the edges of the cliffs. It is mournful country when the storms come, but when the sun shines the sand and the hills are ablaze with pale gold light.

The bus took us up the last hill, past the flocks of immense Liberators, waiting to patrol the entrance to the Channel when 'D' Day comes. We stopped with a jerk before the camp cinema. Four thousand of us marched in—all the strength of St. Eval —to be told something of the plans for invasion. I felt curiously sly at breakfast this morning when some of the pilots were guessing by which way the invasion forces would cross the sea. Some thought Norway. Then someone said, "I bet old Bolitho knows something: he never says a bloody word." I felt guilty and embarrassed because the secret has been a menace to my peace of mind: I have been afraid that I might talk in my sleep.

The four thousand almost made the walls bulge. There was a station 'hop' in the cinema last night: the dust of the dancers still hovered in the air, so that we coughed. Then Group Captain Mead[1] came to the microphone. He is thirty-five, but looks twenty-five; erect as a drill sergeant and showing no signs of having been eleven days in a rubber dinghy, last summer, drinking three ounces of water a day and sustaining himself, before he was rescued, by squeezing the liquid from jelly fish to slake his thirst.

Mead introduced Air Vice-Marshal Baker[2], who commands the Group operating in all the West Country. He is a short, dark man, with quick movements and a passionless voice. Of the four thousand in the cinema, one thousand will be flying on 'D' day: they leaned forward, more anxiously, perhaps, to listen to what the Air Vice-Marshal said. He spoke coldly, as if he were reading a laundry list:

"As everybody in the South of England must now be aware, a most daring and highly organized movement of troops and equipment, which has taken months to prepare and perfect, is very shortly to take place in the shape of an invasion of the Continent of Europe. This enterprise must not fail—whatever the cost. . . . Many lives and vast quantities

[1] Air Commodore R. C. Mead, D.F.C., A.F.C.
[2] Air Marshal Sir Brian Baker, K.B.E., C.B., D.S.O., M.C., A.F.C.

of equipment will depend upon your efforts, not only during the passage of the ships in the initial assault, but during the period of build-up of the bridgehead afterwards."

The Air Vice-Marshal did not reveal the date, or the exact stretch of the French coast chosen for the landing, but he said, "There are four Narvik destroyers and one Dutch destroyer to be accounted for. You have already dealt a shrewd blow against the one and only *Elbing* left in Brest, which put her into dock— and into dry dock at that. The destruction of the Narviks is of vital importance and Coastal Command must do its part in getting them out of the way early in the proceedings."

We were then told something of the impending tasks. When 'D' day comes, the enemy will obviously bring the surviving U-boats out of their Bay ports and try to get them into the Channel, to attack the invasion ships as they cross to France. The plan to prevent this is simple. The 'Unclimbable Fence' of patrols will be moved to the entrance to the Channel, from a line between the Scillies and Brest, to a line between Portland Bill and Cherbourg.[1]

Air Vice-Marshal Baker explained these problems to us, as we stood in the cinema, and he pleased us with a piece of news: the first U-boat had already tried to break through, into the Channel, but an aircraft of 407 Squadron spotted it, and sank it, soon after it turned the corner at Ushant. After this exciting announcement, of what is really the beginning of the Battle of the South-Western Approaches, the Air Vice-Marshal said, "Good luck and good hunting," and stepped away from the microphone.

.   .   .   .   .   .

I walked from the cinema and back to the bus with Eric Batchelor, a six-foot-three British Columbian who knows what the German fighters based on the Brest Peninsula can do. Last

---

[1] See chart, opposite p. 207.

September, when he was flying his Liberator home from the Bay, he was attacked by six Ju. 88s for more than an hour—with a ten-minute break during which he was able to hide in a cloud. He was decorated for his 'masterly evasive tactics' against the six fighters, but he admitted, on the way to the bus, "I was frightened all the time: an hour and ten minutes is too long to be frightened. It is like having your stomach filled with butterflies."

I was not certain of his name up to then. I said, "You are Batchelor, aren't you?" He answered, "Yes, but call me 'Batch'. They do at home."

We agreed that the scene we had shared in the cinema was 'very English', and Batch said, "Yes, I guess that's the way they take these things."

The bus filled: in ten minutes we were back at Watergate, by the sea. Batch told me that, a few months ago, an American aircraft crashed into the near by cliff, at night. Three British airmen saw the flames of its destruction, but they were too far away to help. About five o'clock in the morning, some other Americans scrambled down to the beach, hoping that their friends might still be alive. They did not know the treachery of the Cornish coast: the tide came in, they could not escape, and five of them also were drowned.

.   .   .   .   .   .

Nobody said much about 'D' day and the invasion when we arrived back at Watergate: nobody said much about anything, because 'Butch' Pugh, a New Zealander, was there, and he has a triumphant voice. He said, "This is what I have been waiting for all the four and a half years. And it will be just my luck to be in hospital with tonsillitis or something when the day comes. If I am, I'll jump out of bed and fight in my underpants."

Butch is round as a tub, and his voice can pierce three floors of solid Victorian brickwork. His chief interest is his astonishing motor bicycle which cost him four pounds. It is just three years younger than he is: he saw it hanging from a hook in a garage, bought it, lifted it down, filled it with petrol, and rode it back to Watergate. As much as anything, it looks like a very old, rusty harp, with handlebars like a pair of Aberdeen Angus horns.

After dinner we walked up to the W.A.A.F. officers' mess and danced until our feet ached. On the way back, Batch, Butch and I talked about the English: we agreed that they have great courage. "And they're so bloody clever," said Butch, as a criticism rather than a compliment.

Butch said that what astonished him about the English was that while people were being killed in London, the Londoners took it calmly, but the moment St. Paul's and Buckingham Palace were bombed the people were indignant. He said, "Directly you hurt their history they blow up."

It is a glorious night: as we came to the edge of the Atlantic we could hear and see the waves coming in, like silver oil against the sand. I can still hear the mild thunder of the breakers, and the purr of aircraft, from my room.

June 3. Watergate is usually gay in the evening, when the air-crews come home, but the rooms seem cramped and shabby during the day. I walked on the beach this morning. A few ships steamed by, towards Land's End—children's toys against the grey screen of water. The air was warm and still, and the scene so placid, that it was not easy to realize the solemn purpose of the ships, laden deep in the sea.

Butch came in after tinkering with his motor bicycle for an hour. His hair was tousled and his hands were filthy. He said, "She's a wizard! She goes like a bird." Pure imagination: we learned afterwards that he had left part of the brake on the hill.

June 4. I worked all the morning and in the afternoon I went for a swim with Hubert Jessell. He is something of a scholar and does his own thinking, in silence. The breakers were like cascades of cracked china being flung at us, but it was exciting, if painful.

I dived and jumped about like a lunatic, and felt very fit as we walked back over the beach and washed our sandy feet in a stream.

There was a haze and the distant surface of the sea was sullen. The haze lifted for a few minutes and the sun broke through: in the gap, which was a curtain of egg-shell blue mist, we could see an immense fleet of ships heading out. We saw them for only those few minutes—a wall of shining ships on the horizon; then the grey haze descended again and we saw them no more. But the sight of them seemed to break the tension, as if something is happening at last.

* * * * *

This is my fourth day at Watergate. I felt shy of the air-crews at first—being a 'wingless wonder', a mere penguin among so many eagles, and twice as old as most of them. This evening, in the bar, Batch and another pilot suddenly picked me up and swung me back and forth in their cradled hands, in front of a window. As it was covered by a black-out curtain, I had no idea of what lay beyond and I was afraid: I imagined panes of glass and a drop of twenty feet to the rocks below. Then they shot me out. There was no glass beyond the black curtain and I landed nicely on a broad concrete ledge outside. I have never been more scared in my life, but I prayed and did not protest. Then Batch hauled me back into the bar and I was told that this was my initiation; that I had proved myself worthy of being a member of the mess. I hope there was no sickliness in my smile as I said how flattered and grateful I was to be accepted into their holy company. Then I said, "As a matter of fact, I think you are a lot of bastards to frighten an old man like that," and I insisted on being given a stiff drink to refresh my shattered nerves.

June 5. I suppose we may now say that the Battle of the South-Western Approaches has truly begun. On May 26 a U-boat stopped the Portuguese liner *Serpa Pinto* in mid-ocean and ordered the passengers, mostly refugees, into lifeboats where they kept them for nine hours. Three people, including a sixteen-months'-old baby, died during the transfer to the boats, and two American passengers were kidnapped by the U-boat captain.

The Navy, and our aircraft, have been trying to kill the German ever since, and last night a Liberator attacked a U-boat that may be the guilty one. But there was a surface haze and patches of fog, and the attack failed.

Johnny Posnett came to my room this afternoon and told me the story. He took off last night, in a thirty-knot wind. While they were in the outer Bay, about three o'clock in the morning, the radar contacted a possible U-boat. Johnny Posnett said, "It was still hazy, but there was a moon and a few stars. We decided that we had enough petrol left to investigate, so we homed on the U-boat, got ready to attack and switched on the Leigh light when we were a mile away. Then the flak came up, good and strong, and tracer from all directions. My navigator, R. E. Smith, had seen what he thought was the U-boat, but when we flew in we realized it was a shadow. We decided to do a second attack, up-moon, so we came in again. Smithy saw a colossal wake and the long, low hull. The Hun captain must have been an old hand because he showed remarkably good seamanship. He was going round in small circles, doing everything he knew to avoid us. The flak was pretty terrible but we were not hit once.

"We flew off and when we were a mile away the U-boat ceased firing at us; but when we were two miles away we must have made a perfect silhouette against the moon for he opened up with his heavy stuff. Again we got away without a scratch."

Then Johnny said, "But let's change the subject. I've read your book about Marie Tempest and I'd like to talk to you about her. When I was working in Hull I used to come up by the midday train, see her play, and then go back by the midnight train. I think she was wonderful."

So we forget about U-boats and talked of the theatre for half an hour, until Johnny looked at his watch and said, "Well, I must be going. My wife is having a baby today and I am catching the eight o'clock train to go up to London to see her."

A telegram came before he went to say that it was a boy.

June 6. Perry Allen[1] walked past my door while I was shaving. "Well, it's begun," he said.

Butch put his head out of the door and asked, "What's begun?"

Perry said, "The bloody invasion."

Somebody along the passage yelled, "Well, I can swim forty miles, what of it?" and Perry answered, "Yes, and put your foot on a bloody land mine just as you step on the beach."

Butch said, "Well, I'm ready when the call comes for me to get mowing."

"Mowing?" I asked.

"Yes, get the old reaper out. You know, Death," he answered.

We went downstairs and listened to the voice over the radio.

"In a moment you will hear the Supreme Commander, Allied Expeditionary Force, General Dwight D. Eisenhower," and then the comfortable, friendly American voice that did not seem to be very belligerent, "A landing was made this morning on the coast of France."

Then followed the astonishing figures; thousands of ships, thousands of aircraft, thousands of men.

I thought again of the lonely pilot who flew back to England during the evacuation from Dunkirk, to fill the bullet holes in his aircraft with chewing gum so that he could return to fight again.

Later. I went up to St. Eval in the evening. On the edge of the aerodrome is an old church with a tower which can be seen far

---

[1] Flying Officer P. Ethan Allen, D.F.C., a direct descendant of the celebrated Ethan Allen who fought in the American War of Independence. Killed June 7, 1944.

out in the Bristol Channel. It is a landmark for our Liberators coming home, as it was for our sailors in the old days when Cornwall was the haunt of lusty wreckers and smugglers. I have not had time to look up the history of the church, but I noticed that the fifteenth-century bench-heads include the arms of Henry VI.

The tower fell in the early eighteenth century and was rebuilt by the Bristol merchants, on the understanding that it should always be painted white, to catch the eyes of mariners sailing home. The old sundial over the south porch bears a melancholy inscription: "We shall all die."

I went to the duty crew room to listen to the eight o'clock news. I could hear the clatter of airmen's boots on the steel mesh of the runway. Big Ben sounded eight. The Flight Sergeant looked up and said, "Sounds bloody mournful, like when the King died." One of the airmen said, "Sounds more like the Abdication to me."

Then a voice announced that 31,000 Allied airmen have been over enemy territory in the last twenty-four hours. Everyone in the hut said, "Phew!"

Outside were the four aircraft due to take off during the night. I went out and waited beside them in the closing darkness. One imagines that aircraft become physical and alive when they have flown many times, as ships that have sailed the seas. There were drops of oil on the lip of the gun; the Leigh lights were ready to be switched on to their prey, and the fish-like bellies of the Liberators seemed stained by salt air, rather than the dry air that blows over the land.

Perry Allen and his crew arrived—Perry on his motor bicycle. He inspected the aircraft, touching it intimately: then he said, "I was born in June, and this is a lucky day for us Geminis." He waved to me as he climbed in and waved once more as he taxied away. Then Batch and his crew took off, then Rayner, and Buchan-Hepburn.

After they had soared up, towards their mission, I walked to the bus with Sidney Drake, who is an architect. While we waited, we sketched our ideas for 'the perfect small house', on a piece of paper.

June 7. I went to St. Eval early in the morning to wait for the four Liberators to come home. The grey clouds were edged with pink sugar floss, but they cleared as Batch's aircraft appeared from down the coast. Rayner landed an hour or so later, but there was no sign of Perry Allen or Buchan-Hepburn.

The station commander told me that more than twenty U-boats were sighted during the night, so it is obvious that they are moving towards the Channel, as was expected, to attack the invasion fleet.

Batch walked with me to the edge of the cliff after breakfast and told me the story of his patrol. After he flew off last night he saw a long chain of ships rounding Land's End, on their way to the Channel. He said, "They went in twos, like couples walking up an aisle."

As he was flying south of St. Nazaire, in 'lavish moonlight', his navigator, Ed. Annis, saw the shadow of what he thought was a U-boat. Batch said, "When we were three hundred yards away, we realized that it was a line of jagged rocks with waves breaking over them. Then a searchlight from the cliffs picked us up; then two from the island, fixing us in a cone of light. At the same time the island sent up a myriad of flares. All colours; a real picture display. And there was heavy ack-ack firing at us.

"We stooged west and began picking up numerous French fishing boats. I don't suppose they even knew that the invasion had begun." The aircraft flew over some twenty of them: then the navigator switched on the Leigh light and exposed a U-boat —too late to drop the depth-charges.

Batch said, "The Germans were also taken by surprise and they did not fire at us as we passed over. But there was fire from about half a mile to the west and we realized that there must be two of them. We kept on our course so that we could turn and attack. . . . They must have known we were coming because

K

they did everything they could to evade us; and they were canny enough not to open fire immediately and give away their exact position. The sea was very rough and there was a twenty-knot wind. We lost contact and did not get it until it was again too late to drop our depth-charges."

So, after an exchange of fire, the U-boat submerged, and Batch made for home. After we had talked for a little time, of other things, we went back to the mess and telephoned to ask if there was any news of Perry Allen and Buchan-Hepburn, but none had come.

This means the loss of twenty trained men from the Squadron, in one day. It cast a gloom of silence over us all, but the air-crews did their best not to show it and some of them went down to play football on the beach.

Later. News has come from Predannack of three U-boats being found by one of their Wellingtons and one of our Liberators, early this morning. The pilot of the Wellington, W. J. Hill, told me the story when I drove over to see him. "We were about three miles north-west of Ushant when my second pilot called out, 'There's something on the water down there.'

"I said, 'Poppycock', but he was right and we were nearly over it."

There were three U-boats, silhouetted against the moon. Hill said, "I could see the Liberator, flying in to attack the second of them. I flew in to attack the third, and we opened up and caught him completely with his pants down. We dropped our six depth-charges amidships and the spray obscured the U-boat. But the wake led right into the centre of the disturbance. We dropped a marker, and resumed our patrol.

"When we were about ten miles away, the rear-gunner saw a terrific fire on the water: I suppose it was Perry Allen's aircraft, shot down and burning in the sea."

But the day has not been all misfortune. Of the twenty-two U-boats sighted, on their way towards the Channel, seven were attacked. A mere sighting is a minor victory: it means that we know how many, where they are, and, having been sighted, they were forced to submerge. This cuts down their speed to one-quarter. So far, not one of them has got through.

June 8. At five o'clock in the morning, while I was in a deep sleep, Butch and Mike Ensor opened my door and switched on the light. Butch said, "Come on, you lazy bastard. Get up and get out that bloody typewriter of yours. K.O. Moore has just made history."

They pulled the bed-clothes off me, so I sat up, blinked my eyes, and listened to their amazing story. K.O. Moore's aircraft had sunk two U-boats within twenty-two minutes. They are absolute kills and it has never been done before.

I could not sleep any more: an hour or so afterwards the mess woke up to such excitement that the gloom of yesterday's losses was forgotten. I found an oil truck going up the hill, so I jumped on and arrived at the aerodrome in time to meet K.O. Moore walking out of the canteen with his crew. His face, which might be described as rugged Canadian, incapable of false expression, was good to see. He was white with exhaustion, but as excited as a child.

"You've made history," was all that anyone seemed able to say.

All the four thousand men and women on the station seemed to catch the spirit of victory, and I have seldom seen so much jaunty walking or heard such whistling. Even Group Captain Mead, usually cool and self-controlled, was rushing about with the photographs of the attacks in his hand.

I travelled back to the beach in the van with K.O. Moore, but he was too tired to talk. When we arrived at the mess he went off to sleep. About three hours later I saw him carrying plates of fish and chips to the other members of his crew, still in their beds.

K.O. Moore and Alec Gibb, his navigator, came to me when they woke up and told me their story.

Gibb: "It was a wizard night; a calm sea and a full moon that just laid a white path down the water. About two-fifteen in the morning we contacted a U-boat, between us and the moon. It was a perfect silhouette, as if it were painted on white paper. We could see the conning-tower quite clearly."

Moore: "We flew in and attacked, opening up with the nose gun. They returned the fire, but we silenced them."

Gibb: "I could see four or five of the crew in the conning-tower and some more of them running along the deck to the guns. Then, as one of our guns opened up, I saw one guy grab his stomach and fall."

Moore: "We passed dead over the conning-tower and dropped six depth-charges—a perfect straddle, three on either side. The rear gunner, Webber, saw the plumes and he squealed with delight. 'Oh, God, we've blown her clean out of the water.' We ran in and passed over the spot once more and saw the heaving waters and distinct patches of black oil in the dark green sea; distinct as ink remains when you pour it slowly into a glass of water. In the oil patches were darker spots. I suppose they were bodies. We sent a message back to the base, 'Definite kill', and then went on with our patrol."

Gibb: "It was then that you said, 'Now let's get another one.'"

Moore: "Yes, and we did. We got another contact so we lost height and I made a weave to port and put the second U-boat on our starboard side. The bomb-aimer, McDowell, saw it first."

Gibb: "It was an absolute duplicate of the first attack. The U-boat was dead up moon, slightly to port, so we did a slight turn and opened fire on him at about one mile. His return fire was heavy and there was a perfect fan of tracer from the conning-tower. As we passed over, the depth-charges straddled a line ten feet behind the conning-tower. Four fell on one side and two on the other."

Moore: "It was another perfect straddle. We did a quick turn to port and flew in again to see what had happened. The U-boat was slowing down and coming to rest with a list to starboard. There was a heavy trail of oil behind him and he was down by the stern, but we had no right to think that we had killed him. Our hopes slackened because we had no depth-charges left. We were just going to send a message to base, hoping someone might come to finish the job, when the mid-upper gunner, Griese, shouted, 'She's going down. It's just like a Hollywood picture.'

"And there she was, at an angle of seventy-five degrees, with her bow high in the air, sliding slowly into the sea. We all felt much better then. There was a good deal of smacking on the back and screaming of delight. We did another turn to port, and, for the first time, we switched on our Leigh light. Both attacks had been made without it. The light revealed three dinghies, shining yellow against the dark water, with the Germans in them, floating among the debris and oil. It had all happened so quickly that the wireless operator, Werbiski, did not realize what was going on. He had been busy sending a full report of the first attack back to base, and he thought we were kidding him."

A Note.—The phrases, 'We flew in and attacked' and 'It was a perfect straddle', which appear in K.O. Moore's story, need explanation, and a quick dip into Coastal Command history. At the beginning of the war, the chief lethal weapon used by aircraft against U-boats was the anti-submarine bomb which was not hydrostatically fused and whose performance was uncertain. Owing to its small blast effect the permissible margin of error was so slight that a direct hit was necessary to produce any serious damage. A direct hit on a small, moving target, often partially submerged, from an Anson flying at something over one hundred miles an hour, from five hundred feet, was not easy.

Coastal Command had therefore to think out some new way of bagging U-boats. The need was for a hydrostatically fused weapon, which would explode beneath the surface, causing damage or destruction by displacement of water rather than by direct impact. Some depth-charges were borrowed from the

Navy, but these were designed for dropping over the side of a ship, and when they fell from the greater height and speed of an aircraft, their cases burst as they hit the sea. Coastal therefore turned to the inventors, who produced the depth-charge which is used today. When correctly dropped from the bomb doors of an aircraft, it will not bounce or break up on hitting the water, and it can be released from a low height with safety to the aircrew.

Then the science of using these depth-charges in a heavy aircraft had to be mastered. A ship on the surface is still there to be attacked again if the Mosquito misses it, and a land target is always waiting for a second visit if a bomber misses it the first time. But a diving U-boat is vulnerable for only a few seconds. If fully surfaced when sighted, it can submerge in half a minute and still be vulnerable. Thirty seconds later it will be out of harm's way. The difficulties are doubled at night, in attacks such as those made by K.O. Moore.

Let us take a representative attack. The contact is picked up by the Radar in the dark. A thin line of amber light is revolving continuously on a dark glass screen, and when this light is interrupted by a blip—by the presence of an object outside the aircraft—the first promise of a U-boat has come. A whale or a shoal of fish may cause this blip on the screen, or one of the numerous fishing-boats that have been such a nuisance during our patrols. When the blip has been received, the next task is divided into two periods. There is the brief interval of darkness while the aircraft is flying in, and the thirty seconds of the actual attack, after the Leigh light has been turned on or after the U-boat has been seen in the moon path. During that interval, the Radar operator must give the pilot accurate information as often as possible and the pilot must plan his approach accordingly. If the approach on the unseen target errs by only as much as three degrees, the attack will be abortive. The drift of the aircraft, the possible zigzagging of the U-boat, and the fact that it may be submerging, must be taken into consideration. This is the problem in judgment for the pilot while he is flying in. From the movement of the blip on the Radar screen the pilot must assess the course and speed of the U-boat, by mental arithmetic and instinct. There is neither time nor light for formulae to be consulted. And the pilot must know exactly how much his Radar operator is likely to err in a crisis.

If the U-boat does not submerge, there is flak to contend with, directly the Leigh light has been turned on. It must be remembered that the pilot is not flying a fighter aircraft which responds delicately to control. A Liberator weighs about twenty-eight tons and it is stubborn to handle.

During the minutes of approach, the drill of the ten members of the crew must be as exquisitely concerted as ten separate instruments sounding one chord in an orchestra. It is here that years of training suddenly manifest themselves in one co-ordinated action.

The pilot is flying his heavy aircraft through the dark on a course calculated from the Radar operator's directions. The Radar operator is meanwhile watching the blip on the screen and operating his complicated set. The second pilot is looking after the engines, putting up the revs and boost as required, and at the same time setting up the automatic camera.

This is an important part of the exercise, for the photographs taken, automatically, during an attack, are not merely souvenirs for an album of victories. They must show the depth-charges entering the water, in relation to the U-boat, two or three seconds before they explode. It is from the position of entry, not the extent of the explosion, that the attack can be assessed.

During these same minutes, the navigator has to set up his bombing panel, check the selection of bombs, and see that the bomb doors have been opened. Then he must be ready to switch on the Leigh light. The wireless operator must flash signals back to base, so that they know of the possible target, and so that, if the aircraft is destroyed, it will not be a 'silent loss'. The engineer lies in the open bomb bay to watch the effect of the depth-charges when they enter the water: the front gunner and the two beam gunners must be prepared to give the U-boat hell the moment the Leigh light is turned on; and the rear gunner must prepare to give them a further burst when the aircraft has passed over.

A good captain expects his crew to perform all these tasks within a matter of seconds, so that, at the right distance, the engines may be set at the speed which will allow the aircraft to drop the depth-charges on target from a height of fifty feet. Then the orchestra pauses to watch for the conductor's baton. It falls, the light is turned on, and the target is revealed for this assemblage of preparation. Then the depth-charges are dropped, in a long stick, by the navigator. The aircraft flies through the flak and over the U-boat and, from his point of vantage, the rear gunner is able to substantiate the report of the engineer in the bomb bay. It has been a perfect straddle. The word *straddle* is important. A direct hit usually causes the depth-charge, which is not fused for contact, to break up. A close miss is therefore the perfect way of exploding the depth-charge, to do the maximum of harm.

Then comes the circuit before the aircraft can fly in and seek for evidence. Little wonder that the crew search the water hoping to see yellow dinghies, and white faces peering up, into the merciless beam of the Leigh light.

All this lies in K.O. Moore's two phrases, 'We flew in and attacked', and, 'It was a perfect straddle'. His crew achieved this incredible precision twice, within twenty-two minutes.

Later in the morning K.O. Moore told the story of the attack again, while we sat about him in the shabby old drawing-room at Watergate. Other officers, who had been sleeping after their night patrols, came downstairs in their pyjamas and crept in, quietly, to listen. At the end K.O. Moore said, "Well, there have been nearly one hundred Huns who bought it. That squares things for Perry Allen and Buchan-Hepburn."

Then he slid from his chair to the floor and pulled faces at Mike Ensor's terrier, to make him bark. The dog had chewed a hole in the leg of Ketcheson's trousers, but he was so exhausted after his patrol, lying back and listening with closed eyes, that he had not noticed it.

Later. The evening was all celebration. We went up to the N.C.O.s' mess where, with pretty wives, dart boards and a good-hearted barman, K.O. Moore and his crew were toasted into a sublime fog of tipsiness. The bond between them is heartening to watch: they are drawn together by all that they share as they fly; their technical perfection, and the alternate boredom, hope and disappointment they endure during twelve or more hours over the sea, with death as their near companion. It is a bond in which rank has no importance.

But there was no hint of this solemn thought in the celebration. The wives were so proud, smiling and silent: and they did not protest when we all drank too much and became noisy. There was kind, intelligent understanding in the way they sat back, with quiet gratitude that their husbands had come home alive: perhaps the gratitude was deeper than the pride.

All that the sergeant, who had seen the first attack, could say to me (as he poured a sly double whisky into my glass when he thought I was not looking) was, "It was a bloody miracle. A bloody miracle."

. . . . . .

The returns for the twenty-four hours up to nine o'clock this morning show that eight U-boats were sighted and six attacked by the aircraft in this Group. We can still claim that not one U-boat has got into the Channel to menace the invasion fleet. In its essential purpose, the Battle of the South-Western Approaches is already won.

June 9. The times when the aircraft should return from their night patrols become fixed in my mind, as on a chart, and I find myself waking from sleep in a state of wordless prayer.

Eric Batchelor's bedroom is above mine. I have talked with him more than the others: we go for long walks and he shares his food parcels with me when they arrive from Canada. I feel no barrier of age with him and his fate concerns me: knowing the time that he should return, I wake up, hearing him throwing his flying boots across the floor, and, realizing that he is safe home, I go to sleep again.

There is no adventure in the war, only anxiety, for those of us who are pinned to the earth like this, with the dread that we might be called in the morning and told that another aircraft has been lost during the night patrols. It means the sudden obliteration of ten men with whom I have walked along the beach and drunk pints at The Traveller's Rest.

The newspapers devote too much space to the heroics and glory of the war, and not enough to the miseries; the days of slow starvation in dinghies, the horrors of mutilation and the cries of men being burned. The mass of readers fight shy of these horrors, naturally preferring the heroism, and the victories over the enemy. They enjoy a legend of which the heroes are unaware.

The aircrews are resilient when news of disaster comes, but they are also more vindictive than in the early days. Their hatred of the Germans is based on a dark bargain: they are to be punished, and killed, because the Perry Allens and the Buchan-Hepburns must be avenged.

.   .   .   .   .   .

Five years of being in the R.A.F. have given me my fill of grief. Only two of the eleven pilots who shared my birthday lunch with me in May before the war are still alive. The dismal ritual goes on: the packing of the dead man's possessions, the stack of luggage in the hall, and the new man arriving, fresh from his training, walking up the stairs to occupy the empty room.

Their resilience makes me ashamed of my own inwardness. I sat in the mess late one night, with three New Zealand pilots who had returned from their patrols. We were talking of the dullness of the mess food; the endless slices of dead Swiss roll, half-covered by cool yellow custard. We then imagined, each of us, the dinner we would enjoy. I asked for "twelve oysters, the breast of a roast duck with apple sauce, new potatoes, and peas fresh picked from the garden, followed by a fresh peach so ripe that you could peel it in one, like taking off your vest."

One of them said, "Oh, that's cruel. I'm hungry. Let's make hogs of ourselves."

They went to their rooms and brought tins of food which we took into the kitchen. Between four of us, we ate a tin of sheep's tongues, spread on slices of thick toast and crowned with mustard pickles. Then we shared a tin of honey, also spread on slices of buttered toast, a tin of peaches, two tins of cream, and a cold plum pudding—all sent from New Zealand. They had been saved for several weeks and we ate them in sheer vicious greed.

We felt rather sick afterwards, so we went to the edge of the cliff and sat in the moonlight, belching, and looking down at the sparkling waves and at the aircraft coming home. Then, in the anonymity of darkness, the three began to talk: with my chin between my hands, I watched their three faces in the moonlight, and listened.

All three have suffered violent experiences: one was shot down over the Mediterranean, but he saved some of his crew with such valour that he was awarded the D.S.O. One fought six Ju. 88s, and emerged alive; the third told us that one night, after being attacked, he switched on his torch and saw, in the little circle of light, what had once been the face of one of his comrades. Each of them said that he recalls his horror, lying in bed in the dark. They all admitted the menace of fear.

June 10. I was thinking of this in bed early this morning and could not sleep. So I took a cold shower and went down to the kitchen to find a cup of tea. The mess servants were just arriving; I sat with them as they stoked the fire and made the tea. One of them began to talk of the aircrews we had lost. He is a quiet, kind man who has been in private service all his life. He said that working for the pilots has taught him the value of gratitude. "They are always grateful," he said.

Equally, I have never heard a grumble from the servants. They will sit up all night to serve the aircrews coming home. Uniforms are pressed; garments are taken away, washed and ironed and put back in the bedrooms without a word being said. I am included in this kindness: yesterday a waste-paper basket appeared in my room, without my asking. The batman said, "I scrounged it up at St. Eval. I thought that all authors need a waste-paper basket." It was more true than he imagined.

·   ·   ·   ·   ·   ·

The weather has been unkind: during the night and day of the 9th, the flying hours for the Group fell from 1,040 to 587. Nevertheless, six U-boats were attacked and not one has yet made its way into the Channel. The U.S. Navy Liberators, at Dunkeswell, and the Australians at Pembroke Dock, also made attacks. The Australians seem to have scored two victories. Flying Officer Sheehan, of Sydney, was flying his Sunderland at 800 feet when he contacted a U-boat. As he approached, his crew saw a light below—the glow from within the submarine as the Germans were coming up to the conning-tower. He told me that "the sea was jet-black, the U-boat pale grey, with a shining white wash astern". Depth-charges were dropped and, nine hours later, another aircraft flew over the scene and reported oil streaks converging to one centre, and floating debris.

Flying Officer Livermore, from Melbourne, also dropped his depth-charges on a U-boat, and gave her 250 rounds. There were two explosions. Two other aircraft, flying near by at one-thirty in the morning, reported considerable wreckage in the water, including a rectangular metal box.

·   ·   ·   ·   ·   ·

Today came news of an enemy destroyer aground off the Ile de Batz, where it had beached after being attacked by our Navy, a few days ago. Beaufighters made a low-level bombing attack, through flak from the shore. They left the destroyer in flames and it will never sail again.

. . . . . .

In the afternoon I walked up and down the beach with Terry McComb,[1] who commands 224 Squadron. We talked of the curious illusion among civilians, that the R.A.F. is a sort of precocious youngster that suddenly showed talent when war was declared. 224 Squadron is twenty-six years old: it was formed in Italy, in 1918, and its crest bears the motto, *Fidele al Amico*. It is rather droll to look at the old copy of the crest hanging in the mess, because it bears the autograph of Benito Mussolini.

Terry McComb told me that the Squadron actually began operations before war was declared, at the time of the Munich crisis. We weren't as dozy as those who deride the *Pax Umbrellica* suppose. All the Coastal Command squadrons were ready at their war stations. 224 Squadron was at Leuchars, on the Fifeshire coast, from which they were to patrol the North Sea in slow, old Ansons. But the Ansons could not fly as far as the Norwegian coast, and return. All the German ships and U-boats needed to do was to cling to the shore and slip into the Atlantic, without being seen. Then 224 were equipped with Lockheed Hudsons and their range was much greater. Two weeks before war was declared, they flew to the coast of Norway and reported on the movements of German naval units, while our Home Fleet was moving from Portsmouth to Scapa Flow.

Terry reminded me again of the importance of photography in flight: he said, "You should write a book about it when the war is over." Then, "I can remember our first nervous little attempts to photograph enemy country, on the other side of the Channel. Today, Mosquitoes fly as far as Stettin to photograph the results of bombing. Recently, a reconnaisance aircraft flew to North Africa and back in one day, taking photographs of Venice on the way."

. . . . . .

[1] Wing Commander T. W. T. McComb, O.B.E.

Johnny Posnett landed back this morning with another disappointment. He was flying about twenty-five miles from the French coast when he contacted a U-boat: he flew in, but before the depth-charges could be dropped the enemy opened fire on the Liberator and wrecked one engine.

The story of the combat reveals what I have already tried to describe: the bond between these men who fly big aircraft and the reason why, when pressed by danger, they stick together like burrs in ones hand. Anyone of them, in the startling second of crisis, might become the saviour of the others.

In this conflict the hero was Keith Bettany, the engineer; a quiet little Welshman who comes from the Rhondda Valley. He was sitting on the flight-deck when the flak shot up at him, from the U-boat.

He talked to me of the combat, in the bar at Watergate.

"While I was sitting there, two cannon shells exploded in the bomb bay. It shook me quite a bit and I thought of my mother and father, as one does at a time like that. I waited for the depth-charges to fall, but they didn't, and I realized that something had been hit. The electric circuit had been broken by cannon fire.

"I looked down at the sea through the open bomb doors; there was a little light, remaining from the sun, which had set, and our Leigh light, still shining on the water. I could see the U-boat two hundred feet below me, and the flak coming up towards me. I tried to close the bomb doors, but two of them had jammed. One depth-charge was hanging down, with its nose through the bomb door, so I pulled the lever and released it. Then I was able to close that door, but the other one was still open. The other depth-charges would not fall so there was nothing to do but set course for home."

He had withheld the end of his gallant story. What Bettany had done was this. When the engine was hit, the crew realized that they would have to return home on three engines. After feathering the damaged engine, Bettany went back to the bomb bay, to release the remaining depth charges with his hands, so that the aircraft would gain height. For twenty minutes, he stood on the twelve-inch wide cat-walk, which was covered with oil. The sea sped past below and a howling gale blew up his legs. He hung on to the bomb rack with one hand and released the depth charges with the other. As each one fell, he could feel the aircraft leap and gain height. As the last one fell they reached 700 feet and came home.

I asked Bettany later what he did after the last depth-charge fell. He said, "Oh, I closed the bomb doors, went back and sat between the two pilots and stayed there until we landed."

June 11. News has come from Portreath of an exciting kill: the first time a U-boat has been crippled almost to death, by cannon fire. Four Mosquitoes saw the U-boat, about one and a half miles away, close to Ushant. They flew in and made twenty-four attacks between them, during eight minutes. They poured five thousand rounds of ammunition into the sitting bird.

I drove over to Portreath to talk to the warriors. Flight-Lieutenant Nunn told me that, as they flew in, he could see the Germans rushing to man the guns. After the second attack, they were silenced and, as the U-boat crew poured up from below, they were shot down by our guns. It was a vicious attack: Nunn saw the dead Germans tumbling into the sea. About twenty of them escaped death and jumped into the oil track astern.

The Mosquitoes left the U-boat with her stern awash and her bows turned towards the coast. Then a Liberator flew in, piloted by Flight-Lieutenant Dundas, and finished the job with depth-charges. Dundas told me that the U-boat heaved out of the sea, then slid back, and sank. He saw only green bubbles, oil, wreckage, and three survivors, in their life-jackets.

.   .   .   .   .   .

Five days of the Battle of the South-Western Approaches have passed and two simple facts emerge. The reaction of enemy aircraft to our attacks on U-boats is negligible: few of the

Junkers fighters, which we feared, have dared poke their noses over the Bay. And not one U-boat has been seen beyond a line drawn from Brest to Looe, in Cornwall.

June 12. I went into Newquay with Hubert Jessell, who returned this morning from a ten-hour patrol over the Channel. We walked along the edge of the cliffs, which I hate and fear. He must have sensed my timidity because he moved between me and the crumbling edge and, when the path became dangerous, he guided me inland for a few yards until the way was safe again. It was a charming, silent kindness.

We watched the gulls, crying as they swung in the upwind from the sea, far below. One of them seemed to be fascinated: it swung to and fro, as if in a hammock, for five minutes— perhaps a young gull who had just discovered the pleasure of being caressed by the wind.

Newquay was dull as a mortuary; nowhere to eat, and clumps of bored American soldiers, lounging at the street corners. The death-watch beetle of an English seaside town was already in their blood. The smell from the only restaurant that was open was like the stink of a slaughter-house. We decided to remain hungry and walked back to the mess, cross and argumentative.

When we came to the cliff again we discussed the folly of snapping back and Hubert J. said, "It was my fault. I am tired." I said, "No, it was my fault. I am old and crotchety." So we argued again and suddenly gurgled with laughter and could not trace our argument back to its source.

There is no library in the mess and we have decided to pool our books. An interesting collection arrived from the bedrooms, including *Anna Karenina*, two Théophile Gautier novels, books by Conrad, Samuel Butler, Negley Farson, V. Sackville West, James Pope Hennessy, Cynthia Stockley, and Baroness Orczy.

Later. I went this afternoon to add one or two novels to the library and saw Jock Muir with a book in his hand. It was

Freya Stark's *The Southern Gates of Arabia*. Jock opened it and showed me the dedication: *To the R.A.F. and especially those in Aden who made the writing of it possible by carrying me in safety from Shibaum*.

Jock said, "That's my old squadron. I used to see Freya Stark in Aden, when she came out with her camera to welcome us home from our flights."

Jock is part of the spine of the R.A.F., and has risen from aircraftsman to pilot officer, with every rank except corporal. He has been in the service nine years: he knows its glory, its faults, its tricks and its spirit. I have tried several times to make him talk to me, but he cocks a canny, Glasgow eye and says, "Have a drink."

He will open his heart and loosen his tongue on only two subjects: his childhood in Glasgow and his service in the desert. Indeed, his stories of the desert become so insistent, late at night, that some of his friends recently spread a bucket of sand on the floor about his bed. "It'll make you feel you're back home," they said.

When I saw him with Freya Stark's book, this afternoon, I said, "I know her."

He cocked his head and said, "You do! Verrry well?"

I answered, "I think I can say that she is a friend."

This melted him: he went for his log-book and told me his story. He joined the R.A.F. in 1935 and three years later he was posted to Aden. He said, "We bombed a hell of a lot of places when the tribes got too big for their boots and raided the caravans." During the Italian campaign in East Africa he flew in 69 raids, and he once bombed Addis Ababa. In March 1941, he was wounded over Diredawa and, in the following May, he was sent home, round the Cape. He had been promoted sergeant in May 1940, flight-sergeant in May 1943, and commissioned in December of the same year. Jock has flown 860 operational hours and, since he came to 224 Squadron, he has flown in 47 trips against U-boats, embracing 550 hours of flying.

These are the facts that make such pilots as Jock of solemn value to the R.A.F. Their valour is fortified by long experience.

L

In his case, valour and experience are fortified by stubborn Scottish integrity, and a belly-laugh that sends gloom scuttling through the door. I have only to hear him to feel ten years younger and take the stairs two at a time.

.   .   .   .   .   .

Note. On June 13 the weather improved and patrols were back to normal. The area of these patrols, the 'Unclimbable Fence', was moved and pushed into the Channel, like a cork—in fact, this change in tactics was described as 'The Cork'. It is explained by the two photographs reproduced opposite page 207. One is of the map in the Operations Room at Group Head-quarters on 'D' day. It shows the area patrolled by our anti-U-boat aircraft when the battle of the South-Western Approaches began. The second photograph shows how the area of patrol was changed, during eight days, from a line drawn between Brest and Land's End, to a line between Exmouth and Cherbourg.

June 15. The weather continues fair and two Wellingtons attacked U-boats during the night. One of them was slinking out on its dark purpose escorted by several fishing-boats, like a wolf among lambs. It fired at the Wellington, but the depth-charges had already been dropped: they fell splendidly and the U-boat was enveloped in explosions. It was left, disabled, on the surface. Beaufighters were sent out to finish the task, but there was no sign of the enemy so they returned home.

June 20. Somebody wrote recently of the life of a Coastal Command pilot that it was "long hours of leisure and luxury, punctuated by moments of intense fear". It is a glib statement and has been made before. I think the 'long hours of leisure and luxury' are spoiled when ninety officers have to share two bathrooms, and eat endless slices of Swiss roll, eight times a week. And it is a little hard when a pilot returns from patrol to find four of his friends occupying the bathroom, on their knees, washing their shirts in the communal tub. But there is a touch of pride in the laundry. A week or so ago one of the pilots received six packets of washing powder, from Montreal. He ran four inches of hot water into the bath, put in a whole packet and invited us all to share.

We rubbed our shirts and handkerchiefs, took Butch's advice that 'the secret is in the rinsing', and then hung our clean linen on a line, where it would catch the sea breeze. Two of the launderers had to depart, and fly on patrol to the Bay. When they returned, they did not speak of U-boats, or the enemy: they hurried to the clothes-line, proud of what they found. One came into the mess saying, "My shirt's a better colour than yours."

Back to the phrase, 'long hours of leisure and luxury'. Few of the men who fly heavy aircraft seem to know how to enjoy leisure. If there is a gay party, they throw themselves into it like boys starting a race. But, most of the time, they seem bored, as if the weary hours of patrol, and the 'moments of intense fear' make it difficult for them to adjust themselves, quickly, to the cramped quiet of a room. Some play games of patience; others stare into space, with the distressed look that people wear in a dentist's waiting-room.

These last few days have revealed this. The U-boats are not appearing, although 170 aircraft took off yesterday and last night. The splendid opportunities seem to be over. There haven't been enough U-boats to go round and when the air-crews return from their thirteen dreary hours over the sea, they throw their flying kit into a corner, and mope. If there is a party, they will drink too much and sing their old songs. Otherwise, all is apathy. They may be white with weariness, but they are too restless to sleep. They do not hurry to the newspapers to see what has happened during their absence: they reveal all as they flop into chairs and say, "I'm browned off."

June 21. Sir Sholto Douglas flew down from Coastal Head-quarters this morning and decorated Roger Thorpe, the first

American in 19 Group to win the D.F.C. It was a pleasant little ceremony, squeezed into the busy programme of war, and all 224 Squadron air-crews and ground-crews polished their buttons and paraded in Roger's honour. He is a short, silent, immaculate man from Chicago, whose flying and courage have been described in the official reports as 'magnificent'.

In December he attacked a 5,000-ton blockade runner which was protected by nine destroyers, and he was chased by fighters on the way home. On the night of April 20, when he was on patrol in the Bay of Biscay, he tried to attack a U-boat. No less than three emerged from the black silence and fired back at him. But he went on, making three more attempts to fly in and kill. His Squadron Commander reported that "each of these attempts was made at night, notwithstanding the intensity of flak", and that he "displayed magnificent airmanship" by going down to fifty feet over the sea, thereby getting under the fire. After this fierce interlude he attacked a merchant vessel in the face of more flak, evaded a force of German night fighters, and brought his aircraft home without a single bullet hole.

The Squadron showed their affection by ragging him mercilessly—telling him that he would have to make a speech in front of the Air Chief Marshal, after he had received his medal. He came to me, in real fear, and asked me to help him write it. I told him that his leg was being pulled, but he was not convinced: he walked up and down as if he were going to the gallows rather than his glory. He came to me again and said that he had never been more frightened in his life. Would I help him? He still would not believe that he was being ragged and he went to the parade in misery. I believe the three U-boats, the enemy merchant vessel, and the German night fighters were so much unimportant thistledown blowing about in his memory.

.   .   .   .   .   .

The Air Chief Marshal came down to Watergate after the ceremony, to meet members of 224 Squadron, on the terrace. It was a delightful picture—tables had been put out and the servants wore smart white jackets. It might have been the poor man's south of France, with the silver beach below and the broad blue expanse of the sea. I sat back against the cliff and watched the social ice breaking slowly. The presence of an Air Chief Marshal has a chilling effect on the young, and Sir Sholto Douglas does not warm easily. K.O. Moore, Batch, and the others were presented. Then the chatter and drinking began and everyone was soon at his ease. But when Sir Sholto departed, we relaxed into the merry freedom that comes when royalty leaves the room. However, he was a success. One pilot said that he looked 'a good sort of bloke', and K.O. Moore referred to him as 'Young Duggie'.

Mike Ensor had recovered from the bad temper he had been enjoying all day. He had been on patrol, near Ushant, and was so bored that he tried to remember all the hymns he had learned as a boy in New Zealand. He was half-way through 'Onward Christian Soldiers' when a shower of flak burst through the aircraft. He complained to his navigator, "A chap can't even sing without being interrupted these days."

June 22. I flew up to London with Sir Sholto Douglas in his princely Hudson, over the summer landscape, gentle and silent. The flying bombs began nine days ago and I wondered how I would take this new horror, but I was more interested than afraid. Sir Sholto Douglas said that the Germans were too late with their new weapon. "The mass of people are confident now of victory: had the flying bombs come last winter, when they were all fed-up, it would have been a different story."

I stayed in London for only a few hours and there were no alerts. Pall Mall and the Strand seemed empty and expressionless, like the streets in the City on a Sunday. Yet I was conscious of an impending menace, like the hurrying feet of a robber following one in the dark.

I returned south and arrived in Devon late in the evening, to stay with one of the American Squadrons. Three months ago, when I first came here, it seemed incongruous to find Old Glory flying against the skies of Devon, jeeps galloping like colts through the lanes, and American voices predominant over an area of perhaps a thousand acres. But it is incongruous no longer. The great American aerodrome has settled into the landscape, Old Glory flies within a few yards of the Royal Air Force standard, and the people of Devon have taken the Americans to their hearts. It is reassuring to hear a man from the village talk of 'our aerodrome' having had 'a busy day', with an unconscious sense of alliance which would be good medicine for the cynics who bleat about the future.

.   .   .   .   .   .

The new excitement in our part of the war has been the first appearance of the *schnörkel*, a device for ventilating U-boats when they are submerged. We knew the secret as far back as the summer of 1943 when the experiments began; when the first few U-boats were recalled to be fitted with the ingenious gadget. It consists of two tubes, about fourteen inches in diameter, fastened together and hinged to the deck. One tube is low, to expel the foul air, under water: the intake tube is higher and fitted with a cowl, to keep out the sea-water.

The *schnörkel*—a nice word, meaning the squiggle at the end of a signature or, architecturally, a scroll—has been anticipated for some months. Now it has arrived, as a surprise for the pilots. They seem so cock-a-hoop with victory that it comes as a novelty rather than a new weapon to be feared. Most of the U-boats are now fitted with *schnörkels*: a pilot who saw one yesterday said it was "as much like the chimney of a field kitchen as anything else".

Although the U-boats can now recharge their batteries under water, without coming up to breathe, the *schnörkel* has not helped them so far. In all the sixteen days since the invasion began, the U-boats have sunk only one destroyer and one frigate. We can still claim that they have not menaced our invasion fleet—thanks to half a dozen naval escorts in the area, and the air patrols of Coastal Command. It is a thrilling realization.

The Americans at Dunkeswell were delighted with their part in the *schnörkel* hunt. The station commander said, "Our morale has leapt up."

Morale is the word; the only word with which to describe this volatile, mysterious quality on an operational station, which appears like a flash of lightning with success and falls like a monsoon of depression when things go wrong. It is feminine in its quickness of mood. Group Captain Mead at St. Eval, who does not admit the existence of anything mysterious on his station, will clear his throat and say, "Morale is pretty good," as if he were a doctor saying, "The patient is out of danger." He does it with a curious lowering of the voice which regular officers often affect to cover up the fact that they are dealing with eccentricities of human nature not provided for in King's Regulations.

When I arrived at Dunkeswell I was too tired to gather stories. But it was pleasant to go to bed in an atmosphere of American kindness and plenty; like escaping from England for a day and taking a little holiday across the Atlantic.

I felt the glow of this the moment I walked into the guardroom to sign my name. A corporal from Kentucky was leaning across the stove. The old law of southern hospitality made him rise from his chair and fill a tin can with coffee for me. "Have a drink," he said, offering me a cigarette at the same time.

I had been travelling all day and I was hungry, so I went to the kitchen in the officers' mess to beg some food. One of the Americans shook the mess sergeant, who was sleeping. He got up without a murmur and made me a sandwich with new bread, a six-inch piece of hot stewed steak, and so much gravy that I had to lean forward at an angle of sixty degrees to save my tunic from the drips. Then came coffee and, as I drank it, we found we had a memory to share.

The mess sergeant is a fruiterer from Ohio: in peace-time he goes shooting with his 'bird dog' in the country about Tiffin, a town I know.

I arrived at Tiffin once, also late at night and hungry. The editor of the local newspaper took me to his flat, gathered eight or ten amusing people, and cooked me ham and eggs. It is catching, this unquestioning American kindness. When the sergeant at Dunkeswell knew that I had been to Tiffin, he wanted me to eat apple cake, strawberry shortcake, cookies and cheese crackers. I just wilted and said I could manage no more. He showed me photographs of his house, his 'bird dog' and his 'very lovely family', and then I went to bed.

June 23. This morning I talked to Lieutenant-Commander John L. Munson, of Medina, New York, who took the first photographs of a *schnörkel* in action. Munson was uncommunicative for an American and he made his story rather bald. Last Sunday he took off in the afternoon and saw nothing but what he described as "the usual round of destroyers, frigates, corvettes and a few battleships", until seven-thirty in the evening when they were flying on their patrol between Alderney and Guernsey. They sighted a U-boat two and a half miles away.

Munson dismissed his adventure with a phrase and a sweep of his hand. "Everything happened in the next thirty seconds."

He turned to port, lost height, flew in and dropped his depth-charges. It was an unfortunate attack because the No. 8 depth-charge did not explode. As No. 7 went off somewhat astern of the periscope, No. 8 might have caught the tail nicely. But the attack at least began an argument because some of the crew said that they had seen *two* periscopes. Munson had kept the aircraft beautifully straight and level as they flew over, and the excellent photographs which were taken cleared up the mystery. They showed both the periscope and the *schnörkel*, with smoke coming out of an exhaust at its side.

June 24. I travelled back to Cornwall in a crowded train with sweaty, tired American sailors who ate great piles of cold tongue and beef, and drank beer from their service water-bottles. Then they slept in the corridors. They had been in trains for ten hours.

I stood next to an American nurse from Georgia who had been bringing wounded men back from the coast in a hospital train. She looked fresh and charming, and we soon became friends. She said, "Oh, I'm tired," but one of the sailors with a mop of damp tousled hair, wrinkled his eyes seriously and said to her, "Don't worry, sister. You look fresh as a lily to me."

She said that there were both American and German wounded on the hospital train. She attended a wretched German boy who had lost his legs and one ear. She said, "I could not help saying to him, 'You are only a boy.' Our boys were angry and one of them said, 'Don't give us that stuff, or there'll be a riot. He's old enough to kill us.'"

The story of the changing waves of hatred since the war began is interesting. Neither the Americans nor the British are good haters; they wish, in their different ways, to live amiably with their neighbours. One would like to believe also that they are too civilized to go on enjoying the gall of old angers.

The hatred they have developed during the war has been different in its focus. Pearl Harbour was to open the floodgates of enmity towards the East. Dunkirk, and then the Blitz, opened the floodgates of our enmity towards Germany. It was part of the lesson both countries were to learn, that both hatreds were the same in their essence.

Britain's hatred of the Germans was lukewarm when the war began, depending upon the negative legend that they are our enemy. In the month of May 1940, when Mr. Chamberlain was still in power, a German bomber came down near Clacton. Its magnetic mine exploded, killing or wounding 150 civilians, and killing all the aircrew. There was little bitterness, it seemed, and some of the women of Clacton put posies on the graves of the dead Germans. About the same time a German pilot came down in a field in Kent. Royal Air Force officers took him to their mess and gave him tea and cigarettes. They learned afterwards that, before he was shot down, the German had fired on one of our own pilots who was descending by parachute.

The tune changed after Dunkirk. Some captured German airmen were marched through the streets of Clacton and, this time, the women had to be held back from revenge. One of the pilots who had given the German a cigarette wrote to me a month later, "I hate their bloody guts." The milk of apathy had become the red wine of revenge.

I asked the nurse from Georgia how she felt when she attended her first German patient in the hospital train. She said, "I didn't feel anything. I am a professional nurse and patients are just there to be helped. They don't have any identity."

She said that the wounded Germans were starving and that they grabbed pieces of bread 'as if it were cake'. But they asked for what they wanted, cigarettes, food and bandages, without being shy. This surprised her. "If I were a prisoner in someone else's country I'd feel a bit humble about it," she said.

She spoke also of homesickness among American soldiers. We all know how easy it is to make an American produce his pocket-book of photographs and tell you about his 'very lovely family'. The nurse from Georgia thinks this is charming, but unfortunate. "They think of themselves too much," she said. "I have known them cry themselves to sleep, thinking of home. You would never find an American girl doing that."

I said this was one reason why some American soldiers imagine they do not like England. They dislike any country in which they cannot find their own patch of garden, their own home street and their own mother in her own kitchen.

A few people left the train at one station and we were able to squeeze into a carriage where five American sailors had been eating until they were flushed. They opened their mouths like hoppers and poured in the rolls and cakes. They had been in the train all day and their clothes were twisted, their shirts rebellious and their hair knotted and wild. The sight of one lovely American girl acted on them like magic. They put away their bags of cakes, combed their hair and sat like good little boys on Sunday. One of them, the toughest of the five, sat in the corner. His gnarled, sea-beaten face was turned away from us and he was lost in a dream.

One of the others said, "Ginger, what are you dreaming of?"

Ginger moved his head: without any self-consciousness, he answered, "Home."

June 25. I arrived back in Cornwall and found several good and cheerful stories. At five o'clock in the morning of the 23rd, Flight-Lieutenant W. A. S. Blackden's aircraft sighted a U-boat and attacked it. The *schnörkels* are now the excitement of the chase: the second pilot, Sergeant McConaghy, said that the one he saw was 'like a field kitchen chimney'. A blot of rainbow-coloured oil began to form on the surface after the U-boat submerged: it grew until it was 100 yards wide, so one more of the enemy was held back from his dark enterprises.

Again yesterday, four more attacks were made, and today four more. At three-forty-five in the afternoon the aircrews were able to claim their century: the one hundredth U-boat for the month was sighted, and attacked. The Navy came in and finished its destruction.

June 26. I had a long talk this afternoon with Philip Hill,[1] who also made an attack, about half-past one yesterday morning. He was flying over a hazy, calm sea when he got a definite radar contact. He was not certain whether it was a U-boat so he maintained course and watched, so that he could estimate its speed and decide whether it was only another aircraft. He then flew in to attack. He has done nine hundred hours of operational flying. I asked him if he felt excited.

He answered, "Yes, I began to wonder what the Leigh light would illuminate. I called to the navigator to turn on the light, looked out and saw a stack-like object. It was a *schnörkel*. Then I heard our depth-charges thumping off, and the explosions. I had no time to think very much, as all my attention was taken up in getting the aircraft round for a second attack. Yet one is able to do some sort of thinking with one's second mind and, while I was calculating each moment what I should do, I was also

[1] Flight-Lieutenant P. M. Hill, missing, presumed killed, November 11, 1944.

working out the possible position of the U-boat under water. We had dropped a flame float, and after I had flown away for about four miles I came in again and realized that we had missed it. For the next four hours I circled that flame float, wondering what course the U-boat had taken and how far it would travel before the surface vessels got to it. We had sent a message to base, and all we could do in the end was resume patrol."

I asked him if he felt anything personal about the Germans in the U-boat when he attacked. He said, "No. The crew is not made up of individuals for me. I might feel different if I saw any of them struggling in the water afterwards."

He told me that he has only once seen a pilot depressed after a victory; one, inclined to be a pacifist, who returned on Christmas Eve from sinking a U-boat and sat in the mess, his head in his hands. Somebody asked him why he was so quiet and he answered, "A fine Christmas present I have given those German wives and mothers."

Phil Hill repeated, "It is important that we should not think too much of the men in the U-boat—just look on it as a target." But we did talk of what it must be like, shut within the vast steel hull, submerged, for long hours of day and night. We went to the Intelligence Office and turned up a solemn description of the conditions in one of our own submarines, written by Wing Commander Romanes:

"Probably the greatest hardship is the lack of space in which to live and breathe. The craft is some 200 feet long, with a maximum internal diameter of 15 feet, the pressure hull being nearly round. Throughout the entire length of the boat half of this space is taken up by two big batteries, six main ballast tanks, two quick diving tanks and many trim, fresh-water and fuel tanks. A third of what is left is occupied by engines and main motors; a quarter of the rest by torpedo tubes and their allied gear. This leaves a very small space to be divided into control room, officers' quarters, crew quarters, galley, petty officers' quarters and lavatory room. Space overhead is further restricted by pipes to all the ballast tanks, with their high- and low-pressure air lines and associated valves, both hydraulic and hand-operated, battery cables and a mass of other gear. The control room has to house wireless, asdic, echo-sounder, steering and hydroplane operating gear, as well as a watch of ten men. The living quarters are therefore minute; the wardroom, where four officers must live and sleep, being some 8 feet by 6 feet, while twenty men live in the fo'c'sle, some 20 feet long by 7 feet wide forward and 10 feet wide aft. The hammocks alone seem to fill all the available space and the only way to get between them is to crawl.

"The lively behaviour of the boat in a seaway makes movement even more difficult; she literally whips about and it is not uncommon for the officer on the shipside bunk in the wardroom to be slung clean out and deposited in the alley-way outside. Moreover, the deck is so greasy with diesel oil that even in a slight sea it is a bit of an art to keep on your feet.

"Normally the submarine dives all day, which during the summer means nearly sixteen hours, from six in the morning to ten at night. During this time the crew of forty is using up the very limited supply of oxygen in the air which is trapped in the boat. It is not long before the effects of oxygen starvation are felt. It becomes even more of an effort to move about, and reading a book is difficult as you find yourself reading the same lines over and over again. The effects are very similar to flying at a great height without oxygen.

"To avoid fouling the air more than is absolutely necessary, neither smoking nor cooking is allowed. The lavatories must be used as seldom as possible, as they are operated by pressure air and when blown they release a bubble of air which may be seen on the surface. Smells are impossible to prevent and crew, engines, diesel oil and batteries all make their contribution, so that when the hatch is opened on surfacing, fresh air tastes foul and you get a heavy coat of fur in your mouth which makes your first cigarette taste disgusting. Moreover, when the boat is submerged, a powder is put down to absorb some of the carbon dioxide in the boat, but it succeeds mostly in making the crew cough violently. Moisture condenses inside the hull of the boat, and after a few days there is a perpetual drip everywhere which is most annoying and which makes all the blankets wet."

When we had read this grim account, Phil said, "Well, I'd sooner be where I am—in a nice Liberator." We agreed that men who serve in submarine craft, on either side, must be blessed with especial courage, and not menaced by claustrophobia. The horror of their lives must be intensified when the U-boat is submerged—as they listen, perhaps, to the distant thuds of other U-boats being bombed—thuds that can be heard fifty miles away, under water.

We slowly built up a picture of the life of the submariners. As the Intelligence Officer reminded us, "Since 'D' day, it has been practically impossible for them to surface, anywhere within the patrolled area, without being sighted."

It has been, for the Germans, a battle of invention against invention. Our perfection of Radar, then the Leigh light, began their doom. Now they reply with the *schnörkel*. We do not know how effective this device will be in the future, but we were told that the air coming into the U-boat by way of the *schnörkel* arrives at a speed of 80 miles an hour—an additional hardship in what must already have been the very hell of discomfort.

June 27. When I was a child in Auckland, there was a windmill that dominated the skyline of the city. It had been there when Auckland was a ramshackle settlement, with a footbridge over a stream which ran where the main street lies today. The sails revolved slowly against the sky, reminding us of the 'forties and 'fifties of the last century when our ancestors crossed the world in windjammers to settle in the strange new country. The windmill was one of the first romantic objects of my childhood, and in later years, when I saw other mill sails revolving, in Holland, in Roumania, or on the flat land of Norfolk, my thoughts went back to the sunny land where I was born.

Yesterday I went to tea with Clem Roebuck, one of the controllers at St. Eval. The other guest was a New Zealand flight sergeant, Kenneth Ibbertson, from Auckland. I asked him if he knew what part of England his ancestors came from, and he said, "Yes, I have traced them to Great Corby, outside

Carlisle. I went there and found my great-grandfather's name in the church register. He attended service there on the day he sailed for New Zealand in 1852. He took the first millstones, for the mill that he built in Auckland. They were quarried outside Carlisle and, as far as I know, they are still being used. My great-grandfather operated the mill for thirty-five years."

June 28. For three days not one U-boat has been sighted or attacked. Almost 400 sorties were flown, involving more than 3,000 flying hours by 4,000 members of aircrews.

The highlight has been the rescue of eight men from a dinghy off the coast between Sidmouth and Lyme Regis. They were the American crew of a Fortress which was on its way back after bombing enemy territory.

At the beginning of the war, 'Air-Sea Rescue' was a phrase with a vague meaning. There were only a few small craft stationed about the coast to rescue aircrews who came down in the sea. During the past five years a splendid rescue service has been built up, with technique for locating men who have ditched, sometimes hundreds of miles from the coast. Lifeboats can now be dropped from aircraft; also dinghies in which every possible gadget and comfort have been fixed. One of the innovations last year was the small radio transmitter, installed in dinghies, with which survivors can signal to base. The rescue on the 25th was a splendid and perfect example of the use of dinghy radio.

The Fortress crew came down in the sea and about two o'clock in the afternoon their radio signals were picked up at Lyneham. The message was sent to Headquarters at Plymouth and other stations were contacted, so that bearings were obtained from four different sources. These were plotted and, in spite of the great distance involved, they gave an accurate intersection.

Two high-speed launches were sent out from Lyme Regis and an Air-Sea Rescue Warwick took off from Davidstow Moor. Two more launches set out from Dartmouth, and a third from Portland picked up the signals and joined in the search.

The clouds were at 200 feet and the weather was foul;

distress signals would not have been seen, nor would there have been much chance of the dinghy being sighted by aircraft or shipping. The rescue therefore depended entirely on the plotting of the radio signals on a navigator's desk in an office. The aircraft found the dinghy and kept in touch with it. The weather and cloud then became so menacing that the Americans had to give up using the radio. But they were saved; a launch came alongside and took them aboard, safe and well, two and a quarter hours after the first signal had been received.

June 30. It is not easy to absorb the entire pattern of the war; to realize what is happening to the Americans in the Pacific, or to the armies in Italy, from our haven on this little stretch of the Cornish coast. These battles are far beyond our horizon, and when we read of them they are already as remote as history. One successful attack on a U-boat, or the award of a decoration, sets us jigging with delight, as if we were winning the war all by ourselves.

About eleven o'clock last night news came that Johnny Posnett has been awarded a D.F.C. The dusty old hotel, with the angry sea moaning on one side and grey mist shrouding the hills on the other, suddenly became like a raucous night club. Johnny Posnett is greatly liked, so everyone who was in bed was hauled out and, in pyjamas and dressing-gowns, we celebrated as best we could, on half a bottle of whisky and a jug full of beer.

There was also Johnny Barling's attack to celebrate. His aircraft sighted a *schnörkel*, just before midnight on the 28th. Benny Benson, our only Chilean, who is Barling's second pilot, told me the story:

"Johnny let out a yell, like an Indian seeing a white man for the first time. I was very pleased: I have done ten trips and have never seen a sausage. We came straight up the moonpath and saw the *schnörkel* making a V-shaped ripple in the water.

"Peter Hurn dropped the depth-charges and Sergeant Hanna-win was so eager to see the explosions that he leaned out too far and lost his ear-phones. They went hurtling into the sea."

Johnny Barling flew in a second time and saw the rewarding signs of victory: a patch of oil that spread until it was a mile wide, with one slim streak, two miles long, marking the course of the crippled U-boat.

The Liberator returned, and the crew sat about the mess, bleary-eyed and weary, but unable to sleep until their kill was confirmed. The good news came: six frigates found the dead U-boat about half-past five in the morning and they are bringing the survivors back as prisoners.

Benny Benson[1] must be described. He is an attractive imp, 5 feet 6 inches high, and the masher *par excellence* of the squadron. His roots are English, but he has flowered in the Chilian sun, and his temper has some Latin gusts in it. He looks so young that he should be swinging a strap full of school books in his hand, rather than flying a 28-ton Liberator over the conning-tower of a U-boat.

When Benny is not on duty, he works at advanced mathematics, in his bedroom. But when evening comes, the band strikes up and Benny goes to town. He emerges from his room, trousers perfectly creased, buttons glittering, cap over his eye, at the right angle for a self-confident Lothario, and jumps on the bus for Newquay.

He deserves the rewards he finds. He comes from the mining district of Chile and was only fifteen when the war began. A few weeks before he was eighteen he sailed away on a cargo boat, for an 'unknown destination' in North America. He earned one hundred dollars as wages during the voyage. He told me, one morning as we walked on the beach, "My first job was to empty the wireless-operator's waste-paper basket, full of thousands of minute pieces of yellow paper—all his secret messages torn into fragments. I did not know much about wind direction at that time and threw them over the wrong side of the ship. They blew back and covered the deck. I hid for an hour after that."

Then he learned the first lesson that might ultimately help him against the enemy. While they were steaming through the Caribbean, then a prosperous hunting ground for U-boats, he

---

[1] He was killed in an automobile accident after he returned to his home in Chile.

M

emptied the garbage into the sea, to the horror of the first mate who explained that a trail of vegetable peelings might reveal their position to a marauder.

Benny landed in Canada: eleven days later he was in the Canadian Air Force. He has had to wait a long time to see his first U-boat. "It was worth it," he said, when I saw him this morning, polishing his buttons for his evening victory.

July 1. I flew up to Coastal Headquarters at Northwood yesterday, to gather one of the most gallant and sad stories since 'D' day. It does not belong within the orbit of my diary, but it must be told.

On the afternoon of June 24 a Canso—a Catalina with wheels —was searching for U-boats north of the Shetlands. The captain of the aircraft, Flight-Lieutenant D. E. Hornell of 162 Squadron, a Canadian, has since been awarded a posthumous Victoria Cross.

The Canso had been searching over the sea for ten and a half hours and her patrol was almost ended. About seven o'clock in the evening, the crew saw a surfaced U-boat 5 miles away. Hornell flew in to attack, but the U-boat saw them, altered course, and opened fire. As the aircraft neared the enemy their aim became more accurate, so Hornell was forced to take evasive action. At 1,200 yards his front gunner was able to open fire on the U-boat, but one of the guns jammed and the aircraft was left with only the port gun to defend itself.

The conning-tower of the U-boat had been hit, but the Germans stayed on the surface and fought back. The aircraft was hit at 800 yards and the starboard wing was badly damaged by two shells. They flew on, at the mercy of intense and accurate fire and with their starboard wing in flames. The flak was hitting them continuously, and Hornell and his crew were in great peril.

The official report of his action stated: "One engine was wrecked and in flames; his aircraft had been holed in many places, it was vibrating violently and almost impossible to control. The fire in the starboard engine might at any moment spread to the petrol tanks. His single effective gun could not hope to silence the fire of the U-boat, and his wireless was damaged, so he could not send any distress signals."

His 'cool determination' never wavered. With 'fine contempt of danger' he brought his blazing aircraft down and dropped four depth-charges in an attack which was precise as a peaceful exercise. The bows of the U-boat were lifted high out of the water; then it sank back and disappeared.

The other men in the crew were equally calm and without fear. One wireless operator was stunned and hurled from his seat by the explosion of a cannon shell, but another took his place. The navigator found that his automatic cameras were not working so he followed the progress of the attack with a hand-held camera. The front gunner continued to fire from his single gun.

When Hornell had passed over the target he managed to lift the blazing aircraft from 50 to 250 feet—an astonishing achievement. The fires spread and the starboard engine hurtled from the aircraft into the sea.

Hornell ditched the burning Canso, turning into wind and bringing it down on the water so skilfully that no one was injured. It bounced twice in the heavy swell, once to 150 feet and the second time to 50 feet.

The aircraft was still burning furiously and settling into the sea. Hornell organized the launching of the two dinghies and the salving of the rescue apparatus. One of the dinghies burst: the remaining one was not big enough for the eight members of the crew, so they took it in turn to slide overboard and cling to the side. During the night the dinghy capsized and the crew had to struggle in the heavy seas to right it and climb in again.

Twenty-one hours passed before the survivors were picked up. At ten minutes to eleven that night another Catalina saw a distress signal on the water and flew towards it. There were seven men with the dinghy then: one had died of exposure and his body had been put over the side to make room for a man in the water.

While the Catalina was circling over the dinghy, one of the crew saw an oil patch 3 miles to the west. They flew over and found between thirty and forty Germans in the water, some dead and some alive. They were survivors from the U-boat: it had definitely been killed.

The Catalina flew over the dinghy all night. The sea and wind were so cold that one more Canadian died and his body was also put overboard. Then a Warwick arrived and dropped an airborne lifeboat which fell 500 yards down wind. The men in the dinghy struggled to reach it, but they were too weak. Hornell wanted to strip and swim to it, but the others held him back: a little time after, he lost his sight. The Catalina then left them, after a heroic vigil of twelve and a half hours. It homed a surface craft before flying back to base and the six survivors were picked up. Hornell was still blind, and so exhausted that he died before the launch could reach Ireland.

July 4. I stayed at Northwood long enough to see my first flying bomb: it passed my window while I was shaving, at what seemed like the speed of a swift motor bicycle. I was not proud of my reaction: I paused, razor in hand, gratified when the bomb passed on and left me to continue my shave. My conscience was soothed afterwards when I learned that it had fallen in a cemetery and disturbed only the dead.

I missed breakfast in the mess, and what must have been a delightful scene. The senior officers at Command Headquarters all eat at the same table, and they hide, in aloof silence, each behind his *Times*. The lesser officers breakfast at long tables, with their lesser newspapers before them, in similar silence. There is a cathedral hush on the mess at this hour. When the flying bomb passed over, yesterday morning, the senior officers lowered their copies of *The Times*, listened to the menacing whirr, and immediately disappeared beneath the table. Phil Davies said it was 'the funniest sight' she had ever seen.

From this mild adventure I returned to Watergate. I met

Tug Wilson and Bill Tye in the hall and asked, "Any news?" Tug pointed to a few gashes on Bill Tye's face and said, "Yes, look at that."

They were flying near Ushant about half-past seven this morning when they sighted what they thought was a ship, among the islands near Ile Vierge. They flew in and saw only a break in the waves, but they were near enough to the coast to see the flak towers of Ushant. Tug said, "We were so fed up that we just felt we had to fire at something. We flew in and Bill opened fire with the nose gun, but it jumped out of its mounting and hit him in the face.

"We were level with one of the flak towers so the side and mid-upper guns opened up: the tracer performed a perfect arc as it fell and it was lovely to watch. Then three flak towers fired back at us, but we were then too high and the tracer flak and red star shells burst beneath us. So we flew over the mainland: it was peaceful, just like England, with green fields and hedge-rows. We saw a motor-car on the road, and people going to work. There was a level strip of open country, undefended and quiet. I was sorely tempted to land and capture it."

The audacity within this story is interesting. The coast of France, over which Tug and Bill flew so amiably, used to be a menace to our aircrews. During the long months of patrol, before 'D' day, they knew that as they flew in towards the U-boat bases, or the ports in the Bay, six or seven Junkers would fly out to intercept them. If there was no big friendly cloud in which the Liberator could hide, it had to face the horrible music, fight off the Junkers for perhaps an hour, and return home riddled with bullets—or not return at all.

The coast of the Bay became the chief horror in the minds of Liberator crews, about to take off on their patrols. An Intelligence officer told me that one day when he was briefing a crew, he heard one of them whisper, "I'm not bloody well going there." Of course, he went, but the whisper revealed the general fear. When 'D' day came, we expected the danger from German fighters to increase, but they were sent north to join the forces over the invasion area. A month has passed since 'D' day and only five enemy fighters have been seen in the Bay, in all this time. And three of these were shot down.

The absence of this old danger has made our aircrews almost cheeky in their contempt for the French coast. They come back full of brass, with stories of flying low over the peasants on the roads, of the seaweed fires at Brest, and of fishermen waving to them from the shallows off the coast.

July 7. Retrospect and Celebration. Twenty-six years ago, on April 5, 1918, a D.H.9 aircraft took off from a base near Otranto, to cross the Adriatic and search for a supposed Zeppelin factory in Albania. It was the first operational flight made by an aircraft of 224 Squadron; the beginning of the history of the squadron to which I am now attached. In the months that followed, up to the end of the last war, the twelve aircraft stationed in the south of Italy made more than one hundred operational flights, to bomb the enemy U-boat base at Gjenovic in Jugoslavia.

The first commanding officer of the squadron was Flight Commander J. S. P. Morrison, now Group Captain Morrison, D.F.C., a dry-humoured, friendly man, devoted to snuff, golf and good stories. He came to Watergate last night as guest of honour at our splendid dinner to celebrate the Squadron victories since 'D' day. A piano, bass fiddle and saxophone played 'Bonnie Dundee' as ninety of us walked in to dinner; tomato soup, Dover sole, chicken, ice-cream and a savoury. Wangling and persistence had produced the feast, the Home Guard chief had sent flowers and lettuces from his garden, and a friendly brewer brought two barrels of beer over the hills.

We were packed so tight at the tables that we had almost to take turns in raising our forks to our mouths. Wing Commander McComb, his hair immaculate and his face beaming like a boy at prize-giving, was master of ceremonies. Group Captain Morrison told us of the old days; of the trips across the Adriatic with nothing but a compass, an Admiralty chart of the coast, and a map cut out of a newspaper to guide them; of flying without wireless; and of the petrol tins, with ropes attached, kept under the seats, to be used as lifebuoys in case the crew came down in the sea. There was no 'telephone service' or intercom. within the aircraft, and the pilot used a stick with the numbers 1–12 on it, for signalling to the observer behind him. The observer had a key to the twelve possible messages and the pilot would hold up the stick and touch the appropriate number when he had something to say—'Engine bad, must return'—'Submarine in sight'—or, 'Are they hostile?'

The aircraft cruised at 70 miles an hour and each trip lasted four hours and fifty minutes. The aircrews of the Liberators of today listened in awe to the Group Captain's story: their cruising speed is over 150 miles an hour, and their trip lasts thirteen and a half hours.

Then we listened to the story of the present: Air Vice-Marshal Baker reminded us that over a month has passed since we went up to the cinema to hear him describe the task of the anti-U-boat and shipping-strike squadrons during the invasion In that month the anti-U-boat aircraft of 19 Group have flown 3,700 sorties, covering 29,477 hours, over more than 5,000,000 miles. This is equal to 200 times around the world.

They have sighted 100 U-boats and attacked 59 of them. Then came the fact that was deeply satisfying to us all: not a single life has been lost or a pound of invasion equipment sunk by a torpedo fired from a U-boat. The 'Unclimbable Fence'—'The Cork'—has been wholly successful in preventing the U-boats from operating in the Channel.

Then we all gathered in the hall, beneath the ship's bell of *The City of Marseilles*, which was mined off the coast of Scotland early in the war. An aircraft of 224 Squadron found it, reported its position and thus helped to save the crew. The bell was the Squadron's first war trophy.

We filled our glasses and sang our songs: 'When there isn't a girl about you do feel lonely', 'Salome', and 'The Ball at Kirriemuir'. Billy Wicht, who won his D.S.O. and D.F.C. with the Squadron, then led us in singing 'Alouette'. I obliged with 'Where are the Lads of the Village Tonight?', a merry blending of song and dance, and 'Home Sweet Home', played on the piano with my nose. The Adjutant slid down the stairs on a surf board and I followed him, light as a bird. Then the Air Vice-Marshal and the Group Captain slid down and Butch sprayed us all with soda syphons. Then we sang more songs and filled our glasses again, and Group Captain Morrison stood on the piano and thanked the Squadron. Then we sang still more songs and filled our glasses again and found that it was three o'clock in the morning. So we cursed Dönitz, wished the few remaining U-boats a long rest on the sea bed, filled our glasses once more, sang 'Auld Lang Syne', and tottered upstairs.

July 9. I drove over to Plymouth Sound yesterday, to stay with the Australians of No. 10 Squadron, who fly Sunderlands. The beginning of this squadron makes a gallant and stimulating story. In July 1939, a contingent arrived in England to fly 9 Sunderlands out, for the defence of Australia. They were here when war was declared and the Commonwealth immediately offered the crews, and the aircraft, to the British Government. A second contingent arrived on Boxing Day 1939, to complete the strength and, during 1940, detachments from the Squadron patrolled from Malta, Gibraltar, Cairo, Alexandria and Scotland. In July 1940 they killed their first U-boat. They have flown nearly 3,000 sorties, over 4,000,000 sea miles, destroying 7 U-boats and damaging 8. Twenty-three members of the Squadron have won D.F.C.s, nine have D.F.M.s, one has the British Empire Medal and twenty-six of them have been mentioned in despatches.

The Australians seem to be at home beside this ancient water, from which Drake sailed to circumnavigate the world, almost four centuries ago. The aircrews work in two hangars where T. E. Lawrence served as Aircraftsman Shaw, from 1929 to 1933. Australians are not history worshippers by nature, but they accept the ghosts of Drake and Lawrence quite amiably.

The first pilot I met was Flight-Lieutenant W. B. Tilley, who comes from Melbourne, and who sank his first U-boat yesterday. We stood on the shore and he pointed to a green slope, beyond where the *Golden Hind* once lay at anchor and where a flock of white Sunderlands floated, in its place. "That's where Drake played his game of bowls," said Tilley. "I play there myself sometimes on warm evenings. It's an old man's game in this country, but back in Australia the young ones play it as well."

He was a reluctant talker, until he trusted me: then we sat back, in the mess, and he told me of his first meeting with a U-boat.

"Before I went on patrol I saw my room-mate, Johnny Mabbett: the next time I saw him was towards the end of my patrol, early in the afternoon, about ten minutes from base. I saw a streak on the water: it might have been a periscope so I called Johnny and told him that I had seen a suspicious-looking object. He circled, saw nothing, and answered, 'You're up a tree, Joe. I'm going back on patrol.'

"I flew over the spot again and also saw nothing. A few minutes later the second pilot—he's Roy Felan, the Australian junior tennis champion—said, 'What do you make of that over there?' I said, 'It's a bloody U-boat!'

"I sounded the warning and we turned in immediately to attack. Before I finished the turn the U-boat opened fire. The flak was pretty thick and we expected to be hit at any moment, so I opened up with my nose guns. I could see by the splashes in the sea that our fire was falling short, so I waited and opened up again when we were 1,500 yards away. It wasn't difficult then to keep the fire on the conning-tower. The U-boat made no attempt to submerge and I kept saying to myself, 'When are we going to get to the bloody thing?'

"We both ceased fire and, flying at 75 feet, I dropped my bombs. We passed over: then pandemonium broke out over the intercom. The tail gunner had given the U-Boat a final burst as we ran over: he shouted, 'You beaut. you've got him!' We circled at a quarter of a mile to see the results of our handi-work. The U-boat was low by the stern, but one gun kept popping at us."

From this moment, the final killing of the U-boat became an international party. An American Liberator from 105 Squadron arrived and fired at the crippled hull; then another Sunderland appeared and dropped its depth-charges. The U-boat had ceased to move: white smoke curled up from the conning-tower and the crew emerged. They lined up on deck, with some fifteen yellow dinghies, and then began to abandon ship.

Tilley said, "The U-boat was sinking fast and it went down tail first, almost vertically. I've never been so thrilled in all my life."

When the survivors were in the water, Tilley flew over them, with his camera. He said, "I kept running over, out of curiosity, and they were waving to us and we were waving back. I felt a bit sorry for them, so I dropped them two food packs and a dinghy."

. . . . . .

The Australians talked to me of 'the English' quite freely, because I am a New Zealander. They arrive in this country inclined to criticize the foibles of English life. One Australian was peeved when his host in Scotland scolded him for shooting a brace of grouse sitting on a fence: another who shot a fox and stretched the skin on the door of a barn to dry was perplexed when his host begged him to bury the skin quickly, before any neighbours could see it.

In Australia, it is no crime to kill a sitting bird, and foxes are shot on sight. These superficial differences in attitude towards 'sport' cause embarrassment at first: then they pass, and under-standing, and affection arrive, slowly. One Australian said to me, "The English know how to live. They are not as restless as we are." Wing Commander Gillies, aged only twenty-four, commanding a squadron and therefore responsible for 450 men, said, "I could stay here: I like the way the English live and the way they think."

July 12. I drove across from Plymouth to Watergate and found my friends depressed and anxious. All the war can suddenly

lose its importance because of some episode within this little
bay, and its high, sullen cliffs. The treachery of the Cornish coast
did not end when the wreckers and smugglers were extinguished
by justice. When the sun shines, the coast is glorious, but when
the gulls fly in, crying on the wings of a gale, darkness falls on
the shore. The waves groan and threaten and the cliffs crumble
into the sea. On Monday, while I was away, an aircraft crashed
into the bay and only a few of the crew were saved. Yesterday,
two servants from the W.A.A.F. officers' mess were drowned.
Their bodies were washed ashore at Newquay. One of the girls
had just been married and her husband arrived to arrange the
funeral. The sea looks horrible: the cliffs are dark and the gulls
cling to the crags, shivering and silent.

July 14. After two days of rain, Batch flew me over the Bristol
Channel, to Milford Haven. It was a grey and white morning,
with low milky clouds, against the glowing light: and below,
thirty ships moving in convoy over the darker grey water,
towards Land's End. There were but two splashes of lively
colour during the flight; the green fluorescence of a target
patch, with the diamond of a sea marker burning beside it in
the sea, and the rich porphyry stone of the Pembrokeshire
coast. It is from here that the nameless ancients carried the
gigantic monoliths to Stonehenge, before time remembered.

We flew in a motherly old Anson. Veteran pilots have
respect, even tenderness, for Ansons. In the summer of 1939,
when the war began, they were the reliable, slow aircraft in
which Coastal Command won its first honours. A civilian can
never imagine the love a pilot feels for an aircraft that has
carried him safely through his first combat; it is like the affection
a highwayman must have felt for his horse. I have seen pilots
pat their aircraft, speak to them, and even blow them a
kiss.

About twenty airmen gathered at the end of the runway at
St. Eval to see Batch take off, with me as his only passenger.
He had not flown an Anson for two and a half years and the boys

in the mess had pulled my leg. "You ought to get a good obituary in *The Times*," said one. Butch Pugh said, "You old toper, you will end up as a gin patch in the Bristol Channel."

Some pilots are clumsy and ham-fisted and they put the fear of God into you the moment they touch the controls. Others inspire immediate confidence. I flew with Batch in the old Anson, happy as if I were in the safety of my arm-chair; I wrote my notes, on my knee, 2,000 feet above the Bristol Channel, and enjoyed the wild sweeps of imagination that come so readily in the air.

Below was the space of water up which mariners have sailed to Bristol during the centuries, bringing home contraband, or honest cargoes, from foreign lands. But the romance has gone; the smugglers' caves on the Cornish coast shelter picnic parties from the wind. From 2,000 feet, the lashing waves that the seascape artists painted so boisterously are mere wrinkles on the water; they give little hint of the treachery one would endure if one ditched into them.

Some years ago I found an old letter in a house in Shropshire; it described the voyage of a Quaker missionary who crossed the Atlantic in a windjammer, in 1793. She wrote of her joy when the sailors caught a porpoise, because its oil could be used for the lamp by which the pilot watched his compass as he steered the ship. It seemed a remote episode as I looked out over the Atlantic which has seen two victories during the war; the annihilation of the U-boats, and the conquest of distance. Pilots land in England, still smoking the packet of cigarettes they bought in New York the day before; Mr. Churchill picks up his telephone in Downing Street and speaks to Mr. Roosevelt in the White House. The old cliche, 'It's a small world', has taken on a new meaning.

July 15. I talked for an hour today with Flight-Sergeant G. R. E. Robertson, who spent eleven days in a dinghy last summer, with Group Captain Mead. He said that the painful memories have gone, but that sometimes, when he lifts a pint of beer in a tankard, he recalls that he had less than this quantity to drink in all the eleven days.

He said that during the first days he worried about his parents; then anxiety, fear and hunger left him and he considered, calmly, whether it would be better to die slowly of thirst, dive overboard and be drowned, or drink salt water and go mad. "But I was quite happy about it," he said.

During the hours when they were fishing over the side of the dinghy, using their scabs and pieces of soft skin from between their toes as bait, he looked deep into the water. He was confused as to what he saw and what he merely imagined; he thought he could see big fish swimming, 'like dolphins, staring from the depths', but he still does not know if the dolphins were really there.

We talked of the power of imagination and the temptation in pilots to exaggerate what happens to them. The sailors of the old days no doubt believed that they saw sea serpents and mermaids, because, staring always at the spaces of sea and sky, their gift for fantasy was encouraged. They wished for some break in the monotony and therefore peopled the emptiness from their own minds.

Robertson recalled the story of an engineer who claimed that he had seen a U-boat blown clean out of the sea, with a space of moonlight showing between the hull and the water. It is impossible for a depth-charge to blow a 540-ton U-boat into the air, but the engineer had been so astonished by the might of the explosion that he expected to see a strip of moonlight, beneath the hull. Nothing would convince him that this was harmless imagination.

I drove to Angle, in the cool of the evening; but there were explosions, and the slow-motion plumes of depth-charges in the estuary, to remind me that the world was not as peaceful as it seemed. They were only practice attacks and their spray soon faded in the wind.

On the way we came to the ruins of Pembroke Castle and I asked the driver to stop and allow me to wander among the old stones. The Great Keep dates from 1200 and there is an amiable legend that, in the cavern below, Bluebeard did away with his wives. Henry II stayed here in 1172, King John came, and in 1456 King Henry VIII was born in the castle. Beneath all these episodes of English history there are Roman ghosts— their coins have been dug from the mound on which the castle is built. Scandinavian sea rovers occupied the rock as a camp, in their time. The ruins looked superb in the afternoon sun. But the driver was impatient for his tea; when I returned to the car and remarked on the beauty of the scene, he grumbled, "It's a bit old-fashioned, don't you think?"

July 16. Before I flew back to Cornwall I met Wing Commander John Hampshire, who commands the Australian Squadron at Pembroke Dock. His experiences make a new kind of story for me. He has been in England only five months and has fought most of his war in the Dutch East Indies. Hampshire was trained in Australia: he began with flying-boats at Port Moresby in 1939, then went to hunt down German and Italian blockade runners in the South Pacific and to open flying-boat bases in New Britain, New Ireland, the British Solomon Islands, and the New Hebrides. As the Japanese advanced, in 1942, he flew men, engines, and guns to aid the Dutch at Ambon and Namlea. Finally, he helped to evacuate members of the Air Force; until the desperate hour when a Japanese force of twenty warships arrived at Amboina Island.

Hampshire's next task was with the Americans; he flew ammunition to their base at Sourabaya. As the Japanese threat grew he had to make his landings at forward points in the dark, without the help of any lighting. He then returned to the New Orleans sector to fly the Chief of the General Staff into Milne Bay, at the time when the Allies and the Japanese were rushing to secure bases in Papua.

It is a big balance-sheet of experience to bring to the gentle waters of Pembroke Dock. Hampshire is the richer for it: he now knows both theatres of war and his judgment is mellow, beyond his years. He made me realize the benefits that come to pilots who fight in the East as well as the West. A senior officer told me that Hampshire's influence was good for all at Pembroke Dock, both Britons and Australians.

July 19. A Liberator came over the Channel to take us back to Watergate. This time, Batch was also a passenger. He sat in the port hatch and I in the starboard; a pleasant way to travel as we each had a big open window at our elbow. We watched the pale blue coastline and threw our cigarette-butts into the sea. We agreed that we might write a book together and call it *The World is my Ash-tray*.

I had never flown in a Liberator before and when we landed I went to Stan Weir, the pilot, and thanked him.

"What for?" he asked, and I answered, "For flying the aircraft so beautifully."

Stan was mournful; he said, "The Liberator is not an aircraft. It might have been produced by the bus designer of the London Passenger Transport Board."

Another Liberator was coming in to land and he pointed to it. "There! They're not even beautiful to look at. I don't like flying ugly aircraft. It hurts."

July 20. When Lofty Lord arrived back from patrol today, he learned that he has been awarded a D.F.C. He was the only one who did not smile with pleasure, but I suspect that he was pleased inside. He is an old hand and has held every rank from A.C.2 to Flying Officer—nine in all. His citation commends him for his 'experience and influence'. Except for bicycle rides over the hills, in search of harmless pints in friendly pubs, he has no diversions; the R.A.F. is his life, and has been, since he was a boy.

Lofty is, of course, very tall, and he has the intolerant single-mindedness of men who always walk along one straight line.

He knows none of the delights of inconsistency, and I suspect that he despises writers, on principle. When I pointed out that I was the Command historian and that it was his duty to tell me his story, he clicked the heels of his mind, obediently, and came to my room, resigned but still reluctant.

When the war began, Lofty was a gunner with a Blenheim squadron in Iraq. He was sent to Amirya, in the desert, to fly sorties in defence of Alexandria. He shot down a Savoia 79 and damaged another at the time when the Italians were trying to attack the *Warspite* and the *Ajax*, on their way through the Mediterranean. He shot down another in September 1940, during the bombing of Mersa Matruh, and another during the bombing of Sidi Barrani.

Then to Greece, in November 1940, with nine fighters and six bombers, to patrol over Athens, and for what Lofty described as 'looking for trouble flights over the Greek Islands and near the Italian front lines'. He added an Italian flying-boat to his score during this enterprise. He took part in covering the fleet, for six days and nights during the evacuation of Greece and, just before the fall of Crete, he returned to Egypt and joined a medium bomber squadron. He did twenty-two raids over the Bardia and Tobruk areas; in the last raid he was chased by Messerschmitt 109's and wounded by a cannon shell. He told the story as coldly as if he were describing a visit to his lawyer. "I was dazed and bleeding at the mouth. Then I was hit again and the bullet passed through my right leg. I was still conscious but I could not speak because of the wound in my mouth, so I had to write my instructions to the others on a piece of paper."

Lofty was brought back to England, and mended. He has been with 224 Squadron since May of last year, and has attacked two U-boats.

When the dry delivery of facts ended, Lofty said, "Is that all?" He thanked me politely, left the room as if he had been on parade and, half an hour later, I saw him jump on his bicycle to search for a pint, somewhere over the hills.

Flight-Lieutenant K.O. Moore, D.S.O. (see p. 161)

From a portrait by Eric Kennington

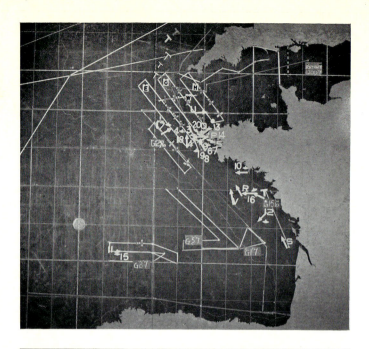

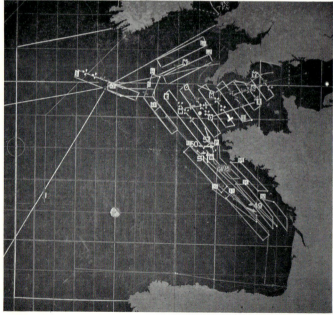

The operations room board at No. 19 Group, on June 7, and June 14, 1944, showing the patrols on those days, and how the 'cork' was placed in the Channel (see p. 176)

July 22. One of the virtues of Coastal Command is that its air-crews and aircraft remain adaptable, and versatile, so that their tasks may be revised as the war develops. This is particularly true of the Mosquito squadrons who have changed their role three times since 'D' day, to cope with the varying tactics of the enemy. In the 'D' day plan they were to provide fighter patrols near Ushant, to protect the heavier anti-U-boat aircraft. But the German fighters, with whom they hoped to do battle, appeared in such small numbers that the Mosquitoes were wasting their time. They were then switched to a new task; to make recon-naissance flights between Brest and the Gironde River. They located the ships and, for the past six weeks, have struck them mercilessly, thus harassing the German transport all along the coast. The attacks took the Mosquitoes right under the nose of the enemy; they had to fly within the entrance to Brest, to bomb the ships, and as far as 10 miles up the Gironde River. They met merciless flak and our losses were depressing. Then our Navy began to prowl in these waters and the Mosquitoes were ordered to provide fighter protection, and to make reconnaissance flights for them.

There was an example of this new task, yesterday, when two Mosquitoes of 235 Squadron attacked Dornier 217's in bad weather. Wing Commander Yonge had been ordered to supply a patrol from his squadron to cover a destroyer escort group operating off Ushant. Dorniers, carrying glider bombs, threatened the destroyers; fighter cover was therefore imperative. Two Mosquitoes were sent off, but the low clouds over the water, and the pelting rain, made their job perilous; one aircraft apparently flew into the sea and the other came home and reported the weather as being 'impossible'. But the destroyers had to be defended. Wing Commander Yonge decided to take off himself, with one other Mosquito, for which the crew must volunteer. Jack Frost and his navigator, Alfie Fuller, offered to go with him.

Wing Commander Yonge, a veteran of thirty-eight, told me the story when I went to see him this afternoon.

"When Jack Frost and I took off, the weather had cleared a

N

little over base, but we had to fly blind, in close formation, to get through the rain and low cloud. We finally broke cloud at 1,400 feet while approaching the patrol area. Then we came into a combination of weather such as I have never seen before. We were in a col, with a thunderstorm to the south, sea fog over Brest and Ushant, and continuous rain to the north. Then we reached the patrol area and it was comparatively clear, but we had to vary our height and fly blind from time to time to keep at our task. At twenty minutes past one, I had not found the destroyers, nor the Dorniers. Half an hour later we sighted two Dornier 217's, with a Mosquito from another wing opening fire on them at long range; it was still trying to attack, after being hit in the port engine. The pilot had to give up and fly home as best he could.

"We jettisoned our wing tanks and attacked the second Dornier. I was just about to open fire when I saw that Frost had already set its port engine on fire. I therefore swung my sight on to the leading Dornier and attacked it with several bursts of cannon and ·303. I closed right behind his tail, although he was doing his best to dodge me. Out of the corner of my eye I saw the first German, diving in flames, and three parachutes floating down to the water.

"My burst was effective; the Dornier blew up in front of me: so close that the streams of his oil blacked me out completely. I had to jerk back the stick to avoid hitting him and to fly on instruments until the windscreen wiper cleared some of the oil away. Then I could peer through the clear spots, between the thick German oil, and see the two Dorniers blazing on the sea, and several of the crew in dinghies.

"It was then that we saw the destroyers we were supposed to defend. I spoke to the Navy and told them that both the Germans had been shot down in flames, and that the survivors were waiting in the water to be picked up.

"Frost and I became separated in the thick cloud on the way back, but we landed at base within five minutes of each other. Then I handed the Mosquito over to the ground crew—always there to make us feel that they are part of the effort. They wiped the thick oil from the fuselage and painted a swastika on it, for victory."

I said to Wing Commander Yonge, at the end. "You have a gift for making a story clear. Are you related in any way to——?"

"Yes," he interrupted, "Charlotte M. Yonge was my father's aunt."

July 27. Jack Brookes is the Flight-Engineer Leader of 224 Squadron—a solemn responsibility, beyond my comprehension. He is one of those people who seem confused by life, except when they are looking into the guts of an engine. Then, his face catches fire with delight. He has done all he should to vanquish the enemy since 'D' day, but, when he has an hour to spare, he seeks his mistress—the motor-car he is building, in a garage on the side of the hill. When others leap on bicycles and pursue dalliance in the town, he climbs the slope with his kit of tools and gets to work. He is tired of 'bought cars'. He said, "You have to remove *A*, unscrew *B*, and lift up *C* to find *D*. I want a car where everything is where I put it."

So far, the engine, wheels and body have cost him £40. Butch Pugh told me that it is so perfectly made that it is 'just waiting to take off and fly like an exquisite bird'.

I know little about the magic within a motor-car, but Jack Brookes is so intense in his love that I decided to pry; I went up to the garage, leaned against the door and induced him to talk. He comes from Birmingham; when he was last on leave he saw an Austin wheel in a scrap yard and bought it for half a crown. He was carrying it along the street when he saw its brother, in the garden of a house. He knocked on the door and said to the man who opened it, "I have just bought this wheel for half a crown. Will you take half a crown for that one?" The man agreed and Jack went off with the two wheels under his arms.

"It was a football Saturday," Jack told me, "and the buses were crowded. I was so exhausted that I went into the local to have one. I rested the two wheels in the fire-place and I was just drinking my pint when a bloke came up, looked at the wheels and said, 'Austin, eh?' I said, 'Yes,' and he said, 'I believe I've got two more of those in my garden, if the dustman has not taken them. I'll bring them in tomorrow.'

"The man brought them in and I gave him a pint of beer."

Jack's first experiment in engineering was to build a motor bicycle. He was not so adroit then, as now—while riding through a suburb of Birmingham, a split-pin became displaced and he lost control of the machine. Let him finish the story. "Well, I just went straight over the island and up the steps into the cinema. The manager was so pleased I had not killed anyone that he thanked me. So I leaned the bike against a poster of Hedy Lamarr, went upstairs with him and had a drink."

August 10. So far, the month has yielded us few prizes. We sat by the radio last night and heard that the U.S. forces had taken Guam; a vague, distant compensation for the lull that has settled on Cornwall. In the first four days of August only one U-boat was seen; on the 5th two were attacked, between Brest and the English coast. But we do not know if they were victories; they fell into the unsatisfactory category of 'probables'.

The pilots report more and more Sperrbrechers in the area of patrol. They are converted merchantmen, strengthened internally so that they will not sink if they hit a mine, and they are heavily armed. The only fat prize was on the 7th when a formation of Beaufighters attacked and sunk a Sans-Souci escort vessel in the harbour of Les Sables d'Olonne. The crews saw two splendid explosions, and fierce fire and smoke as the ship went down.

I decided to move on for a day or two, so I drove up the coast to Tintagel and arrived yesterday afternoon. It was a sublime day and when I came to the great headland, joined to the coast by a narrow ledge, I paid threepence to the gatekeeper and walked into another world. This hard-bitten earth is heavy with legends and, standing by the ruins of the Castle, I willingly believed that King Arthur was born in Tintagel—that 'this Star of wonderful magnitude' lived here; and that Merlin's ghost, 'plentifully endowed with the spirit of divination', haunts the shore; where bells ring in the sea and the birds cry with sailors' voices, on the wings of the storm.

The illusion of ten minutes' escape into legend was enchanting; I drove on to the aerodrome at Davidstow Moor with a curious sensation of having turned centuries over in my hand, easily as pennies.

.   .   .   .   .   .

I was waiting in the Intelligence Officer's room when I noticed a circular box, rather incongruous among the confidential papers. On the lid was printed *Camembert, fabrique en Normandie*, and a pretty coloured scene of a cow, a stream, and a tree. I leaned over and smelled deep; sure enough, there was a *camembert* inside. So the days of anaemic 'mouse-trap' were over; at last, cheeses were arriving from France. This one had been brought back by Wing Commander Gatward, who walked into the office just as I was watching the cheese with a greedy look. He sat down and told me the story.

On August 7, he was ordered to take two aircraft on a reconnaissance flight over the harbour at St. Helier, to gather information needed by the American units in France. (Gatward is no stranger to the French; in June 1942 he flew a Beaufighter, below roof-top height, along the Champs-Élysées, to the Arc de Triomphe, where he dropped a stream of cannon shells into the German Military Headquarters.) He flew over St. Helier, 'had a squint and made some careful notes', and then flew on to Normandy with his information.

He landed at an aerodrome six miles from Cherbourg, and was driven into the town by an American sailor. "The country was very pretty," he said, "rather like Devon: but the telegraph wires were down, hanging drunkenly from the poles. The road was cratered by bombs and the jeep bounced two feet in the air as we drove on. The civilians were cheerful, not particularly interested in us, and going about their business. The Americans put us up. There was no electric light, and no water, so we shaved and washed next morning with a bottle of Vichy water from a shop near by."

Gatward went into the streets of Cherbourg in search of wine to bring home, but there was none, so he bought six boxes of *camembert* and flew back to Davidstow Moor.

Yesterday afternoon, he led twenty-four Beaufighters to search for enemy ships between Belle Ile and the mainland. He told me, "We saw a few old fishermen who waved to us, and there were children in one of the fishing boats; they waved, too. Then we flew south and, just as we approached the extreme end of Bourgeneuf Bay, I spotted four German minesweepers, hunched together, still, in a calm sea. I gave the old cry, *Attack!* *Attack!* Flak came from the shore, and the minesweepers also opened fire, keeping it up until we opened with our cannon at 1,000 yards. Then the fire from the ships died down, but it still came fairly thick from the shore. One of our aircraft bought it. I had seen their tracer coming in with mine, so they must have been shot down during the attack; their aircraft crashed into the sea, close to the ships.

"As we closed range to about 400 yards, we fired off our rockets; three of the ships were soon on fire and the fourth was smoking. It was all very satisfactory.

"We went over the tops of the ships and broke out to sea. Then one of our pilots called up to tell me he had lost an engine and to ask if I would escort him home. At that moment, one of the others called up and said, 'It's all right, I'm with him,' and a third signalled, 'I'm with you, old chap. Carry on.' "

So the Beaufighters returned—the crippled aircraft escorted on either side—leaving the minesweepers in flames. Gatward said, "We just toddled home along the coast, seeing nothing but a few fishing boats on the way."

When he finished his story, Wing Commander Gatward leaned forward and drew his *camembert* towards him. "Here," he said, "a souvenir—that is, if you like good cheese."

(I kept it until it was no longer possible for us to share the same room. The batman said, "I like a nice piece of cheddar, sir, but not *that*!" So I found three people to share the *camembert* with me and we scraped the rind until it was almost transparent.)

.   .   .   .   .   .

From Davidstow Moor I drove along the coast into Devon. The only sign of war was a splendid convoy of ships, moving over the blue satin water. I was to spend the day with Poles, and South Africans, based at Chivenor.

It is not easy to imagine the difficulties that beset pilots who have come all the way from Poland to fight for their country, from an English field. They are not flying over the hills and rivers whose freedom they seek; they have to learn new geography, and a new language. We try to help them by putting sign-posts, in Polish as well as English, on the aerodromes; even the instructions in aircraft, and rescue dinghies, have to be in both languages, so they may appreciate the advantages of the simple words, *Climb in Here*, in their own tongue.

The Polish crew of a Wellington told me of a U-boat they killed on the night of June 18. There was something fierce and almost frightening in their voices as they spoke of the utter destruction, parts of the U-boat being blown into the air, and the wreckage. They are pleased by revenge. The stories of at least two of the Poles should be set down, to remind us of the fortitude of mind of these exiles: introspective, persistent, sullen warriors, who believe that Poland may be freed, and Germany punished, from this island.

The first of them is Flight-Lieutenant Antoniewicz, the pilot; he comes from Bilaystok, which was freed by the Russians two weeks ago. After a year in the Polish army, he joined the air force and was still a cadet when the war began. When Warsaw fell, he fled to Roumania where he spent three miserable months in a concentration camp. One night he escaped; he made his way to the coast of the Black Sea where a friendly Roumanian helped him to board a ship for Syria. Then he travelled to Marseilles and trained as a pilot with the French. When France capitulated he went to Oran, and then to Casablanca where he found a ship to bring him to Liverpool. He has been fighting with the R.A.F. ever since. "I have attacked three U-boats," he said to me. "One we have killed; I saw the oil and the wreckage, and the Germans, in the water."

The navigator of the Wellington, and Antoniewicz's friend, is George Moller, who was a pilot cadet, stationed near Warsaw, when the war began. His school was bombed and he tried to escape to Lublin in one of the aircraft, but it crashed within a few miles and Moller had to walk back. He then hitch-hiked into Hungary where he became very ill. He was sheltered by a Jewish family who were kind to him; they fed him on oranges until he was well enough to escape to Jugoslavia, and then into Greece. He also made his way to Marseilles; then to an aerodrome at Lyons where he was bombed, twice. When France fell, he walked to the Atlantic coast where he found a ship to bring him to England, and the R.A.F. It was the *Arandora Star*, which was sunk four days after it landed George Moller in Liverpool.

From my long, solemn talks with the Poles, I was taken to drink beer with three South Africans; B. D. Miller, W. T. Wilkins, and R. C. Naude. The mood of the talk was very different; theirs is a merry war, with more jokes and less submerged desire for revenge. "Where do you come from?" I asked Miller, and he answered, "Johannesburg." Then Wilkins said, "I come from Zululand." "And I come from East London," said Naude, "but if you are writing it down, please add *South Africa*, or they will think that I come from the East End of London."

They agreed that they all wished to see some 'nice German dinghies with lots of Germans in them'; and then Naude said, "But in the meantime, let's have another drink."

August 11. As I write the stories of attacks on U-boats, I am worried lest the details, so frequently the same, will bore the average reader. The variations between them are slight: the ultimate photographs so often alike. My writer's mind therefore seeks some touch of surprise, to keep the narrative awake—to make the landsman aware of the adventure in U-boat hunting. I think I can claim that an attack the day before yesterday suits my purpose.

U-boats are picked up on the Radar screen, or they are actually seen on the surface. In the Mediterranean, with its deeper distances of vision, aircraft are often able to see a sub-merged U-boat, but this is seldom possible in our colder, northern waters. During the afternoon of August 9, the crew of a 53 Squadron Liberator saw a U-boat, beneath the surface, off the Ile de Noirmoutier, forty miles or so south of Belle Ile. There was a kill—especially pleasing to the commanding officer[1] as this was his last operational flight before departing for a desk at Coastal Headquarters.

Pilot Officer A. S. Dantzic, the mid-upper gunner, told me the story. "We were tootling along, to look at an oil slick, covering about a mile and shimmering on the sea. The beam gunner suddenly called out, 'Skipper, there's a sub down there.' It was a submerged U-boat, looking like a nice long greenish cigar, with a darker green circle, which was the conning-tower. The pointed nose was quite clear, but the stern was low. You know how the painted line around the edge of a swimming-bath trembles in the water, well, the U-boat seemed to shiver like that.

"The C.O. gave the order to attack. The first time we went over, the bomb doors failed to open, so we had to come in a second time, dropping the depth-charges nicely between the end of the immense oil slick and the stern of the U-boat. The explosion was so terrific that I seemed to be looking up, instead of down, towards the column of water."

Oil surged to the surface and, later, the Navy picked up some U-boat planking and samples of oil, after the Liberator had resumed patrol. The U-boat had apparently gone down and was struggling with its injuries.

[1] Group Captain R. T. F. Gates, D.F.C., A.F.C.

About two-thirty next morning, Johnny Barling, of 224 Squadron, saw the same U-boat, with our own frigates at hand. The survivors were climbing into their one-man dinghies—some thirty of them, who were afterwards picked up and brought home as prisoners. When they were interrogated they said that they had left Lorient the previous afternoon, with supplies for fourteen weeks. Their enterprise was therefore well nipped in the bud.

August 13. It is fascinating, and satisfying, to watch the map in the ante-room day by day, as John Stratton marks the conquered territories with red pencil—a rich, porty red, good for measuring victories. All that Air Vice-Marshal Baker described as our 'D' day task has been accomplished: one after another, the U-boats have joined the ghosts of the Spanish galleons on the ocean bed. The few that have escaped are creeping out of Brest, for the uncertain haven of ports in the south. The ships also are trying to save themselves: fifty-one were sighted off the French coast during the last twenty-four hours, and one of the surviving three destroyers in the Bay was blown up by a direct hit. The attacks went on, mercilessly, all day and night. Yesterday morning, a 1,500-ton vessel was seen, with branches of trees tied to the sides and rigging. It was hugging the coast, trying to pass itself off as an island.

The reports of the attacks are horrible to read: ship after ship has been left in flames. The U-boats also continue to suffer: the crew of one, picked up and taken prisoner, included members of shore-based administrative staff, who had hoped to get away with their documents to safety in the south.

August 14. The Beaufighters and Mosquitoes made three brilliant attacks, but we lost five aircraft as the price of sinking two Sperrbrechers, and hitting a destroyer, another Sperrbrecher and two smaller vessels. The Beaufighters came back with a melancholy photograph of the *Magdeburg*, blazing under cannon fire, before it sank, quickly, in a tower of flames.

Later. The crews of three of our aircraft were saved. The last, from a Mosquito, baled out and were captured by the enemy, but the Maquis set them free and they all returned to England.

August 15. Gilbert Potier came home with another victory for 53 Squadron. Each pilot tells his story with his own self-revealing phrases, so that his narrative becomes a slight autobiographical sketch. Potier is not afraid of words: he told me his life story when we first met, early in July. In peace-time he was a chartered accountant, but his horizon has expanded since then. He was trained in Canada, and his first operational task when he returned was to fly members of the British Military Mission to Russia. Next, to the Shetlands; then in search of the *Tirpitz*, near the Lofotens.

His growing world of adventure is fascinating when one relates it to the map. In May 1942 he made a reconnaissance of Spitzbergen, and in July his squadron was based on Archangel, from which he searched again for the *Tirpitz*. He returned to England, and in September he flew again to Russia; in October he was in Gibraltar, and a few weeks later he was in Northern Ireland. The Bahamas, Texas, and Montreal followed; then he came back to England to hunt for German submarines. He told me the story of his first attack, five weeks ago, and revealed the pleasure in his heart when he said, "I saw my first, nice, juicy U-boat."

Gilbert Potier came back today after seeing his second 'nice, juicy U-boat'; one of the few trying to escape from the pens in Brest. "It was a lovely sunset," he told me, "and the stars were peeping out. As we passed Brest I saw a thunderstorm ahead. I summoned all my courage because I do not like thunderstorms. In peace-time I used to put my head under the bed-clothes.

"The stars went out and the night became black: the lightning was terrific, each jagged fork seeming to run from the sky to the sea. Every time there was a blinding flash I thought it would hurl our thirty-ton aircraft into the drink. Then we were through and beyond it all. I relaxed and soon the stars peeped out again.

"Just before midnight, the Radar operator said, 'Hullo, Skipper. Contact just appeared!' "

Gilbert described the attack that followed and then told me that the Navy found the crippled U-boat at seven-thirty this morning. He said, "They finished what we began, and one more of the bastards went to the bottom."

.   .   .   .   .   .

The real drama of the week has been on our own doorstep. A few days ago, two navigators were strolling along the cliffs near Newquay when they saw what looked like the periscope of a U-boat, out to sea. They were afraid that it was planning to attack shipping in the Bristol Channel, or escaping to the cooler waters of the north. There were hundreds of people bathing or paddling on the beaches, unaware that the enemy was near. The navigators hurried to Newquay railway station and tele-phoned the aerodrome at St. Eval. Aircraft were sent out to search the sea, but the U-boat evaded them.

Then came the only blow to our local pride, for some time. A ship in a convoy steaming from Hartland Point to Tintagel was attacked and crippled by the U-boat, next day.

Sometimes, during the past two and a half months, we have stood on the cliff and counted as many as thirty ships steaming by. This armada has continued, day after day, and not one of the thousands of ships has been menaced, until this unfortunate merchantman was torpedoed by the impudent invader. About eight o'clock last evening, the pilot of a Sunderland, crossing the Bristol Channel, saw the wounded ship being attended by three others. Five miles away was the periscope of the U-boat,

making up the coast towards Hartland Point. The aircraft was
on a peaceful flight and was not carrying any bombs, but the
sight of it was enough to make the U-boat dive, thus saving the
crippled ship and its escort from further attack.

The nearness of the U-boat, within sight of the Cornish
beaches, gave me a strange sensation of danger. Then news
came that it had been caught, and sunk, by the Navy, as it was
passing near the Scillies.

August 18. As I walked into the mess at Portreath today I saw
Lord Trenchard, just leaving after talking to the aircrews. I do
not suppose there is any man in Britain who quickens the blood
of the R.A.F. as he does: even the youngsters, who have been
in the Service only a year or so, are aware of his influence. His
uniform is old-fashioned; drain-pipe trousers, with cuffs, and a
flat cap which the young ones do not think at all elegant; but his
face, flashing from fierceness to laughter, suggests the rugged
liveliness of his character.

When he had gone I heard two pilots talking of him with
respect and affection. One of them said, quite naturally, "Of
course, he is the father of the R.A.F."

Lord Trenchard has a talent for saying the right word with
such sincerity that his anecdotes are always fresh. Perhaps his
greatest flash of imagination came in Egypt, when he was
talking to airmen working in the vast caves dug by the Pharaohs,
and converted into engineering workshops for the R.A.F. He
said to them, "The Pharaohs would be pleased that they dug
these caves if they could come back and see a generation as fine
as yours working in them."

        .   .   .   .   .   .

The most interesting note for the day comes from a U.S.
Navy Liberator that sighted a U-boat beneath the surface, in the
north-east corner of the Bay of Biscay. On August 11, I wrote

of an attack made by a Liberator on a U-boat also spotted while submerged, in the same part of the Bay. These are the only two occasions on record and must surely be due to some eccentricity in the tides, or the light, in these waters. Both were about forty miles from the coast, and only fifty-five miles apart.

August 19. Thirteen years ago a French boy, living in a village near Cherbourg, fell in love with a girl who went to the same school. He was so young that he still wore short trousers, and she still wore her hair in pig-tails down her back. His name was Jean Lecouté, hers was Marguerite Duchemin. Jean lived in the village of Les Pieux, where his father was a confectioner, and Marguerite lived some twenty kilometres away, but they met every day at school.

Jean's father, Alexandre Lecouté, had worked in Amiens during the 1914–18 war; when peace came he sold his shop and moved near the coast, to be as far as possible from the German frontier, with his wife and children.

When they were old enough Marguerite and Jean were sent to Paris. She was to be a teacher of English, and he was to be a mathematician, but the war began and Jean was sent to Le Mans to be trained as a pilot. There were too many pupils and too few aircraft, and when the Germans approached, Jean could not fly away: he was packed into a railway wagon with the others and taken to Laval, then to Douarnenez, where they found a tunny fishing boat with a crew of eight. It bore the valiant name of *Trebouliste*. One hundred and twenty-eight officers and pupils boarded the little boat and sailed for England. Their last sight of France was the town of Brest, in flames. Jean did not see his country again for more than four years.

The *Trebouliste* crossed the Channel and paused off Penzance, where Jean saw St. Michael's Mount for the first time: but a fisherman came out in a little boat and told the Frenchmen they would have to sail on and report to the authorities in Falmouth. So the *Trebouliste* rounded the Lizard and a trawler, the *Lady Estelle*, came alongside and guided them into port.

"Ninety-five per cent of us were seasick," Jean told me, pleased to be able to measure even his hardships in terms of mathematics. "We had nothing to eat except some old dry bread and cheese, and water coloured with rum. But one of the pupils was still gallant: he raised his head and said, 'You see, we are real Frenchmen still; all of us are following *Lady Estelle* like one man.'"

They reached Falmouth in the evening, and in black-out darkness they went to sleep on the quay. When Jean woke in the morning he found the wharf crowded with sleeping Frenchmen: the *Trebouliste* had not been the only fishing boat crossing the Channel the day before.

Some British workmen walked by and gave the pupils their food, and tea from their thermos flasks. It was the first kindness Jean met in England: he said, "I shall never forget that."

At noon they were fed on bully beef and apples; then they were taken by train to the Midlands and to Trentham Park, some of them still carrying the obsolete 1874 rifles they had brought, in case they had to defend themselves. There were 2,000 Frenchmen in the camp: those who could read English opened the newspapers and told the others of the armistice in their country.

The commanding officer called them together and told them they must choose; to stay in England and fight under General de Gaulle, or return to France. Only the very young ones went back; those who were afraid for their parents.

Sixteen of the boys, including Jean Lecouté, spoke good English, so they were sent to an elementary flying training school, and when summer came Jean was able to fly twin-engine aircraft. There was an interlude in Equatorial Africa and Syria; then he returned to England and became a Sunderland pilot, hunting U-boats in the Atlantic and in the Bay. But he always flew at night, so he never saw the coast of France.

All this time, Jean had no news of his family, or of Marguerite, who had escaped from Chartres to Bordeaux on her bicycle, being machine-gunned and bombed on the way. When she arrived in Toulouse she found her sister-in-law and her nephew in the market place, by accident. They told her that her eldest brother had escaped to Morocco. She went on, to Port Vendres where, again by accident, she met her father, who encouraged her to cross and join her brother in safety.

Marguerite made the journey, and, soon after she arrived in Morocco, she learned that Jean was flying with the R.A.F., in England. She wrote to him and, a month or so ago, they were married, by proxy.

Jean has flown 350 hours in Sunderlands and has sighted 2 U-boats. One fired back at the aircraft and then submerged quickly, leaving its gunners to drown. Two weeks ago, Jean was second pilot when his aircraft attacked another U-boat: he told me, "We dropped our depth-charges and saw the bows lifted high in the air, before it settled and made for the coast of France."

A few weeks ago, after the Americans entered Cherbourg, the Navy offered to take Jean across the Channel in a destroyer, so that he could see the beach-head and perhaps land to search for his mother. Jean approached the shore of France, but there was a haze and he could not see far over the water. Then the destroyer moved in close and he stayed on deck all day, peering at the barren hills and coast; but he did not see even one Frenchman, and the captain decided that it would not be possible to put him ashore. In the evening, he was brought back to England.

Jean was preparing to fly on operations again when I met him yesterday. A letter had just come with good news: his mother and family are safe, and his brother has not been sent to work in Germany, as he feared. And the house in which he has always lived was not injured during the bombardment. Jean said to me, "When I read the letter, I breathed again."

.   .   .   .   .   .

The battle is becoming pale: during the twenty-four hours up to nine o'clock this morning, only one U-boat was seen and attacked; and only one German aircraft—a Junkers 88, flying 100 miles out to sea.

U-boat being depth-charged by a Sunderland of No. 10 Squadron, R.A.A.F., on July 8, 1944 (see pp. 198-90)

The same U-boat, sinking. The crew are crowding to the conning-tower, preparing to escape (see p. 200)

"The *Magdeburg* . . . sank quickly, in a tower of flames" (see p. 217)

The attack, by a Sunderland of 201 Squadron, should be described, for it confirms what I have written before, of the precise co-ordination achieved by the nine members of an air-crew, during the few seconds of combat. The crew of the Sunderland flew with a strange captain, Flight-Lieutenant Baveystock, who took over at the last minute. When the U-boat was sighted, at half-past five in the afternoon, Baveystock was below: he climbed to the bridge and controlled the attack from the second pilot's seat—an unusual performance. The straddle was perfect: three depth-charges fell on either side of the conning-tower and there were nice signs of a kill; compressed air bubbles followed by debris, a wooden wheel, and sheets of paper—the navigator's charts—scattered over the sea.

Some U-Boats are escaping to the north, but very few. They have to make the perilous journey around Ireland and on to Norway, where they will do battle with our aircraft based in Iceland and Northern Scotland. But that will be another story.

August 22. In late July and early this month, the U-boats were inclined to stay on the surface and fight it out with our aircraft, but about two weeks ago they changed their tactics: they submerged by day and moved at *schnörkel* depth during the night. The *schnörkel* has not been the salvation the German inventors expected and, in its present form, it can be used only when the weather is kind. Also, prisoners tell us, the *schnörkel* sometimes fails mechanically, and the air in the U-boat then becomes so foul that they are forced to surface, and expose themselves to attack.

About midnight on the 21st, three audacious U-boats surprised a Halifax by remaining on the surface. They were close together, making for the Gironde River. The U-boats and the Halifax exchanged fire, but the captain of the aircraft, Wing Commander J. B. Grant, lost his targets in the darkness. About two hours later, while he was still seeking them, there was a violent explosion within the aircraft. It lost height rapidly and struck the sea, in a succession of leaps. The crew were so stunned that those who have survived are still hazy as to what happened. Water rushed in and Grant escaped through the emergency hatch, with two other members of the crew: two more broke clear through the rear escape hatch. Grant climbed on to the port wing, but he was soon swept off by the high waves and had to swim about for half an hour before he found the other survivors.

Only five of the crew of nine had escaped. They watched the aircraft, which suddenly caught fire; when it sank, they clung to pieces of wreckage and swam as best they could, in turbulent water, slimy with petrol and oil. After two hours one of the five sank into the water; and another, a navigator, became delirious, imagining that he was still flying and asking for orders. He died about six o'clock in the morning.

When dawn came, the sun was still hidden, but the three knew that land was some twenty miles to the east, so they set course with a hand compass, hoping to swim slowly towards the coast. A Sunderland passed near, but did not see them. Then a Liberator and another Sunderland appeared and Grant waved a piece of metal, trying to make it reflect the stingy morning sun. But they also passed. Grant went on waving the reflector until it was seen by a warship—the frigate *Saint John*.

The three who had survived the horrible night were taken aboard and, after being fired on by the shore batteries, the frigate turned out to sea and brought them home.

.   .   .   .   .   .

There were two good shipping strikes to compensate for this disaster. Twenty-one Beaufighters attacked two armed trawlers in the harbour of Les Sables d'Olonne on the 20th: they were hit so violently that parts of them were flung 200 feet into the air, and both were burning when the Beaufighters turned for home. The Mosquitoes also enjoyed a victory, after an attack on two minesweepers and an armed trawler, near Le Verdon. The trawler was left on fire and both the minesweepers exploded. Four of our aircraft were damaged, but all the crews returned unharmed.

The crews of Beaufighters and Mosquitoes respond to victory like children. It is interesting to watch them as they make their report to the Intelligence Officer after an attack, and see how their manner, and even their appearance, is affected. If the strike has been abortive, they look weary, and the younger ones are pale and unnaturally wrinkled: if they have been successful, they are young, fresh, and cock-a-hoop. The crews of Liberators, as if burdened by the monotony of their long patrols, are less wild after victory; but the Mosquito pilots sometimes celebrate in a sort of heathen ceremony. They turn the metal stools in the bar upside down and beat them like tom-toms; then they will light a fire of old newspapers on the floor of the mess and dance about it until the flames die down.

August 25. The day before yesterday was fruitless. About one hundred sorties were flown, but no U-boats were seen; only a few ships in the Gironde River. The last considerable prizes left are the two destroyers still lurking in the Bay.

Later. The Beaufighters have bagged the final prizes. About nine o'clock yesterday morning, 20 aircraft of 236 and 404 Squadrons, led by Squadron Leader E. W. Tacon, a New Zealander, located the destroyers in the mouth of the Gironde River. They had been ordered to attack a supposed U-boat and they flew in over the flat farm-land north of Bordeaux, then down the river. They found the target, but it was only the hull of a Sperrbrecher that was attacked some days ago. The 20 aircraft then came to the mouth of the river and saw the two destroyers, opposite Le Verdon. Then, after having flown so far without any interruption, the flak suddenly came up at them.

The leader brought the aircraft into position for a beam

attack. The destroyers got under way and tried to escape out to sea, but they were too late. The cannon fire from the aircraft was accurate and the rockets fired perfectly, leaving both ships shrouded in flames and smoke.

But Tacon had to lead into the heart of a merciless barrage, from the ships and the shore, and only 3 of our 20 aircraft came through unharmed: 2 were so badly hit that they had to finish the attack on one engine. Three of our damaged Beaufighters had to land in France and one crashed into the Bay. But the end is satisfying: the crew were all rescued from the sea by one of our destroyers, and those who landed in France were flown back to England today.

August 26. One of our aircraft flew up the Gironde River this morning to photograph the results of the attack on the 24th. The pictures they brought back celebrate the final victory against the enemy destroyers in the Bay: one showed an oil streak leading to the open sea, where the first of the two must have fled before it burned and sank; another oil streak led towards the wharf, where the second destroyer no doubt moved, in flames, hoping to land its crew before it went down.

August 27. Victory does not seem to be as exciting as the battle itself. We all sat in the mess, moping and wondering where the Squadron will be sent for its next task. Some of the boys said, "Old Hector is Intelligence," with a rather damning note in their voices. Then—"Why don't you go up to Group and see what you can find out?"

Obediently, I drove up to Group Headquarters and behaved like a ferret. Air Commodore D'Aeth, usually helpful and not a bit entangled in red tape, smiled amiably at my subtle questions but told me nothing. I hovered outside Air Vice-Marshal Baker's office, hoping he might open the door and say, "Hullo, Bolitho, buying some warm woollen underwear?", or "Hullo, Bolitho, you'd better get your sun-helmet out of store." But the door remained closed, so I went to see the Intelligence Officer. He was friendly but not helpful. After five years in the Service, I know how to twist my neck and scan the secret documents in anybody's tray, but I learned nothing.

I returned to Watergate. "Any gen?" they asked me. "I am afraid not," I answered. So we sat deep in our mouldy arm-chairs and talked of the rigours of winter in Iceland, windy headlands in Scotland, and lazy noons in the Azores.

September 3. The theme changes, with news of two rescues from the sea. A Wellington of 172 Squadron attacked a U-boat on the night of August 26. Only three of the crew were saved—picked up by a Sunderland, two days later. And a Liberator of 53 Squadron crashed into the sea, at three o'clock in the morning of the 27th. Again, only three of the crew survived, among them a gallant and experienced pilot, Flight-Lieutenant Cameron Forbes, D.F.C.

I have waited six days before going to see him, because I was told that he is shaken and silent. "He paints better than he talks," one of the other pilots told me. "The walls of his room are covered with his pictures."

Inducing pilots to talk is an art and I am learning it slowly. One must allow enough time to pass for their unhappy experience to assume the shape of a story in their mind; time for them to recover from physical shock and to achieve mental detachment, so that their disaster is separate from their immediate self. Some eleven months ago I helped to write the story of a pilot who had spent seven days in a dinghy, with his companions mad or dying. He wrote the narrative in four thousand desperate words: when he finished, he cried in my room. But he smiled afterwards and said that when he read the pages and saw the ghost that had been haunting his peace of mind, in terms of the written word, he felt free of his melancholia for the first time.

I had been told of Cameron Forbes, "He comes from Aberdeen: he's pretty dour, and silent." But I had seen two or three of his pictures—painted on the Cornish coast. His talent was young, but the colours, imagination and courage in his landscapes belied the accusation of dourness.

The afternoon came when we first met, in my room. My pen and paper were on the table, but Cameron Forbes sat very straight in his chair and his lower lip had a sullen tilt. He *was* silent, and the words would not come. Then I said, "Paint it for me: tell me the story in terms of colour, as you would see it on a canvas." Slowly, at first, then without a halt or tremor, he told me what had happened.

"It was very black and the moon had gone down; not the blackness that is full of colour—an unpleasant blackness. There was a haze. The Radar got a contact and we flew in, but there was nothing to see: we flew in again, but still nothing. Perhaps it was a fish. Then I heard a harsh New Zealand voice over the intercom. It cut through my head. He said he thought he saw something, a slick or a swirl, so we decided to go in as it might be from a periscope. We turned and let down to one hundred feet. It calls for accurate flying when you can't see the horizon and you can't see the sea.

"There was no more talking on the intercom. I might have been by myself. Then the voice said 'Level'. The bomb doors were open and the Leigh light was turned on. The beam was sweeping out in front of us: purplish light. The light on the altimeter—red, green, amber. Mostly amber. Then there was a tug on the aircraft and I had the sensation of something being wrong. Then a long, tremendous crash.

"I have an extraordinary recollection of the period between the crash and the realization that I was out of the aircraft, under water; the feeling of being swung forward, and pressure on my right side. I remember saying to myself, 'Well, Forbes, you've gone a complete circle.' I thought of a surrealist picture by Dali, of myself curled up in the pre-natal position. I was curled up and I had completed a cycle. It was dark and I had my eyes closed. Then I was in the water and I thought, 'Which way is up?' because I was under and it was dark. I inflated my Mae West, kicked away and came up. It seemed ages, but it must have been only a few moments.

"I want to paint it, when I can—the moment when I broke through the surface of the water. We had dropped flame floats before we crashed and they made a sad light on the water in the night. There seemed to be two of them. I struck out for the dinghy. It was inflating, upside-down, moaning. . . .

"That's the picture: just the dark sea, the two flame floats and the dinghy, upside-down. I'd like to paint that, with pieces of the aircraft floating, pieces of wreckage, and the flashes of light on the water.

"I thought a little. The front part of the aircraft where I had been must have broken off, like a biscuit, and with me in it. And I must have gone down with it and been released when it was deep.

"It must have been about three in the morning. My hand was cut where something had grazed past and taken my watch with it.

"I yelled, 'Dinghy, dinghy here,' and I heard two voices, one calling, 'It's Al,' and one calling, 'It's Ted,' but I didn't know then how many of them were in the water. Al and Ted swam towards the dinghy and I got there too and found it upside-down. Al still had his watch but something had shaved off the glass and one of the hands, and buckled the other one, so we still could not tell the time. The three of us did not say much. I said, 'How the devil do you get this the right way up?' but it sounded as if somebody else was speaking in the darkness—like your voice coming back to you when you speak through a microphone. This is all that was said until we got the dinghy over.

"I managed to crouch on the piece of aircraft to which the dinghy was still attached, and to help Al turn it over. One of the boys hadn't much joy in his arms as his collar bone was broken. The other had pretty ropey legs. I felt the piece of aircraft shudder under me: I kicked it away and jumped into the dinghy. Al said, 'Give me a hand with Ted,' so we hauled him in. I wound the cord around my hand, to break the dinghy away from the piece of aircraft. The cord was strong, but it broke easily and we were free.

"Then the last part of the aircraft went down. I could see it, white in the faint light of the flame floats. It seemed small and insignificant. We were much bigger than it. I had flown it once before and disliked the feel of it. It was very final when it went down.

"We paddled with our arms and legs as best we could, and gathered all we saw from the water, while the flares were still alight. It was our friends we really wanted to find. We found two 'K' type dinghies, still in their packs, some wreckage, a cushion and some flame floats. The flame floats were of inestimable value so we took them in. We grabbed everything. Most of the regular dinghy equipment must have fallen out: there was comfort of a sort in just having things. There was no sign of anyone else, and that meant seven lost. I felt terrible about it.

"Then began our five hours in the dinghy. Some aircraft passed over us; we could hear them throbbing in the black. We used some of the distress signals that fire two red stars, but the aircraft just flew on into the night.

"I never lost control of my thoughts. That is what I was afraid of, because I did not know how much the other two were damaged. The co-ordination in my mind was good: I knew what I wanted to do. The sea was very, very kind. It had taken seven of us so I suppose it was ashamed. It was quite calm and gentle, just rocking us easily. We'd hear the aircraft coming closer, closer. Then I'd screw the cap off a star cartridge, quickly, and fire it when the aircraft was near us. Then I fired a second one when the aircraft went away. It was difficult to screw off the caps as my hands were oily and I hadn't an awful lot of pull in them. The cartridges would go *pop* and nothing would happen. It was a crushing feeling: only five out of thirteen went off.

"We also threw the flame floats out, at intervals, so we could tell which way we were drifting, and to attract any aircraft. Then we fixed up the weather curtain because the wind was cold. We snuggled together, deep into the dinghy as we could. I tried to keep doing something all the time so that I would not pass out. I told the others to go to sleep and they closed their eyes, but I do not think they slept. We switched on our lamps occasionally, to see each other's faces, as we waited for the first light of morning. We talked while we were baling out the dinghy, to keep up our spirits. It was good to see the flame floats alight on the water. Sometimes we heard the splash of fish that were attracted by the flames.

"We weren't too badly off really, although the nearest coast might still be in the hands of the enemy. The worst that could happen would have been for us to drift on to the rocky shore and not be found. So it was best for us to keep on the area of patrol and hope to be picked up in the morning.

"Then came the first glimmer of light. It was quite pleasant. We could see each other better. Ted's jaw was broken in two places and his eyes were puffed up. He had two gorgeous circles under them. We said to him, 'Where were you last night?' and, 'What was her name?' But he couldn't laugh because of the breaks in his jaw. Al had lost his shoe and sock and he asked me to cover up his foot as it was bad. Ted had lost the sole from his shoe. He put his shoe on Al's injured foot and Al asked him politely, 'Do you mind? Can you move your foot a wee bit, Ted? That's all right, it's only my foot.'

"It was a slow, green dawn; I thought the sun would never come. It was pale but we could see the rising swell. Then it was light, and we pepped up again. We were two or three hours overdue and we wondered whether they would tell our people we were missing. We hoped we would be picked up before the Adjutant got to his office, so that no news would be sent to our families.

"It was good to see the water: cool, bluish, with glints coming off it. We then compared our appearance in the morning light; it was something to talk about. We could see Les Sept Iles, but we didn't wish to go there, with shoals and reefs to puncture our dinghy.

"I was looking at the dawn and Al was looking down-Channel. He said, 'What's that?' and I saw four dots that might have been more islands. Then one made smoke and that cheered us immensely. Then, 'Are they nearer?' 'Are they coming towards us?' 'Are they going away from us?' 'They *can't* be going away from us.' Then the dots seemed to change course, as they came close, three or four miles away, and we saw that they were minesweepers.

"One aircraft had passed over us in the first light, but it had not seen us. Then a second one came: one of our own gull-coloured Liberators, flying at 1,000 feet. The pilot was Bob Dobson. He turned towards us and flew over us: then over the minesweepers, and he must have been signalling because we saw a ship flashing back. Al waved the red sail and I waved the yellow weather apron; we waved like mad.

"Then the second minesweeper altered course towards us; it was rather frightening, seeing the big minesweeper bearing down on us. They came alongside, hove to very nicely, and put out a scrambling net.

"Then one of the fellows on board produced a new piece of rope with a horrifying, red four-pronged hook at the end. He cried out 'Catch!' It came aboard and I saw that the prongs were turned in, so they could not hurt us. Then sailors came down the scrambling net to help us up. I shoved the cushion between the ship and the dinghy, because there were barnacles on the ship, and I felt we ought not to be outdone in seamanship. The other two were helped up: then I made to scramble up, but I was very stiff. I was led to the Executive Officer's cabin where I took off my clothes and was wrapped in a nice warm blanket. They took our names and flashed them back to the Liberator. I drank pints of coffee and I didn't even taste the first three or four cups. Then they sent a whaler to one of the other ships for a surgeon, and he came and checked us over. Those Naval types were kindness itself. 'How about some soup?' Dozens of cigarettes appeared. I said, 'Sorry, I smoke a pipe.'

" 'Have you got it?' one of them asked. I answered, 'Yes, it's in my battledress.' Within a minute my pipe was cleaned, dried, filled, in my mouth and lit. They just couldn't do enough.

"It was a Canadian minesweeper, which pleased me no end, because I served in Canada and fell in love with it. I am enormously fond of almost everything that comes from that country."

September 6. The excitement is fading again; so many German ships are now submerged hulks along the coast, or are hiding in the recesses of the rivers. No U-boats have been seen for some days and our patrols have been reduced. The aircrews sit about the mess, bored, guessing where they will be posted next. Butch Pugh wonders if he will get his four pounds back for his motor bicycle; he says, "I cannot take it to Iceland or the Azores."

There has been only one drama in our day—the return of Frank Chew from adventure in France. During an attack on shipping in the Gironde River, twenty-five days ago, his Mosquito was so badly hit that it lost both engines and broke in two as it ditched in the river. Frank, and his observer, Jock Couttie, swam free of the wreckage and saw that their rescue dinghy had drifted fifty yards away. They swam to it, climbed in, and considered their chances of escape. Frank had lost his shoes in the river and there were no paddles in the dinghy: so they broke two pieces of wood from the wreckage and then decided to make for the open sea, with the hope of being picked up, rather than land on the river bank and risk being captured.

Frank Chew told me, "After paddling for half an hour we heard the chug-chug of an engine; a sixty-foot trawler manned by Germans came alongside and threw us a rope. I quickly sank my French money over the side of the dinghy, as I didn't see why they should have it." After being overturned into the river —when Jock also lost his shoes—they were hauled aboard. "The Germans weren't rough with us," Frank said. "I had bruised two of my finger-nails and one of the sailors bandaged my fingers, quite gently.

"Just as the trawler touched the wharf at Royan, a funny little German officer with blazing blue eyes jumped on board and called us, 'Swine, bastard, gangster.' Then he thumped me in the kidneys. When he had pounded me about a dozen times he packed up and had a couple of bangs at Jock. I said, 'Never mind, Jock, take no notice of him.' The German officer was glaring mad; he said, 'Swine, bastard, gangster,' again, and then left us. Then another officer motioned us on to the pier: he flourished a big automatic, so big I thought it ought to be on wheels. They took us to separate rooms. Some hours passed and then we were put into a small van, closed all round. We were not allowed to talk, but we could see past the blanket hanging in front of us, as it swayed a bit. We saw the same buildings two or three times and realized that they were running us round and round the streets to confuse us.

"After about an hour of this we left the town and drove to a Luftwaffe base in the country, where an officer took everything from us: fountain-pens and cigarette-cases—all except the gold ring on one of my wounded fingers. He was kind about that. Then they let us sit in the sun to dry our clothes, with nice open farming country about us."

In the afternoon, Chew and Couttie were taken to what was left of Cognac aerodrome. The hangars were down, and there were no aircraft. Frank thought the German officers 'well dressed', but not 'a very bright bunch of fellows'. Late that evening they were put in separate cells, in the local gaol.

Frank Chew went on with his story. "It was Saturday night, August 12, when they locked us up. On Monday afternoon a guard came in with bread, coffee, greasy soup, and a meat ball swimming in gravy . . . the smell of the meat ball was all over the cell so I picked it up with the spoon and threw it out of the window. The guard was about my own age and he was mad at me. I just prowled up and down, looking at the bars of the window. There were seven of them, with two cross-pieces, and the cement that held them was new.

"When night began to fall I used the spoon to dig the cement away from the bars. I soon wrenched one of them free. While I was working on the second I heard a noise outside the cell, so I quickly shoved the concrete back and put the spoon on the table."

The guard came in and took Frank from the cell, before his work on the window was finished. He joined Jock Couttie in the passage and they were led towards three trucks, and a car in which two German officers and two girls were sitting. For the first time, in the jumble of German talk, which he did not understand, Frank Chew heard the word *Maquis*. He said that the officers and the girls had a 'frightened' look when they said it. Frank and Jock were 'pushed' into one of the trucks and 'the procession set off for Bordeaux'.

There was one adventure on the way, when they stopped with a puncture. 'A French chap' overtook the little convoy on his bicycle, and, as he passed, he bowed politely and said, "*Bonjour, bonjour.*" When he was some yards ahead of the car and trucks, he jumped off, whipped out a revolver, and took a few shots at the Germans in the front truck. Then he jumped on his bicycle again and made off, pursued by the officers and girls in the car.

The trucks drove into the Luftwaffe headquarters at Bordeaux. Frank said, "We were still without shoes and one of the officers made signs to us, apparently asking what size we took. I said 'eight' and he said *acht*, and then we were marched into the Bordeaux gaol and put into a cell with three other prisoners. The cell was 7 foot square; when I climbed on Jock's shoulders I saw that we were four storeys up . . . there was no chance of escape. Every now and then a guard came in and tapped the bars with a piece of metal. Perhaps they had found out about the bar I removed in the last cell and were taking no chances.

"They let us out for half an hour and we met some of the other prisoners; ten Americans, a Canadian, and an Englishman, who had been in France since last December. . . . We got into the good old argument with the Americans as to which were the best aircraft: theirs or ours."

Frank and Jock were moved to still one more cell, so small that there was just enough room for them to lie down, side by side. "We didn't talk much," Frank told me. "We'd known each other for so long, there was nothing left to say."

On Wednesday, August 16, the crew of a Lancaster were brought to the prison, after being shot down during an evening raid on Bordeaux. "There were so many of us then," said Frank, "the Germans had to put us into the prison chapel, where we were quite gay, talking our heads off.

"The officer had not forgotten about our size *acht* shoes: on Wednesday morning they were brought to us. It was just like home: forms to sign, in triplicate, vouchers, bags of paper, exactly the same as home."

The chapel was used as a gaol for Germans also, and next day Frank Chew heard, once more, the whispered, fearful word *Maquis*. Again they were moved on, by the Luftwaffe, to Merignac aerodrome. "They seemed quite friendly and treated us well," he said. "I suppose they knew their number was up, with our armies moving over the land, and the Maquis advancing. . . . They took us to the hospital to sleep, where we waited three days. . . . We had one little trick that annoyed them. On the wall was a photograph of Hitler and one of Goering. When the guard came in he always found us staring at the photographs without saying a word. They did not like that, so one of them took the photographs away."

Again, the prisoners were moved: a convoy of 3,000 men left in 'the most terrible trucks' Frank had ever seen. "Some of them had no tyres and travelled on the wheel rims; all of them used charcoal because they had no petrol."

The Maquis were coming 'nearer and nearer'. The prisoners passed truck after truck 'blown off the road'. They arrived outside Chateau Neuf and stayed beside a farm for four days, the trucks camouflaged with sods of earth piled against the wheels. While they were in hiding, nine Spitfires flew over. "They did not see us and no one fired at them," said Frank, "but we were proud to see them.

"The Germans were a poor lot: they put us in a barn and when the Spitfires flew over they hid in the woods. I wasn't impressed by what I saw of those Germans at all. There was one, a tall chap of about twenty-four, from Munich. He would come up to us, put his finger to his lips and whisper, 'No Hitler'. And one of the guards, a little chap, said he wanted to see England and learn to speak more English, so we told him, 'You'll learn plenty of English in one of our prisoner-of-war camps; we have special classes for chaps like you.' We laughed, but he didn't.

"Whenever the truck stopped, the little German would hand one of us his rifle while he jumped out after us . . . and he would drowse off to sleep with his rifle and bayonet at his side. We could have slit his throat, but it would have been foolish.

"Then came the day when five of them took out a map and began jabbering very quickly. They told us of the landing of our troops in the South of France, and what parts of the country they had taken. But they weren't bitter . . . at least, those who came near us weren't.

"Just about this time the rain and the hardships got the better of some of our boys, and they had stomach trouble, dysentery, and rashes . . . fourteen of them were sent to the civilian hospital in Angouleme.

"Then the Maquis attacked the camp. It was dusk and there was great shouting and yelling going on, and bursts of gun-fire all along the woods. We were put back in the barn and the door was locked . . . next day we heard a rumour that the Germans were fighting their way out and that they intended leaving the sick behind. Of course, the rest of us went sick immediately. They sent us to the civilian hospital, so we were all together again.

"We hadn't been in the French hospital five minutes when the whole town knew. Oh! You should have seen them! They came with flowers and wine and champagne: they even smuggled a radio into our room so we could listen to an American dance band, then the English news. That was good to hear. We were told that our soldiers had taken Rheims.

"Everybody in the town seemed to visit us. Some of the girls came and we got a Marine lieutenant, who could speak French, to write a few phrases on pieces of paper for us. When the girls said *"Bonjour"*, we said, *"Bonjour, enchanté"*, so quickly they thought we could speak French. So they rattled on, but we didn't understand a word.

"On the evening of August 31 we heard firing in the streets: the Maquis had arrived . . . and at three o'clock in the morning a Maquis officer came to our beds and said, 'You are free.' "

So Frank and Jock got out, put on their uniforms and joined the parade in the streets. There were 'hundreds of flags', and 'bonfires', and everyone 'went mad'. "They cheered us," Frank said, "because of our R.A.F. uniforms, and they just showered kindness on us. They gave us breakfast in a big hotel."

On September 3—the fifth anniversary of the war—Frank and Jock landed back in England.

"There was only one sad bit after that," Frank Chew said. "Jock had got a bottle of brandy in France and he had nursed it all the way, like a baby. After we arrived in London we went to the R.A.F. Stores, and as we walked in Jock dropped the bottle of brandy and broke it. As long as I live I shall not forget the expression on his face."

Conclusion. The end of a battle is like the fizzle of a dying rocket, after all its force and splendour are spent. My recollections of 224 Squadron during the last days of the Battle of the South-Western Approaches are ridiculous rather than heroic: I recall Butch selling the motor bicycle that had bored us all so much, for the four pounds he gave for it; and an obdurate old man arriving at the mess to re-cover the billiards table, just as everyone was moving out.

"You're six months late, chum," he was told. "We're on our way."

"I've got my orders," he answered, and went on covering the table, while our luggage was being carried down the stairs. The great exodus was watched, between the banisters, by the sinister, dusty cat that seldom appeared after sunset. It was our belief that it became a witch at night and made excursions on the kitchen broom.

So I think of Watergate as it was after the warriors departed: torn wall-paper flapping in draughts coming through broken windows, and the creature—cat by day and witch by night—walking around the billiards table with the pretty green cloth that arrived too late for Lofty and Jock to prove their prowess at snooker.

The task I had been detailed to report came to an end in mid-September; there were no more German ships to attack and the few surviving U-boats had escaped. Fourteen weeks had passed

Flight-Lieutenant Cameron Mc. A. Forbes, D.F.C.
(see p. 227)

Flight-Lieutenant E. T. Bachelor, D.F.C.
(see p. 152)

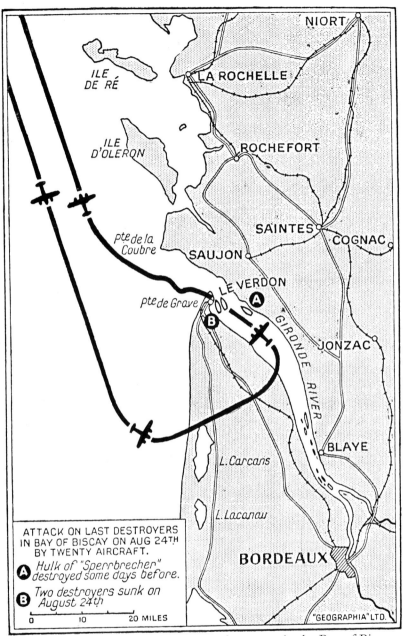

ILE DE RÉ

ILE D'OLERON

NIORT

LA ROCHELLE

ROCHEFORT

SAINTES

COGNAC

SAUJON

pte de la Coubre

LE VERDON

pte de Grave

A

B

GIRONDE RIVER

JONZAC

BLAYE

L. Carcans

L. Lacanau

BORDEAUX

ATTACK ON LAST DESTROYERS
IN BAY OF BISCAY ON AUG 24TH
BY TWENTY AIRCRAFT.

A *Hulk of "Sperrbrecher"
destroyed some days before.*

B *Two destroyers sunk on
August 24th*

0   10   20 MILES

"GEOGRAPHIA" LTD.

Chart showing attack on last enemy destroyers in the Bay of Biscay,
August 24, 1944, by twenty aircraft (see p. 225)

since 'D' day, when the incredible armada of 4,000 ships and several thousand smaller craft crossed the Channel, within twenty-four hours.

We knew, by September, the full value of our own part in this mighty attack—since described by Sir Winston Churchill as 'the greatest amphibious operation in history'. The part had been considerable, and victorious. During the four days following the first invasion, thirty-six U-boats were sighted as they made their way from the Biscay ports, to molest our ships within the invasion area. Twenty-three of them had been attacked, six had been destroyed and six seriously damaged. All had been held back from their sinister purpose. As far as the aircraft in the south were concerned—those based in Cornwall and Devon to fight the Battle of the South-Western Approaches—not one U-boat had broken through the 'Unclimbable Fence'. Throughout 'the greatest amphibious operation', from first to last, only nine of the many thousands of British ships were sunk by the enemy.

This victory was won in spite of the unceasing industry and invention of the Germans, with the new *schnörkel* device: even in November 1944, after the airborne attack on Arnhem and after Calais had been retaken, the output of U-boats was greater than in any other month of the war.

The German surface fleet had suffered similar defeat. Early in June the enemy had tried to strengthen his forces by bringing three destroyers north from the Gironde River, but our aircraft attacked them and sent them back to port. Two days later they slunk out again, hoping to fulfil their task, but the Navy sank one of them, drove one ashore and forced the third back to Brest. The attack by our Beaufighters on August 24 finished the kill and all the destroyers were then out of the picture.

The E-boats were also held back from the invasion area, or were sunk. German prisoners, brought to England by our Navy, told us that the E-boat bases were partly destroyed by Bomber Command, in the early raids; and that when the boats dared the open sea, the Navy and Coastal aircraft attacked them so mercilessly that not one got past to hamper the invasion.

P

The success against these major units of the German Navy were so immediate and sure that, by the end of June, our aircraft were able to concentrate their fury on German merchant shipping. As early as June 15, they had their biggest victory in one day when Beaufighters sank an 8,000-ton merchantman, a 4,000-ton naval auxiliary and a minesweeper, and damaged four escort vessels.

The story of what followed is told in these pages, leading to the events at the beginning of August, when our tanks were sweeping through France. The enemy forces on Brest Peninsula were cut off and every possible ship in the Bay was called to their aid. But the pathetic little rescue fleet was bombed from the air and could do little to feed, or re-arm, the remnant of their defeated army.

.   .   .   .   .   .

The members of 224 Squadron showed no pleasure or satisfaction over their part in this triumph. Looking back on the scene of farewell, I recall a curious nervous melancholy as Watergate emptied; as the cat-witch took over and the labels on our luggage fluttered in the sea wind that blew up, over the sand and the tamarisk, to the façade of the hotel. There had been a scene of forced merriment in the bar and I had been made to sing and dance, for the last time, 'Where are the Lads of the Village Tonight?' Mike Ensor had taken off in his dejected old car, on the journey of 700 miles to Elgin. When Batch and I got into our car, to drive off, the others came to the door and, standing on the slope of dusty shingle road, they sang 'For They are Jolly Good Fellows'. This was too much for my spontaneous tear ducts, so I whispered, "Drive off, quickly."

We made our way to Dunkeswell, where we stayed with the Americans, for the night. They were very kind, filling us with steaks and giving me, as a special gift, a beautiful binding file for my manuscript. "With love from Uncle Sam," said the pilot who filched it from the stores.

Then a glance over our shoulders as we departed next morning, and the lively colours of Old Glory and the R.A.F. Standard, still flying within sight of each other, in a Devon field.

.   .   .   .   .   .

I returned to Coastal Command Headquarters in October 1944. After a few weeks I went to stay with 224 Squadron again, at Banff in Scotland: but the spirit and fun of Watergate had become pale, and the patrols and encounters yielded few of the stories my Commander-in-Chief required. So I was recalled to my tasks, within the small horizon of a desk at Headquarters— to tasks that give no touch of gallantry to the end of my story.

I am writing these last pages within the quiet safety of the Close in Salisbury, in April 1955—almost ten years after the war ended. The airmen who come into the Close, with their cameras and their sketch books, belong to the new, young generation; the aircraft that fly so perilously near the Cathedral spire make the Liberators of my day seem like amiable old buses, in comparison. These are the birds of hell, flying at 650 miles an hour.

During the past ten years I have been to America, Canada, Australia, New Zealand, India, Pakistan, Italy, Switzerland and Portugal, and the war seems very far away; it is assuming the shape of history, and the remote look of an experience from which all emotion has faded. But the egocentric impulses, so natural and dangerous in a writer, urge me to think back and wonder what lessons I learned, as a human being, from my work as a civilian caught up in the extrovert pattern of an armed service.

These lessons were given form and made intelligible to me by an accident during my last months in the R.A.F. For more than a year I had endured insomnia that was destructive to a man of my age. Introspection and self-pity are the children born of such sleepless hours, and I became so ill that the doctors sent me to the Medical Rehabilitation Unit at Loughborough. Death may be the last enemy, but self-pity is the foulest and most constant: and it was to cure me of this, as well as insomnia, that

I made the dreary journey to the incredible hospital in Leicester-shire—a requisitioned school, set in fields on the edge of the town.

I had begun the war believing that courage and heroism were one: that they were both inspired by crisis—by sudden, dangerous circumstances. At first, I did not pause to analyse the stories that came in to the Air Ministry. I saw courage in terms of action; the soldier holding his machine-gun post, the stoker in the depths of the doomed ship, and the wounded pilot in his burning air-craft, still flying in to drop his depth-charges on a U-boat. I think that the story of Jimmy Ward,[1] the New Zealand V.C., made me dig deeper and realize that courage is more than will-power during a dangerous crisis. Jimmy Ward had climbed on to the wing of the bomber to put out the flames in the engine, and for this he had been given the Victoria Cross. But the noble moment in his story—the moment of spiritual courage—was in the train, when he tore up the letter that would have excused him from flying in combat ever again.

I was able to think and become a little wiser about this mystery of courage while I was at Loughborough. Imagine the big, pleasant park, and two sham-Elizabethan structures—ugly, vast and efficient: and a quarter of a mile away the modern gymnasium, with the biggest swimming-bath in England, and every gadget and contrivance to nurse limbless men and tortured bodies back to health, and self-confidence.

On my first morning, I looked out of the bedroom window and saw about fifty maimed men, some hobbling on crutches, some walking with slow, unnatural erectness, because they were sheathed in plaster; some with their shattered arms in cradles that kept their hands at a perpetual salute.

The first sight of them stirred pathos, but when I opened the window and heard them singing 'Lili Marlene' as they walked towards the gymnasium through the snow, I realized that the pity was a selfish emotion entirely within myself and that they were not in need of it.

In the afternoon, I also walked to the gymnasium; the doctor

[1] See pp. 79-82.

had decided that exercise and discipline were the pills I needed, and I joined the crippled men in a syllabus that exhausted me.

On the balcony were the 'leg cases' being drilled by a sergeant who led them in singing 'Jingle Bells', while they fixed heavy chains to their thin weak ankles, and then raised and lowered them, so that the jangling links added a sound effect to the music.

The men recently fitted with artificial legs walked up and down, with goose-step stiffness, singing 'Deutschland über Alles' in a lusty chorus, to the surprise of a Polish navigator who shrugged his shoulders as best he could within a plaster-cast, and said, "The English sense of humour is fantastic. I do not understand."

The officer in command, Group Captain O'Malley,[1] was a great man; a rugby player in his youth, a doctor by profession, a bluff man to look at, a scholar by instinct, and a genius at teaching men to emancipate themselves through a ruthless, realistic acceptance of their physical handicaps. I was horrified the first time I heard one of his instructors say to a maimed pilot, "Come on, up those stairs, you lazy cripple." The pilot climbed the stairs on all fours, like a tortoise, and when he reached the top he put his fingers to his nose at the instructor, laughed, and said, "Lazy cripple your bloody self."

The simple truth remains with me that Loughborough was the happiest place I have ever known: and the happiness could not be resisted. I recall one officer whose forbears had been soldiers since Wellington's time. He had served three years in the army before he joined the R.A.F. He won his D.F.C. for bombing Channel ports and his D.S.O. for long-distance flights, in Marauders, from Suez to Athens and back. But a string of miserable Italian railway trucks were to blame for his ultimate injury; they crashed into his jeep and one of his legs was cut off. He was bitter, aloof and disillusioned when he arrived at Loughborough, but the example of courage about him—the eager grasping at every hope and sign of improvement—seemed to be absorbed into him, like heat, and he slowly learned to laugh again. One saw his despair fade, like a conquered fever.

[1] Group Captain C. J. S. O'Malley, C.B.E., M.B., M.R.C.., L.R.C.P.

Then I think of Jimmy Nelson, the last Eagle Squadron pilot to fight with the R.A.F. He had learned to fly when he was studying at Denver University and he came to England long before America was at war. He was more at home in the sky than on the earth—a 'natural flyer', whose kingdom was lost when he crashed, lost a leg, broke fourteen bones and eleven teeth. He arrived at Loughborough about the same time as myself, nursing the stump of his leg on the back seat of a motor-car, bitter and thwarted, like a boy who had just been told that he would never play again.

After a month, Jimmy was learning to run up and down the balcony with his artificial leg. Then he dared to play in a game of basket ball; then the day came when he did a hop, skip and jump along the balcony with the sergeant, playing pat-a-cake with their hands at the same time.

I think also of an Indian from Lahore, who told me that one of his ancestors migrated from the Balkans to the Punjab before the birth of Christ—perhaps he was a soldier in Alexander's army. The Indian was in England when the war began, so he joined the R.A.F. as a navigator and made nineteen flights, bombing Germany, before he was hit by flak, over Hamburg. When he arrived at Loughborough one of his arms was useless, and he began his long months of drudgery with dumb-bells and medicine-balls, to teach his arm to work again. I used to tease him, "That's what happens when you get mixed up with our useless wars: you should be sitting on spikes under a banyan tree, contemplating your navel."

Slowly, I learned that courage is more than physical valour; that it is a spiritual force which lifts men out of the slough of despair and disillusionment, and that it cannot be defined. It became ludicrous for me to think of my own mental ills with such a miracle happening about me: I left Loughborough, no longer sorry for myself, and sleeping like a child.

.   .   .   .   .   .

Then I recall the morning of May 8, 1945, when I was shaving in the bath-room of a house in Hampstead, with the electric light on because the window glass was still covered with black-out paint. The bells began to ring, from all the churches and towers of London, and one knew that the war was truly over. I remember picking up a used razor blade and scraping fiercely at the black paint, to let the light in through the window, for the first time in almost six years.

I dressed and walked from the house, across Hampstead Heath. The bells continued their jubilee—among them the bell in the Abbey tower that was rung in Elizabeth's time, for the victory over the Armada. And a murmur of delight seemed to rise from London—seven miles away: all the sounds of triumph, where there had so recently been the ugly thump of guns. I walked on, paused to enjoy the view Constable painted, between the trees, and then past gardens where carnations and roses were in bloom. Exactly one hundred and twenty-six years before, Keats had walked along the same path, to drink with his cronies at The Spaniards, on the night when he heard the nightingale. I followed his ghost, into the bar, and ordered half a pint of beer. Then I moved to the fire-place and read the lines of the poem, in a frame above the mantelpiece:

> *Darkling I listen; and, for many a time*
> *I have been half in love with easeful Death . . .*

I walked on to the Heath again and, as I listened still to the bells and the singing, I mumbled through the rest of the poem. As I said:

> *Through the sad heart of Ruth, when sick for home,*
> *She stood in tears amid the alien corn . . .*

I looked down the slope and saw an American nurse, in uniform, making her way up to the path, waist-high in the tall dry grass. She was a pretty, radiant girl, neither in tears, nor alien, as she walked amid the English corn.

.   .   .   .

I wandered the world for three years when the war was over, glancing at a hill-top in Connecticut, a bay in Sydney Harbour, and a lofty slope above Auckland, where I was born, imagining the house I would build to escape from the bitterness of Europe and the exhausted, strained poverty of England. On second thoughts, all these enterprises lost their charm, and I am back again, settled unto death, I hope, within the shadow of the spire in Salisbury; waiting for the poppies to glow on Harnham Hill, and watching the lively old canons walking across the grass to Evensong. But there is one last episode, associated with the war, that seems a suitable and true end to my story.

In November 1945 I crossed the Atlantic on a dingy troopship, with plans to see Batch in Vancouver and Butch in New Zealand. The bond of Watergate had not weakened and I boarded the ship at Liverpool with as much heart as John Cabot must have enjoyed when he sailed from Bristol, four and a half centuries before. The hawsers hit the water and we moved out, to cross the ocean that had been sour with war for six long years. As evening came I asked to be allowed to go to the bow, and I leaned over, watching the sea being sliced and tossed aside in spray.

The Battle of the Atlantic, and the Battle of the South-Western Approaches, suddenly became real to me as they had never done on paper, or even in the stories told by the air-crews, after their long vigils and combats over the sea. I stood as far forward as possible, so that I had the sensation of flight, as the spaces of dark water sped by on either side.

I was about to circumnavigate the world, in peace, and the freedom of the particular stretch of ocean I was crossing had been won by the pilots I had known, and seen come home from battle, to laugh and drink in the mess at Watergate. The waves, stretching, without anger, as far as the setting sun, became the symbol of what the warriors had fought for—something infinite and beyond themselves. As the ship cleaved its way west, I looked over the bows for a long time and played with a quotation I half-recalled. I have since confirmed the phrases that had become confused in my memory: they were written by William Collins, in 1746.

> *How sleep the brave, who sink to rest,*
> *By all their country's wishes blest!* . . .
>
> *There Honour comes, a pilgrim grey,*
> *To bless the turf that wraps their clay,*
> *And Freedom shall awhile repair,*
> *To dwell a weeping hermit there!*

INDEX